Tolstoy As Man and Artist with an Essay on Dostoevsky

Tolstoy As Man and Artist with an Essay on Dostoevsky

Dmitry Merezhkovsky

MINT EDITIONS

Tolstoy As Man and Artist with an Essay on Dostoevsky was first published in 1901.

This edition published by Mint Editions 2021.

ISBN 9781513283104 | E-ISBN 9781513288123

Published by Mint Editions®

MINT
EDITIONS

minteditionbooks.com

Publishing Director: Jennifer Newens
Design & Production: Rachel Lopez Metzger
Project Manager: Micaela Clark
Typesetting: Westchester Publishing Services

Contents

Life of Tolstoy

1828	Born August 28
1843	Went to Kazan University
1851	Enlisted in the Artillery and went to the Caucasus
1852	Published *Childhood, A Landlord's Morning, The Invaders, The Cossacks* (a novel)
1854	Published *Boyhood*
1855	Became Divisional Commander in the Army
1854–1856	Published *Sevastopol Sketches,* after serving in the war
1855	Published *Youth*
1857	Visited Germany, France, Italy, and England, after resigning his commission
	Published *Memoirs of Prince Nekliudoff* (Albert: Lucerne)
1859	Published *The Three Deaths* (an allegorical story), *Family Happiness* (a novel)
1860	His brother Nicholas dies in Tolstoy's arms. The long novel *War and Peace* is begun
1861	Renewed rupture with Ivan Turgenieff. *The Story of a Horse* is published
1862	Married Miss Behrs (he, thirty-four, she, eighteen years old)
1863–1878	*The Decembrists* (published in fragments)
1864–1869	Published *War and Peace* (his chief novel) written at Yasnaya Poliana
1869	Published *A Prisoner in the Caucasus; Stories and Translations for Children*
1870	Learned Greek. Spent six weeks in the Bashkir Steppes
1873	Described the Samara famine in newspaper articles. Began *Anna Karenina*
1873–1876	Published *Anna Karenina* (his second masterpiece)
1879–1882	Published *My Confession*
1880–1881	Published, in Russian, at Geneva, a *Criticism of Greek Orthodox Theology*

1880–1882	Published *The Gospels Translated, Compared, and Harmonised*
1881	Published *What Men Live By* (folk-tale)
1884	Published (abroad) *My Religion*
1884	Published *What's to be Done*
1884–1886	Published *The Death of Ivan Ilyitch*
1885	Published folk tales, such as *The Candle, The Two Pilgrims, Ivan the Fool, The Long Exile*, etc.
1886	Published folk legends, *The Three Old Men*, etc.
	Published *The Power of Darkness* (a play)
1887	Published *Life*
1888	Published *Work While You Have the Light*
1889	Published *The Kreuzer Sonata*
	Published *The Fruits of Enlightenment* (a comedy)
1892	Deposited his Memoirs and Diaries in the Rumiantzoft Museum, Moscow
1893	Published *The Kingdom of God is Within You*
1894	Wrote a preface to Guy de Maupassant's work. Eng. trans. (1898) *Guy de Maupassant and the Art of Fiction*
1895	Wrote *Master and Man*
1898	Published his treatise on Æsthetics, *What is Art?*
1902	Serious illness at Yalta

Note.—For a fuller list of dates, see Mr. G. H. Perris' admirable study, *Leo Tolstoy* (Fisher Unwin, 1898).—*Ed.*

Life of Dostoevsky

1821	Born (October) in Moscow, the son of a surgeon, in a hospital for the poor
1843	Left the Military School of Engineering as a sub-lieutenant
1844	Obtained his discharge from military service to devote himself to literature
1846	Wrote *Poor Folk* (at the age of twenty-four), a remarkable psychological novel
1849 (April 23)	Arrested, with thirty-three others, for Fourierism, as an opponent of marriage and property
1849 (Dec. 22)	Reprieved, when at the scaffold
1849–1859	Wrote nothing. Spent four years at hard labour in Siberia, and four years in service in the ranks
1858	Returned from Siberia to preach the morality of the "divine spark" even in the pariah, and the Christian "morality of the slave": of pure unselfishness. He brought back from Siberia a young wife—the widow of a prisoner
1860	Published *The Injured and Oppressed* (an inferior novel). Became contributor to various Slavophile newspapers
1862	Published *Recollections of the House of the Dead* (a masterpiece, describing his exile)
1865	Falls into the direst poverty. Loses his first wife, his brother, and child; and escapes abroad to avoid imprisonment for debt. Visits Florence and Baden-Baden
1866	Published *Crime and Punishment*; a great picture of the poorer classes in Russian society, teaching the possibility of preserving purity of soul under any circumstances. His penury continues
1868	Wrote *The Idiot*
1870	Began to write *The Brothers L'aramazov*, a great psychological novel, of which the first part only, in four volumes, has been finished.
1873	Wrote *The Possessed*

1873	Published *An Author's Note Book.* He spent his remaining years in comparative comfort in St. Petersburg
1880	Delivered a great speech on the future of Russia, on the occasion of the unveiling of a monument to Pouchkine
1881	Died, and was followed to the grave by forty thousand people.

PART FIRST

TOLSTOY AS MAN AND ARTIST, WITH AN
ESSAY ON DOSTOEVSKY

I

In the case of both Tolstoy and Dostoevsky, but especially in the case of Tolstoy, their works are so bound up with their lives, with the personality of each author, that we cannot speak of the one without the other. Before studying them as artists, thinkers, or preachers, we must know what manner of men they are.

In Russian society, and to some extent among critics, the opinion has taken root that about 1878, and in the early years of the next decade, there took place in Tolstoy a deep-seated moral and religious change; a change which radically transformed not only the whole of his own life, but also his intellectual and literary activity, and as it were snapped his existence into halves. In the first period, people say, he was only a great writer, perhaps too a great man, but at any rate a man of this world with human and Russian passions, grievances, doubts, and foibles; in the second he shook off all the trammels of historical life and culture. Some say that he is a Christian champion, others an atheist, others still that he is a fanatic, a fourth party that he is a sage who has attained the highest moral illumination, and, like Socrates, Buddha, and Confucius, become the founder of a new religion.

Tolstoy himself, in his *Confession* written in 1879, confirms, and as it were insists on, the unity, unchangeableness, and finality of this new religious birth.

"Five years ago something very curious began to take place in me: I began to experience at first times of mental vacuity, of cessation of life, as if I did not know how I was to live or what I was to do. These suspensions of life always found expression in the same problem, 'Why am I here?' and then, 'What next?' I had lived and lived, and gone on and on till I had drawn near a precipice: I saw clearly that before me there lay nothing but destruction. With all my might I endeavoured to escape from this life. And suddenly I, a happy man, began to hide my bootlaces, that I might not hang myself between the wardrobes in my room when undressing alone at night; and, ceased to take a gun with me out shooting, so as to avoid temptation by these two means of freeing myself of life."

From this suicidal despair he was saved, as he conjectures, by becoming friendly with simple believing folk, with the labouring classes. "I lived in this way, that is to say in communion with the people, for two years; and a change took place in me. What befel me was that the life of our class—the wealthy and cultured—not only became repulsive to me, but lost all significance. All our actions, our judgments, science and art itself, appeared to me in a new light. I realized that it was all self-indulgence, that it was useless to look for any meaning in it. I hated myself and acknowledged the truth. Now it had all become clear to me."

The most guileless, and therefore most valuable and trustworthy of the biographers of Tolstoy, his wife's brother, S. A. Bers, in his *Reminiscences*, also speaks of this "transformation" during this decade of his life, which seemed to "wholly alter the mental activity and consciousness of Leo Nicolaievich."

"The transformation of his personality which has taken place in the last decade is in the truest sense entire and radical. Not only did it change his life and his attitude towards mankind and all living things, but his whole way of thinking. Leo became throughout his being the incarnate idea of love for his neighbour."

As conclusive is the testimony of his wife, the Countess: "If you could know and hear dear Leo now!" she wrote to her brother early in 1881. "He is greatly changed. He has become a Christian, and a most sincere and earnest one."

It would be difficult to doubt such forcible and reliable testimony, even if we had not at command a still more trustworthy source, his own artistic creations, which in reality from the first to the last are nothing but one vast diary of fifty years, one endless and minute "confession." In the literature of all ages and nations there can scarcely be found another writer who has laid bare the private, personal, and sometimes delicate aspects of his own life with such noble and unreserved candour. He seems to have told us everything that he had to tell, and we know all about him that he knows of himself.

It is impossible not to have recourse to this artistic, and consequently unintentional and unforced confession, if we wish to ascertain the real significance of the religious transformation that took place in him at the age of fifty, that is, in the part of his life immediately preceding old age.

In his first work, *Childhood, Boyhood, and Youth*, a book written when he was twenty, he gives us his still fresh recollections from the age of fourteen to fifteen.

"In the remainder of the year, during which I led a solitary and self-centred moral existence, all abstract questions as to the destiny of man, a future life and the immortality of the soul, already planted themselves

DMITRY MEREZHKOVSKY

before me: and my feeble and childish intelligence struggled with all the ardour of inexperience to solve those questions, the putting of which constitutes the highest task which the mind of man can set itself."

Once on a spring morning, when he was helping the servants to put out the garden frames, he felt of a sudden the joy and contentment of Christian self-sacrifice.

"I felt the desire to mortify myself in doing this service to Nicolas. 'How foolish I was before, how good and happy I might have been, and may be for the future!' I said to myself. 'I must at once, at once, this very minute, become another man, and begin to lead a new life.'"

To set to rights all mankind, to exterminate all the vices and miseries, began to seem to him "a thing worth doing." And he decided "to write down for himself all through his life the tale of his duties and occupations, to set forth on paper the object of his existence, and the rules by which he would always and invariably act." He at once went upstairs to his room, got a sheet of writing paper, ruled it, and having defined his duties towards himself, his neighbour, and God, began to write.

With a mournful, sensitive, and yet superficial mockery, as if not suspecting all the depth and morbidity of what was passing in his own soul, he proceeds to recount the intellectual life which then, in the phrase of the Apostle James, became "doubleminded in him." The impression conveyed is a strange one, as if there were in him two hearts, two beings. The one absorbed in Christian thoughts of death, who, to inure himself to suffering "in spite of terrible pain, held out for five minutes at arm's length the massive lexicons of Tatishchev; or went into the pantry and with a rope lashed his bare back so hard that tears streamed involuntarily down his face." The other self, impelled by the same thoughts of death, would suddenly remember that death was awaiting him every hour, every minute; and determine to give up all study and "for three days do nothing but lie abed and revel in reading novels and eating gingerbread and Kronov honey, which he bought with his last few pence." The one Leo Tolstoy, self-conscious, good and weak, controls himself, repents, and cultivates loathing of himself and his vices; the other, unconscious, wicked, and violent, "fancies himself a great man, who has discovered for the welfare of all mankind new truths, and with a proud consciousness of his own merit looks down on other mortals," finding an especial, subtle, and bitter-sweet gratification of pride even in self-contempt, humiliation, and self-chastisement.

In telling us these boyish thoughts, he concludes that at the root of them were four feelings: "the first, love for an imaginary woman, or the 'gratification of the flesh'; the second, 'the love of love' of mortals, i.e. pride or the gratification of the spirit; the third, the 'hope of unwonted and glorious fortune', this special passion being so powerful and firmly rooted that it grew to be a madness; and the fourth, repulsion for myself and remorse."

But in reality these are not four feelings, but two—for the first three amount to one—i.e. love for self, for the body, for the physical life of his own "ego": the other, loathing or hatred for himself, is not love of others or of God, but simply self-hatred. In both cases the primary cause and link between these two apparently conflicting feelings is the "ego" either asserted to the utmost or denied to the utmost. All begins and ends with self. Neither love nor hatred can break through the encircling wall.

So we come to the question, which of the two combined and blended Tolstoys is the more real, sincere, and lasting—the one that lashes himself with a rope on the bare back, or the one that, in Epicurean fashion, gobbles gingerbread and Kronov honey, lulling himself with the thought of death, that everything under the sun is vanity of vanities and vexation of spirit, that better is a live dog than a dead lion? Is it the one that loves, or the one that hates himself? He who begins all his thoughts, feelings, and aspirations in a devout Christian way, or he who weakly gives them up to finish his days like a heathen? Or is it perhaps—and this would be for him the more terrible conclusion—that both alike are real, both sincere, and both to last as long as the breath in his body? In any case he judges himself and his boyish thoughts, which he calls "lucubrations," with more severity and justice in this first of his books than in the sequel he ever does again, even in the famous and hotly repentant self-scourgings of the *Confession*.

"From all this heavy moral travail," he says, "I carried away nothing but an ingenious mind, which weakened in me the power of the will, together with a habit of constant moral introspection which destroyed the freshness of feeling and the clearness of judgment. A natural bent towards abstract speculation had so greatly and abnormally developed self-consciousness that often, when I began considering some simple matter, I fell into an unescapable round of analysis of my own thoughts; I gave no more heed to the question before me, but pondered over my own reasoning. When I asked myself of what I was thinking, I answered, Thinking over my methods of thinking. And again, of what am I thinking? I think I am thinking of what I am thinking, and so on. Dialectic took the place of reasoning."

In reference to his first failure with "Rules of Life," when, meaning to rule the paper, and using instead of the ruler, which he could not find, a Latin dictionary, he smeared the pages with a long drawn smudge, he remarks plaintively, "Why is all so fair and clear in the mind, yet comes out so shapelessly on paper and in life, when I attempt to put theory into practice?" Is this only the helplessness of a childish intelligence, of a childish conscience, which will grow with time to full consciousness and maturity? Scarcely so. At any rate, even when he wrote *Childhood and Boyhood* as a young man of twenty-four, he realized that this immaturity of his was independent of age, and that its ineffaceable stamp would remain on him all through life. "I am convinced of one thing, that if I am fated to live to an advanced age and my recital catches up my years, as an old man of seventy I shall dream in just as childishly unpractical a way as I do now."

In these calm and simple words there is more Christian resignation, if we can ever speak of such a trait in Tolstoy, than in all his subsequent loud-voiced and passionate professions of repentance. Is it not easier to say of oneself in the face of the world, as he afterwards did, "I am a parasite, a flea, a prodigal, a thief, and a murderer," than in calm self-consciousness to acknowledge the actual limits of one's powers, to say, "I am still just such a child in my old man's thought as I was in my boyish reflection. In spite of all the boundless force of artistic genius that is in me, in my searchings for God I am not a leader, a prophet, the founder of a new religion, but just such a weak, morbidly dual man as are all the men of my time?"

The Squire's Morning, next in the chronological order of his productions, which fully corresponds to the actual order of his life, is a sort of sequel or continuation of his huge journal. Prince Dmitri Nekhliudov is none other than Nicolai Irteniev, the hero of *Childhood, Boyhood, and Youth*, after leaving the University before the end of his course, where he realized the vanity of all human knowledge, and settled in a village as its squire in order to help the common people. In Nekhliudov there takes place just such a moral and religious transformation as in Irteniev. "All that I knew is foolishness, and all that I believed and loved," he says to himself. "Love and self-sacrifice are the only true happiness, the only kind of happiness that is independent of circumstance."

Reality, however, does not satisfy him. "Where are these dreams?" he reflects. "It is more than a year that I have been seeking for happiness on this path, and what have I found? True I sometimes feel that I am self-contented, but it is a barren and merely intellectual satisfaction."

Nekhliudov is forced to the conclusion that for all his wish he does not know how to do good to his fellow men. And the peasants show their suspicion of the Christian sentiments of the *barine*. The only outcome of this unsuccessful, and in reality, childish attempt to combine the virtues of a Lord Bountiful with those of the Gospel is a painful and fruitless envy of the young peasant Iliushka, and that, not of his spiritual, but his bodily force, his health, his freshness, the unruffled slumber of his mind and conscience. We know from the biography of Tolstoy that after the failure of his Nekhliudov-like experiment with the tenants of Yasnaia Poliana, being disappointed as to his capabilities as a country squire, he quitted his property, and went to the Caucasus, where he entered the Artillery as a cadet inspired by romantic dreams of military glory, and with the charms of the primitive life of the mountaineers, like Olenine, the hero of *The Cossacks.*

Exactly like Irteniev and Nekhliudov, Olenine is conscious that he is boundlessly free. This is the characteristic liberty of the young and wealthy Russian gentleman of the forties, for whom there are neither physical nor moral restraints. He could do anything; he lacked nothing he wanted, and nothing curbed his impulses. He had neither family, nor country, nor religion, nor unsatisfied wants. He believed in nothing, he acknowledged nothing. He loved thus far himself alone, and could not fail so to do, for he expected goodness of nobody else, and had not yet had time to become thoroughly disenchanted with himself.

But although he believes in nothing, and owns no superior; though he loves himself only, and that with a simple and childish cynicism, this student, still at his books, this cadet of Artillery, is already making his "philosophical discoveries," and setting his primitive life among the Cossacks of the "Stanitsa" (settlement, military colony) over against the inferior civilized life of the rest of mankind.

The deceptions in which he had hitherto lived, and which even then had pained him, and which now he began to feel inexpressibly contemptible and ridiculous, seemed clearly demonstrated to his mind. "How pitiable, how feeble, you appear to me!" he writes to his Moscow friends. "You do not know what happiness is, or in what life consists! You want for once to experience natural life in all its unadulterated

DMITRY MEREZHKOVSKY

glory. You want to see and understand what here I see every day before me: the eternal inaccessible snow of the mountains, the majesty of woman in all her primitive beauty, fresh as when she came from the hands of her Creator. Then it will flash on you which of us is ruining himself, which lives in the truth or in falsehood, you or I. If only you knew how pitiful, how paltry all your delusions seem to me!"

"Men live as Nature lives: they die, are born, couple themselves, again fructify, fight, drink, eat, enjoy themselves, and die again; and there are no conditions except those invariable ones which Nature has imposed on the sun, the grass, the animals, the trees. They have no other laws. Happiness is to be one with Nature."

This primitive philosophy is incarnated in the real hero of the story, the old Cossack, Uncle Yeroshka, one of the finest and most perfect creations of Tolstoy, a character who enables us to look into the darkest and most secret depth of the author's being; a depth, perhaps, never laid bare to his own consciousness. Here for the first, and, it would seem, the last time, with artistically perfect and deliberate clearness, stands out one of the two persons always at issue within him, the person that is always acting, but saying little of himself, and still less realizing himself. This familiar, and yet unfamiliar, this unfathomed and unillumined being within Tolstoy, seems to writhe and dart in the character of this giant, who, with the child-like eyes, an old man's deep and weary wrinkles, and a young man's muscles, bears about him a strong savour of new wine, brandy, powder, and ebullient blood; I refer to Uncle Yeroshka. His life, like the life of the half-savage Chechenetses, is replete with "love of free independence, idleness, plunder, and war." He says of himself with simple pride, "I am a fine fellow, a drunkard, a thief, and a hunter. A merry man with women; I love them all, I, Yeroshka!"

Here we have the unconscious Russian cynic philosopher. He feels himself as boundlessly free as the Russian *barine* Olenine. He too respects nothing, and believes in nothing. He lives outside human laws, beyond good or evil. Tartar Mullahs and Russian Old Believers awake in him the like calm and contemptuous jibes. "To my mind it is all the same. God made all for the delight of man. *There is no fault in anything.* Take example of the animals. They live alike in Tartar thickets and in ours. What God bestows, that men gather. But our people say that instead of enjoying this freedom we are to lick saucepans. I think that everything is alike a cheat. You die, and the grass grows: that is all that's real."

He has the old pre-human sagacity, the clear-eyed and bottomless, yet morbid soul of the Wood-god, half-divine, half-beast, Faun or Satyr. He can be, in his own way, good and tender. He loves all that lives, all of God's creatures. And this love has a sort of flavour of Christianity about it, perhaps because in the utmost unconscious depth of heathenism there is the germ of the future change to Christianity, the organic germ of Dionysus—of self-abnegation, self-elimination, the fusion of man with the God Pan, the Father of all being. We must not, however, forget the historical, and still less the psychological gulf that separates this first wild, and if we may say, heathenish Christianity from the later civilized Christian spirit. If they approach one another, it is in such unlikely fashion as extremes sometimes meet.

Uncle Yeroshka drives away the night-moths which flutter over the flickering fire of the candle, and fall into it.

"'Fool, fool! Where are you flying to? Fool, fool!' He rose, and with his great palm began to drive the moths away."

Does not the tender smile of Uncle Yeroshka at this moment recall that of St. Francis of Assisi? He has a touch of hot blood in him too, a touch not merely animal, but human, because on the conscience of the old "thief" there is, after all, no murder. Like Nature, he is at once merciful and cruel. He himself does not feel or suspect this anomaly. That which in the sequel curdles off into evil and good, in him is as yet blended in a primitive, unconscious harmony.

Olenine, too, in his own heart, which so eagerly desires to turn to Christianity, finds inborn in him an echo of Uncle Yeroshka's cynical philosophy. In the stillness of the noon hush, in the depths of the southern forest, with its awe-striking superfluity of life, he suddenly learns an unchristian self-abnegation, a half-animal, half-godlike fusion with Nature, the holy but savage love of Fauns and Satyrs, which seems to men madness, full of enthusiasm and the terror which the ancients called "panic," born of the God of the universe.

"And suddenly on Olenine there came such a strange feeling of causeless happiness in his love for the All, that he, from old childish habit, began to cross himself, and mutter thanks to some one." As he listens to the buzzing of the gnats, Olenine thinks, "Each of them is just such a separate Dmitri Olenine as I myself am." And it became clear to him that he was in no wise a Russian gentleman, a member of Moscow society, the friend and relative of such-an-one or so-and-so, but simply just such a gnat, or just such a pheasant, or deer, as those that at the moment had their being about him. "Like them and Uncle Yeroshka I shall live awhile and die. And what he says is true: '*only the grass will grow better.*'"

But he also is twy-natured, and the *other* Olenine, Irteniev, like Nekhliudov, keeps on making the assertion, "Love is self-sacrifice! It is not enough to live for oneself; one must live too for others." He tries to reconcile the unearthly love of the Wood-god and Satyr, with the modest, profitable, and reasonable Christian virtues. He sacrifices his own love for Mariana, in favour of Lukashka the Cossack. But nothing comes of this sacrifice, any more than of Irteniev's rules of life, or Nekhliudov's seigneurial Christianity.

"I am not to blame for beginning to love," is the startling confession that breaks from him in a moment of desperation; "I have saved myself from my love by self-sacrifice; I have pictured to myself delight in the love of Lukashka the Cossack for Mariana, and I have only excited my passion and jealousy. I have no will of my own, but some elemental force loves her through me, all God's world, all Nature forces this love into my soul, and bids me love. I wrote formerly of my new (that is, my Christian) convictions. No one can know with what trouble they were worked out in me, with what joy I recognized them, and saw a new path opened to me in life. There is nothing in me dearer than these convictions, nor has been. Well, love came, and they exist no longer, nor do I regret them. Even to understand that I could value *such a one-sided, cold, reasoning frame of mind* is difficult for me. Beauty came, and scattered in the dust all the pyramidal edifice of my inner life. And I have no regrets for what has vanished. Self-denial is all nonsense. It is all pride, an escape from merited misery, a refuge from envy of the happiness of others. To live for others, to do good! Why should I, when in my soul there is only love for myself?"

"Only love for himself": in that all begins and ends. Love or hatred for self, for self only; such are the two main and sole axes, sometimes latent, sometimes manifest, on which all turns, all moves in the first, and perhaps most sincere of Leo Tolstoy's books. And is it only in the first?

II

Olenine the cadet dreams of becoming A.D.C. We know that an artillery cadet, Count L. N. Tolstoy, also dreamed of being A.D.C. and getting the Cross of St. George. "When serving in the Caucasus," says Bers, "Leo passionately desired to get the Cross of St. George." At the commencement of the Crimean campaign he was at first before Silistria, but afterwards went to Sevastopol, where he was under fire for three days and nights in the Fourth Bastion, and took part in the assault, displaying great valour. The soldierly ambition of those days he afterwards expressed with his usual candour in the secret thoughts of one of his favourite heroes, Prince Andrei Volkonski, in *Peace and War*, making him dream of becoming a Russian Napoleon.

"If I desire this, desire glory," says the Prince to himself before the battle of Austerlitz, "wish to be known to my fellows and be loved by them, well, am I to blame for willing and living for this alone? *I will never tell any one this*; but, my Lord, what am I to do, if I love nothing but glory alone and the love of my fellows? Death, wounds, the loss of my family, nothing has terrors for me. And however dear, however sweet, many people are to me—father, sister, wife, for they are the dearest to me—yet however terrible and unnatural it seems, I would give them all at once for a moment of glory—of triumph over other men, for the love of other men towards me."

Tolstoy was actually recommended for the decoration he so passionately desired, but he did not receive it, as Bers declares, "on account of the personal ill-will of one of his superiors." This failure greatly grieved him, and at the same time "changed his attitude towards bravery," as Bers further asserts with his invariable frankness. It was to him that Leo once confessed "his pride and vanity, for when after the failures of his youth, that is in military matters, he achieved a wide-spread fame as a writer, he declared to me that this fame was the greatest delight and happiness to him. In his own words, there was in him "an agreeable consciousness of the fact that he was at once a writer and an aristocrat." Sometimes he said jocosely, that he had not "won his way to be a general of artillery, but he had become a general in literature."

No doubt some of the coarseness and want of restraint in this admission is not to be ascribed to Tolstoy: in all probability, even in joke and familiar intercourse, he managed to express himself more delicately and modestly. But, on the other hand, we need to see how deep was the simple and, as it were, unconscious devotion of Bers to his great kinsman in order to realize how totally incapable he was of any malicious or satirical fabrication. He writes his life of Tolstoy in all simplicity of heart like the compilers of ancient fairy tales; and though, in truth, Bers' *naïveté* is worse at times for his hero than subtlety or irony, to the inquirer it is perhaps more valuable than the highest intelligence.

However this may be, having got sick of war and warlike courage, on which he afterwards took such immortal and pitiless literary revenge, he retired as lieutenant of artillery, and went first to St. Petersburg and then abroad. "St. Petersburg," remarks Bers, "never pleased him. Neither by hook nor by crook could he make a show in the highest circles there; he had, of course, neither official career nor large fortune, and his great fame as a writer was not yet achieved."

Coming back from abroad in the year of the liberation of the serfs, Tolstoy found employment as communal arbitrator, and also undertook to teach in the village school at Yasnaia Poliana. For a time he contemplated devoting his whole life to this work, and finding lasting content in it. But little by little he got tired of the school, as he had of all his former attempts to do good to his fellows. And at last he got so far as to see "something faulty and wrong," as he himself calls it, in his relations to the children. "It seemed to me that I was corrupting the pure and primitive souls of the little peasants. I vaguely felt remorse for a sort of sacrilege. I remembered the children who are made by idle and corrupt old men to contort themselves and represent voluptuous scenes in order to excite their worn out and jaded imagination."

The remorse, as always in his case, was sincere, but unbridled and morbidly excessive. From his school diaries of that period one thing at least is clear, that he really was not as much concerned about the children as about himself. When he made Fedka and Senka write compositions, which he afterwards, in his journal of pedagogy, declared more perfect than his own works, or Pushkin's, or Goethe's, he made on the minds of the children experiments with his own intelligence, that were, perhaps, too much in his own interest and not without danger for them. He admired, like some new Narcissus, his own reflection in the children's ideas, as in the mirror of a deep and virgin spring. He, the teacher, so terribly, so fatally influential, loved in the children himself and himself alone. "Things seemed to go well," he admits in his *Confession,* "but I felt that I was not wholly sound mentally, and this could not go on long."

A fresh transformation was already in process in him. "I felt ill," he said, "more spiritually than physically, threw up everything, and went off to the Steppes, to the Bashkirs, to drink koumiss, and live the life of an animal."

When he came back he married Sophia Andréevna Bers. All his former attempts to settle in life, his Nekhliudov-like philanthropy of a country-gentlemanly kind, his barbaric life in the Cossack colony, war, the school, were only curiosity and dilettantism (in the widest and older sense of the word), that is, done for the love of the thing; for throughout his life he has been like Uncle Yeroshka, above all, a great lover of endlessly-varied sport. But this step of marriage was neither sport nor play, but his first business of real importance, renewing all things, and transfiguring them. It was a business to which he not only wished to devote himself, but actually did devote himself. He was thirty-four and she eighteen. Directly after their marriage they retreated to Yasnaia Poliana, and spent there, almost without a break, some twenty years in complete isolation, never getting tired of their quietude or feeling the want of anything beyond it. These were his best years, and in them he composed *Peace and War* and *Anna Karenina,* reaching the highest pitch and expression of his powers. "Her love for her husband was boundless," writes the Countess's brother; "the nearness, amity and mutual love of the couple were always a model to me, and the ideal of conjugal happiness." It was not without reason that her parents said "We could not wish our Sonia greater bliss."

We see in the *Reminiscences* of Fet this Natasha or Kitty, one of the most faultless and perfect feminine types of the cultured Russian Squirearchy—"all in white, with a huge bunch of keys at her belt," simple, quiet, always gay, and generally *enceinte,* for she has no less than thirteen children. "She seven times wrote out *Peace and War,* and at the same time that she was so working," adds Bers, "and went through the cares of the mistress of a house, even to the minutest kitchen matters, she found time herself to nurse, teach, and clothe the children, to their fifteenth year." When their second daughter was born the mother fell ill, so that she was at death's door, and after several attempts found herself unable to nurse the child; but when she saw another woman suckling her daughter she wept for jealousy, suddenly dismissed the nurse, and caused the child to be fed with a bottle. "Leo found this jealousy natural, and was delighted at the matronly qualities of his wife."

"Love of children and the bearing of children,"—the words will not seem too grandiloquent, or reminiscent of the old patriarchs who received commandment from the God of Israel, "Be fruitful and multiply, and replenish the earth."

Whatever we may think of Tolstoy's domestic happiness, all must admit that there is in this connexion something solid, firm and well founded, if not complete. At any rate, it is a compensation,—it has balance, and is consequently beautiful, or as the people would say, wholesome; in other words, exhibits what is rarest nowadays in Russian Society. Russian life is neither vigorous and alive, nor quite dead. It is not wholly moribund, but only eaten into and maimed, as by some shameful disease, which lays waste the family by subtle poison.

Cowardly, or bold, all too earnestly intent on the future, we are apt to rate too low the perfect patterns and exemplars of past times, that "comeliness" and "shapeliness," those clinging zoöphytic roots of all human culture, deep seated in their subterranean, native animal warmth and darkness; roots by which the golden-fruited tree life alone is fed, and in spite of all "grey theories," blooms for ever. To us the following outspoken, it may be, too outspoken words of Nicolai Rostov, in the Epilogue to *Peace and War,* seem, perhaps, cynically coarse and *bourgeois.* "It is all sentimentality and old wives' fables, all this good of one's neighbour! I want our children not to be vagabonds on the face of the earth; I want to secure and protect the existence of my family so long as I am alive; that is all."

Pierre Bezukhov looks down on Nicolai Rostov, fancying himself destined by means of his "philosophisings" to give a new tendency to all Russian Society—perhaps to the civlized world. Levine, too, like young Irteniev, considers the salvation of mankind "a thing that is easily accomplished." As he busies himself with the ordering of his stewardship, or in what Rostov more candidly calls "the ordering of his own property," Levine reflects, "This matter is not merely my own personal concern, but the common welfare is at stake. There ought to be a radical change effected in the management of property, and particularly in the position of the lower classes. Instead of poverty, there should be general comfort; instead of hostility, concord. In a word, a bloodless revolution, yet the greatest of revolutions, at first within the narrow bounds of our district, then spreading over the Province, over Russia, and over the world." Yet none the less both Levine and Pierre Bezukhov, though they talk, do not act. They live still in precisely the same manner as Nicolai Rostov says he himself lives. And in the *Confession,* Tolstoy lays bare with true Tolstoyan, Rostovian, or Levinian candour this last cynical secret of his favourite heroes.

"The whole energy of my life at that time was centred in my family, in my children, and therefore in my anxiety for the increase of the means of living. The striving after protection was already directly subordinated to the endeavour to make circumstances as good for my family as possible."

He even declares that he took to authorship at the time, that is, when he wrote *Peace and War,* and *Anna Karénina,* simply as a means of improving his material position, and draws the moral that for him "there was only one truth, that you must live in such a way as may be best for you and your family."

When he used to come home from shooting, or his brief and grudging business excursions, Bers tells us, he never failed to express his excitement in the words, "If only all is right at home!"

This is not Philistinism. It is of course an instinct immeasurably more primitive and profound. It is the eternal voice of Nature, the insuperable instinct of self-preservation, which bids the beast keep his lair, the bird its nest, and man kindle fire on a hearth. "I have been married a fortnight," he writes to Fet, "and am happy, and a new, a totally new man. Now how can I write you a letter? Now there are invisible, nay, visible efforts to be made, and with it all I am over head and ears in farming, and Sonia is as deep in it as I. We have no steward, and she herself plays bailiff and keeps the accounts. I have bees and sheep, and a new garden, and spirit distillery."

He is working for the purchase of the Yasnaia and Penzeno property, and six thousand *desiatines* of land at Samara, where he is going to form a stud: he is buying up about one hundred Bashkir mares and counting on profits from the abundance of milk; means to cross them with trotters, riding horses, English, and other breeds. The old housekeeper at Yasnaia tells us of his passionate fondness for a breed of swine, a particularly fat and hairless kind, without a bristle and short-legged.

He above all fell in love with his pigs, of which he kept three hundred head in couples, in separate small styes. In these the Count would not allow the slightest dirt. "Every day I and my assistants had to clean them all out, and rub the floor and walls. Then as he went through the piggery of a morning, the Count would be vastly pleased and shout, 'What management! What excellent management!' but Lord deliver us if ever he saw the slightest dirt. He would straightway fly into a fit of passion. The Count was a very hot-tempered master."

Anna Seyron, who was governess to the Tolstoys, in her jottings, *Six Years with Count Tolstoy* (St. Petersburg, 1895), a volume apparently intended to be spiteful, though in fact it is rather frivolous and clumsy, says ironically that their famous sucking pigs were "looked after like children." The joke is hardly a good one. What of it, if a good economist found time to look after his children, who, besides, were surrounded by Swiss, German, or English *bonnes,* as we know, and after, inspect sucking pigs as well? There is nothing despicable in farming, any more than in the care of the body. What we have to notice is that on Tolstoy's property all is to the purpose and well ordered, one to this post, another to that, and this applies to his people, animals and plants alike.

And even if, like Levine, he, while caring for his warm and sheltered lair, and looking after sucking pigs, consoled himself with the notion that he was caring for the good of mankind, and taking part in the slow and bloodless revolutionizing of the world, in sober truth, he was only following the deep and true instinct of animal self-preservation, what of that? Pigstyes and nursery, and stud, aviaries or wine-presses and Sonia Andrevna's ledgers, these "impalpable and palpable efforts," were in conformity with the dictates of Nature, the weaving of the nest, and a very fine nest too. Above all, you see here his great and simple love of life, that eternally childlike joy of living which there was in Goethe. "Leo," Bers tells us, "every day praises the day for its beauty, and often adds, quite in the spirit of the great heathen, 'How many riches God has! With Him, every day is set off by some beauty or other.'" "The wondrous dawn," he writes to Fet, "the bathing, the wild fruit, have put me in the state of mental languor which I love; for two months I have not stained my hands with ink, or my mind with thinking. It is long since I have delighted in God's world as I have this year. I stand gaping, wonderstruck, afraid to stir for fear of missing anything." And yet these were his most wearisome and terrible years, when he contemplated suicide, and was planning the *Confession.*

Perhaps he was never more natural, more true to himself, more worthy of the brush of a great painter, more as God created him, than at the Baskhir festival which Bers describes. Through Mohammed Shah Romanovich notice had been given that Tolstoy was getting up at his place in Samara a steeplechase of fifty versts (thirty-four miles). Prizes were got ready, a bull, a horse, a rifle, a watch, a dressing-gown, and the like. A level stretch was chosen, a huge course four miles long was made and marked out, and posts put up on it. Roast sheep, and even a horse, were prepared for the entertainment. On the appointed day, some thousands of people assembled, Ural Cossacks, Russian peasants, Bashkirs and Kirghizes, with their dwellings, koumiss-kettles, and even their flocks. The desert Steppe, covered with feathery grasses, was studded with a row of tents, or huts of branches, and enlivened by a motley crowd. On a cone-shaped rise, called in the local dialect "Shishka" (the Wen), carpets and felt were spread, and on these the Bashkirs seated themselves in a ring, with their legs tucked under them.

In the middle of the ring a young Bashkir poured koumiss out of a large cauldron, and handed the goblet in turn to the squatting figures, a sort of loving cup. The feast lasted for two days, and was merry, but at the same time, dignified and decorous, "for Leo knew," says Bers, "how to inspire a crowd with a respect for decency." What an unforgettable, antique, pastoral idyll we get in this feast under the sky of the waste, among the waves of the desert grass! Even now, in the figure of Tolstoy at seventy, that harsh, material, almost coarse peasant visage, that figure which he himself, and others have tried in vain to make appear that of a subdued repentant, and ethereal leader of modern thought, I recognize the not unfleshly sanctity, the comely dignity of one of the old patriarchs, who led their flocks and herds from well to well, through the desert, and rejoiced in their posterity, "more numerous than the sands of the sea." "I undertook great things," he says in the *Confession,* in the words of Ecclesiastes, "I built myself houses, and planted vineyards, I made gardens and groves, and placed in them all manner of fruit trees, I made myself cisterns for the watering of the groves, I got myself men-servants and maid-servants, and there were attendants in my house; also great and small cattle; I had more than all those that had been before me in Jerusalem. And I became great and rich, and wisdom dwelt with me. Whatever mine eyes desired I did not deny them, or grudge my heart any gladsomeness."

One day Count Sologub said to him, "What a lucky man you are, my dear fellow! Fate has given you every blessing of which man can dream, a strapping family, a good and loving wife, world-wide fame, health, everything." And certainly if not in the things of the spirit, yet at least, outwardly, his was at that time, the happiest life imaginable. "If a genie had come," he himself admits, "and offered me the world to choose from, I should not have known what to choose."

And see! when he has reached this summit of the welfare attainable by mortals he looks out over the "evening valley" before him, as if

DMITRY MEREZHKOVSKY

the gods had at length grown envious of a too happy man, and were reminding him, not in the startling voice of misfortune or bereavement, but the low whisper of one of the Fates, that over him, too, destiny was hanging.

He saw that he had been pursuing his life's journey on and on, till suddenly aware of the closeness of the abyss, and that destruction yawned before him. He realized, like Solomon, that all was vanity and vexation of spirit, and that the wise man must die even as the fool. "I felt terror at what was awaiting me, though I knew that this terror was more terrible than my position itself, but I could not patiently wait for the end. My horror of the darkness was too great, and I felt I must rid myself of it as soon as possible by noose or bullet." Before dwelling on this last turning-point of his life, the heights from which he began the descent to "the plains of evening," we must examine the trait always as strong in him as the love of life, namely, its obverse, the fear of death.

III

"I am sorry for those who attach great importance to the mortality of all living things, who lose themselves in the contemplation of earthly insignificance. For is not life ours merely that we may make what is perishable imperishable, a task accomplished only when things mortal and immortal are rightly discerned and appraised?"

That is what Goethe says *(Maxims and Reflections)*.

In the conclusion of *Faust* he refers to the same thought, almost in the same words, though still more succinctly and clearly:

> *Alles vergängliche*
> *Ist nur ein Gleichniss.*

"All that is passing is but a semblance, is only shadow, or symbol. We must combine," Goethe says, "must value both treasures—*beide Schätzen*—must combine (συμβάλλειν, from which comes σύμβολον, a symbol—that is, fuse, weld together, make one)—we must fuse the idea of the non-enduring with that of the enduring, must, without abasing the transitory and the mortal, see in it and beyond it, what is immortal and unfleeting. We cannot attain what is supernal save by comprehending and growing to love to the end, to the utmost limits, what is earthly; not despising nor shrinking from the nothingness of the earthly: we must remember that we have no other ways of rising, no other stepping-stones to God, save "likenesses," "manifestations," and "symbols," not devoid of flesh and blood, but clothed in the most living flesh and blood. For the mystery of our God is not a mystery merely of spirit and speech, but also of flesh and blood, since for us the Word was made flesh. "Who eateth not my flesh and drinketh not my blood, he hath not eternal life." And so, not without flesh, but through flesh to that which is behind it, such is the greatest symbol, the most glorious union; "Ah! to how many is it still unattainable!"

This teaching of Goethe's as to the holiness of what is earthly and transitory, of the incorruptibleness of the corruptible, is the best answer to despair and terror; to the words of Sakya Mûni and Ecclesiastes, on the corruption of all that has being; the best answer to the Nirvana, and the "vanity of vanities," quoted by Tolstoy in his *Confession,* as the profoundest expression of his own despair.

It is strange that the old Hellenes, and the new Hellene, Goethe,

DMITRY MEREZHKOVSKY

certainly did not love the world and worldly delights less than Solomon or Tolstoy. But the fear of death did not annul for them the meaning of these delights. On the contrary, the blackest darkness and the terror of the abyss even increased for them the charm of life, just as the blackest velvet enhances the splendour of diamonds. They did not shrink from that darkness but, as it were, deliberately out-gazed it, that they might overcome it. Tragedy, the boldest illumination of the dreadful in human fate, did not arise in the most radiant period of Hellenic culture by an accident. The despair of Œdipus, confronted by the Sphinx's riddle, is more unbounded than that of Sakya Mûni or Solomon. But even in sight of the Parthenon is the brightest temple ever erected by man, the theatre of Dionysus, god of wine and delight. Sophocles, serenest of mortals, exulted in the sight of this deep despair. "Is there not," asks Nietzsche, "a special leaning of man's soul towards the cruel and enigmatical, proceeding from the thirst for enjoyment, from the overflow of health, from fulness of life, a special and seductive daring, full of the keenest insight, demanding the terrible as a foe, a worthy foe, in wrestling with whom it can try its strength to the uttermost?"

The tragedy of Will, as "Prometheus," the tragedy of Thought, as *Faust*, were just such appeals full of "tempting hardihood"—*versucherische Tapferkeit*—to the fear of death and the mystery of life. Only the strongest of the strong, the coolest of the fearless, ventures with impunity on this cup of terror, of which Pushkin too, strongest and most intrepid of the Russian race, speaks, when he says:

> *In battle there is rapture,*
> *Rapture in the giddy darkness of a gulf;*
> *In the tempest-scarred face of ocean,*
> *The gloom and madness of waves:*

> *Where the desert heaves in hurricane,*
> *Or the breath of plague is warm;*
> *Yea, rapture in all that threatens to destroy,*
> *For the heart of a mortal still hides*
> *Black magic that none can divine.*

> *So, Pestilence, praise be to thee,*
> *Fear we not gloom of the grave,*
> *Thy death-boding cry appals not.*

When an excessive fear of this "darkness of the grave" is present, a too vivid and sobering consciousness of bodily decay, of the nothingness of all things earthly, is the first sign that of a surety the divine sources of that particular civilization are exhausted or polluted, that in it the vital force is declining. At first sight the despair of Sophocles in *Œdipus* seems akin to that of Solomon in "Ecclesiastes," but in reality they are at opposite poles. One is an emotional ascent, the other a descent; one is a beginning, the other an end. In the *Lalita Vistara* of Buddha, in the Ecclesiastes of Solomon, we hear the voice, not of the soul awakened, but of the flesh dying. In the weariness of sated Epicureans, in the *taedium vitae* of Rome's decline, in the skull placed by philosophers among the wine-cups and the roses, there is a coarse fleshliness, alien to the Hellenic body and spirit, the senile materialism of a culture bereft of its soul and its gods. For the purest and most perfect Christianity is as confident of life and as fearless of death, and has as great a power of making the mutable immutable as perfect Hellenism. What though the lilies of the field tomorrow wither, and are cast into the fire? None the less today the sons of the Kingdom of God rejoice that "even Solomon in all his glory was not arrayed like one of these." The smile of Francis of Assisi, as he chanted a hymn to the sun, after the crucial torments and the vision of Mount Averno, recalls the smile of Sophocles, chanting a hymn to Dionysus, god of wine and happiness, after the bloody horrors of the tragedy of Œdipus. In one and the other there is youthful fervour, and yet the calm of perfected wisdom. It is only those who have stopped half-way, no longer what they were, and not yet what they shall be; who have pushed off from one shore, and not yet made the further, who are "adrift," in Goethe's phrase, "in the contemplation of earthly nothingness." Excessive fear of death generally serves as proof of religious impotence, or religious imbecility.

In Tolstoy's *Childhood* he describes the impression made on a child by his mother's death. He looks at her as she lies in her coffin. "I could not believe that that was her face. I began to look at it more closely, and gradually discovered in it the familiar and beloved features. I shuddered with fear when I became sure that it was indeed she, but why were the closed eyes so fallen in? Why was she so terribly pale, and why was there a blackish mark under the clear skin on one cheek?

The service came to an end: the face of the dead woman was uncovered, and all those present, except ourselves, went up, one after another to the coffin, and made their reverence. One of the last to go up and take leave of her was a peasant-woman, with a pretty five-year-old girl in her arms, whom she had brought with her, Lord knows why. At that moment I carelessly dropped my wet handkerchief, and wanted to pick it up, but no sooner did I stoop, than I was startled by a terrible and piercing cry, full of such horror that if I lived to be a hundred I should never forget it, and when I think of it a cold shudder runs over my frame even now. I raised my head; on a stool by the coffin knelt the peasant-woman, with difficulty holding the little girl in her arms, and her child, wringing her little hands, turned behind her a face full of terror, and, fixing staring eyes on the face, shrieked terribly, wildly. I, too, cried out, in a voice which I fancy was even more fearful to hear than that which had so startled me, and rushed from the room."

We may here say that this unreasoning cry has never, since then, been hushed in Tolstoy's works. He has infected the minds of a whole generation with his own terror. If, in our day, people are afraid of death, and that with such shameful and hitherto unheard-of panic; if we all, in our inmost hearts, in our flesh and bones, have this cold shudder, the marrow-piercing chill of which Dante speaks on seeing the sinners shivering in the infernal lake—"Then an icy chill passed over me. Even now I feel it when I remember them"—then we are, in a very large measure, indebted for it all to Leo Tolstoy.

However, he had not taken his account of the death of Irteniev's mother from his own recollections; for Tolstoy's mother died when he was three years old. He neither could remember her nor was present at her death. But, apparently, in his description of the hero of *Childhood*, the awfulness of death which he depicts with almost cynical minuteness of realism, was innate in himself, exceptional and peculiar to himself, at least in that degree, had dawned in him with the first flashes of consciousness, and never quitted his side through life. Many years later, when a mature man in the full light of knowledge, he finds that same dread overhanging his spirit, and is as helpless, or more so, in face of it than he was as a child.

He writes to Fet, from Hyères, near Nice, in a letter dated October 17, 1860, with regard to the death of his brother Nicolai: "On the 20th September he passed away, literally in my arms. Never in my life has anything had such an effect on me. He was right when he said to me that there is nothing worse than death, and if you remember that death is the inevitable goal of all that lives, then it must be confessed that there is nothing poorer than life. Why should we be so careful, if, at the end of all things, nothing remains of what was once Nicolai Tolstoy? He never said that he felt the approach of death, and yet I know that he followed it step by step, and was well aware how long he had to live. Some minutes before his death he dozed awhile. Suddenly he started up and murmured in alarm, 'What is this?' *He saw that he was passing into nothingness.* And if he did not know what to cling to, what shall I find? Assuredly even less."

In this letter, astonishing, yet alarming in its outspokenness, what most of all strikes one is the simple unconscious materialism displayed to the verge of cynical coarseness; it is a soulless callousness. There is no wavering, no possible questioning, no doubt as to the fact that death is a "passing into nothingness." He feels no mystery. Shunless, fruitless terror is there, senselessly destroying and drying up the very springs of life. It is like what the heretical, Judaizing, Russian Nihilists of the fifteenth century said, "And what is the Kingdom of Heaven? What is the Second Coming? What is the resurrection of the dead? There are no such things. If a man dies, his place knows him no more." Or as Uncle Yeroshka puts it, "I die, and the grass grows the better." It is a blind wall, or, in true Russian phrase, "dead emptiness."

Twenty-five years later, long after his conversion to Christianity, he expressed the same feelings of unreasonable animal fear in "The Death of Ivan Ilyich." "He remained once more alone with it. He was eye to eye with it, and there was nothing to be done with it. He could only look at it and shudder."

We know that throughout his life, in many contingencies of actual danger, Tolstoy has shown remarkable personal courage and even foolhardiness. He almost loved the whistle of bullets in the deadly fourth Bastion at Sevastopol, and took a delight in mastering the fear of death by his vital energy, and it was of death that he thought least when at the Piatigor "colony" he fired at arm's length at a mad wolf, or, when, in hunting, he was borne down by a she-bear, which all but throttled him and tore the skin from his skull, so that "the flesh hung down in tatters over my eyes," and there was as much blood on the snow "as if a sheep had been killed." Getting up from under the animal, forgetting his wounds and feeling no pain, but trembling with excitement, he shouted with a sportsman-like keenness, reminding us much of Uncle Yeroshka, "Where is the bear? Where has the brute gone?"

No, the fear of death in him in no way proceeds from bodily timidity.

That fear, though at times it may amount to cowardice, is more inward and deep-seated. At its original source, in spite of all animality, it is yet abstract, and, so to speak, a metaphysical fear. Yet all the more are we alarmed at these sudden black gaps, in that they occur in his soul and in his works, side by side with the most passionate love of life. They are like those deceptive mantled pools in marshes, on the surface covered with the greenest, freshest, most alluring grass and the brightest flowers. Soon as the traveller sets foot on them they give way and the quagmire engulfs him. What is this frail and subtle filament, which makes all the wheels of the machine suddenly leave their axles and turns order into chaos? Whence this drop of venom, warping his soul, so that life's sweetest honey turns to gall?

Recalling the passionate psychological exercises of his youth, which destroyed in him, as he said, the freshness of feeling and clearness of judgment, and even then brought a morbid dread of death, in consequence of which he now, with the remorse of a Buddhist devotee, scourges his back with seven-fold cords, now, in the hopelessness of Solomon, throws aside lessons for gingerbread, novels and Kronov honey. He himself declares the cause of this temperament to be a preternaturally developed self-consciousness. And in fact, if we trace the spiritual life of the man throughout its course, it is impossible not to arrive at the conclusion that between the conscious and unconscious side of his mental growth there is a want of correspondence and equilibrium. To say, however, that this want of correlation consists precisely in the exceptional strength of his self-consciousness is, I think, to miss the truth. All Europeans, at any rate, have had the opportunity of beholding how a much greater force of consciousness than that of Tolstoy, namely Goethe's, did not in the least disturb the harmony and balance of that spiritual and intellectual life, nay rather enhanced it. No, it is not to superfluity of consciousness that we must look for one of the most fertile causes of faultiness and morbidity in the moral and religious development of Tolstoy, but rather to the want of, and incompleteness of such consciousness. In him, consciousness is exceptionally trenchant, or at least acute and strained, but it is not all embracing; it is not all-penetrating. It shines brightly, but not from within, like the sun from behind the transparent atmosphere, thoroughly penetrated by light, but from without, as a beacon lights dark surfaces of sea. However bright and widely shed are the rays of this beacon-like perception, the unconscious elemental life in the waters is of such unfathomable depth, that a defiant, subaqueous darkness remains impenetrable by any rays. But what I would lay stress on is that his consciousness has developed, not only from without and separately, it has grown, not only in another, but in a wholly opposite direction from the trend of his unconscious, his sub-conscious existence, so that there are always in him, as it were, two or more men, one of them always opposing violently the other. This internal rift and discord, like the flaw in a bell, at first scarcely perceptible, gradually widens and causes a jarring sound. Alas! the louder and more powerful the voice of the bell, the more excruciating and fatal is the note of the flaw!

The fit of the fear of death, which, at the end of the seventies, brought him to the verge of suicide, was not the first and apparently not the last, and at any rate not the only one. He felt something like it fifteen years before, when his brother Nicolai died. Then he felt ill and conjectured the presence of the complaint which killed his brother—consumption. He had constant pain in his chest and side. He had to go and try to cure himself in the Steppe by a course of koumiss, and did actually cure himself. Formerly, these recurrent attacks of spiritual or physical weakness were cured in him, not by any mental or moral upheavals, but simply by his vitality, its exuberance and intoxication.

Olenine at the thought of death, just like Tolstoy among the cannon-balls at Sevastopol, recognizes in himself "the presence of the all-powerful god of youth." Now, what is the real reason why the transformation of the later seventies had for Tolstoy such decisive and unique importance? He himself explains it, it is true, upon spiritual grounds. But were there not, as in his former nervous crises, also physical causes? Was it not that special feeling, proper to people in later middle age, when they realize throughout all their mental and physical organization that so far they have been going uphill, but from that time onward they will be going down? "The time had come," he says in his *Confession* about this very period of his life, the beginning of its sixties, "when growth in me came to an end; I realized that I was no longer expanding, but contracting, that my muscles were growing weaker, and my teeth falling out."

Here we hear the profoundly sensual Anacreontic lament, without the Anacreontic clearness:

> *Grey have grown, ay, grey have grown*
> *My curls, the glory of my head,*

And loose my teeth are in my jaws,
And dimmed the fire of mine eyes.

In just the same way, Levine, alone at night in his room at the wretched inn where his brother Nicolai is dying (how closely this death-scene resembles the dying scene of Nicolai Tolstoy!) is seized with this sense of approaching old age, the animal dread, the marrow-piercing chill of the bones, and suddenly realizes throughout his physical being "that all is coming to an end, that this is death." "He lit a candle, and got up cautiously and went to the looking-glass and began to examine his face and hair. Yes, there was grey hair on his temples. He opened his mouth: his back teeth had begun to decay. He bared his muscular arms. Yes, they were pretty strong. But Nicolinka too, who was breathing yonder with the remnants of his lungs, had a sound frame."

"What is the meaning of getting on in years?" asks Tolstoy in 1894. "It means that your hair is coming out, your teeth decaying, wrinkles are coming, your breath unpleasant. Even before all comes to an end, or becomes dreadful and repulsive, you become conscious of red and white in the wrong places, sweat, bad odour, loss of bodily shape. Where is that of which I was the servant? Where is beauty gone? All is gone; nothing left. Life is over." In her letter of 1881, where the Countess assures her brother that Leo is wholly changed, and "has become the most sincere and devout of Christians," she also says that he "has grown grey, has lost his health, has become quieter and more low-spirited than he used to be." This remarkably close connexion between the mental crisis and the gain or loss, the ebb and flow of his physical health, runs through his whole life.

The "all-powerful god of youth" had taken flight, the ecstasy of life had evaporated. "We can live," he owns, "only as long as we are drunk with life, and when we grow sober, cannot help seeing that all is deception, illusion, and a stupid illusion too. If not now, then tomorrow there will come disease or death on those I love, and on myself. Nothing will remain but putrefaction and worms."

The variance and duality of his conscious and unconscious life, the flaw, at first scarcely perceptible, had gradually widened into that "yawning gulf," of which he speaks in the *Confession,* and drawing near "he clearly saw that there was nothing before him but annihilation."

"And what was worst of all, was this, that Death took him (Ivan Ilyich) to itself, not in the heat of action, but while he was simply looking it straight in the eyes; he had looked, and passively undergone the torture." And he remained alone with it, "eye to eye with it, and there was nothing to be done with it. He could only look at it and shudder."

"And being saved from this state, he sought consolation; screens, defences, were found, and for a short time sheltered him. But these once more were destroyed or shrivelled up, as if that gaze had penetrated everything, and nothing could turn it aside."

Then began that last terror which was so great, that "he longed to free himself from it as quickly as possible by noose or bullet."

Tertullian maintains that the human soul "is, of its very essence, Christian." But are all souls Christian? Are not some of them naturally pagan? It seems that Tolstoy, in particular, has the soul of "a born Pagan." If the depth of his consciousness corresponded to the depth of his elemental life he would ultimately have understood that he had no reason to fear or be ashamed of his pagan soul, that it was given him by God; that he would find his God, his creed, in fearless and exhaustless self-love, even as people with souls that are naturally Christian find their God in endless self-sacrifice and self-denial.

But owing to the profound incongruity, the want of equilibrium, between his consciousness and the unconscious element, only one of two things is now left him, either to subordinate his consciousness to the real elements of his nature, which he did during the first half of his life, or on the other hand to subordinate his elemental nature to his consciousness, which he tried to do during the second half of his life. In the latter case, he would inevitably come to the conclusion that all self-love, all life and the development of an isolated personality, is something fleshly and animal, and consequently sinful, wicked and diabolical, the sheer destruction of which should be our highest good and our sole good. And, in fact, that is the conclusion he has come to. He is determined to the uttermost to hate and mortify his own soul in order to save it. When the *Confession* was written it seemed to Tolstoy that he had already finally arrived at, and discovered, absolute truth; that there was no occasion to search further. In the concluding pages he calls to the bar and judges no longer himself, but only others, calling all human culture "self-indulgence," and the men that practise it "parasites." He says point blank, "I grew to hate myself, and now all has become clear to me."

But three or four years after the *Confession* the "clearness" had once again grown dim and confused. Even in 1882, at the time when he wrote a certain well known series of letters from Moscow; and after inspecting the night-refuge at Liapino, when he was persuading all his acquaintance who were well-to-do to combine, in order, by private Christian benevolence, to save that city in the first place, and then all Russia, and lastly all the human race, his conscience was ill at ease. The tension, the diffidence, the discord of the cracked bell, is heard in this summons, so far from simple, and couched in language so unlike his own, so reminiscent of Rostopchin's placards of the year 1812. "Let us give like fools, like peasants, like labourers, like Christians; we pay taxes, we recognize the universal duty of paying taxes; why not also of showing brotherly kindness? Prove your friendship, brothers, and all together!"

When, while collecting money for the poor, he expounded in his friends' houses this new plan for saving the world, he fancied that his hearers grew uneasy. "They were perturbed, but it was mainly for my sake, and by my talking nonsense, though that nonsense was of such a kind that it could not be frankly called nonsense. It was as if some external cause had bound my hearers to assent to my folly." And after a speech in the Senate, when conferring with the conductors of the correspondence, he again came to feel that their eyes said, "Why, out of respect for you, they have wiped out your folly, but you are returning to it!"

At length the all-important and, as he thought, novel truth that private charity is an absurdity, was revealed to him by the simplest arithmetical calculation. One Saturday evening Semyon, the carpenter, with whom Leo was chopping wood, as he came near the Dorogomitov bridge, came upon an old beggar, gave him three kopecks, and asked for two back again. The old man showed his hand with two three-kopeck pieces and one kopeck in it. Semyon looked, and wanted to take the kopeck, but then changed his mind, took off his hat and crossed himself and went on, leaving the old man the three kopecks. Semyon, as Leo knew, had savings amounting to six roubles, fifty kopecks, and he, Leo, had six thousand roubles. "Semyon," he reflected, "gave three kopecks and I twenty. What did he and I give respectively? How much ought I to give in order to do as much as he did? In order to give as much as Semyon, I ought to have given three thousand roubles, and asked for two thousand back, and if I could not get change, left that couple of thousand as well to the old man, crossed myself and gone on, calmly talking about life in factories." A further and final inference from this calculation was irresistible. "I give a hundred thousand kopecks, and am still in no position to do good, because I have two hundred thousand left. Only when I shall have *nothing at all* shall I be in a position to do some little good. That which from the first an inward monitor told me when I saw the hungry and shivering at the Liapino house, namely, that it was my fault, and to live as I live is wrong, wrong, wrong—that alone is the truth." The whole moral edifice, raised with such infinite pains, such desperate struggles, at once tottered and fell, and he had once more to own himself wrong, and publicly to repent. "I am a wholly enervated parasite, good for nothing whatever. I, too, although an insect, feeding on the foliage of the tree, am attempting to further the growth and soundness of the trunk, and to cure its disease." A new transformation, a new second birth, had now therefore to take place in him.

It became clear that he had not only entertained no proper hatred for himself, and had not found the truth, as he thought, when penning the *Confession,* but had not even begun the real search for it. And at the same time he became convinced that this time the final and everlasting truth had been revealed to him; the putting of it into practice seemed easy. "A man has only got not to desire lands or money, in order to enter into the Kingdom of God." He was convinced that the evil which ruins the world is property; "It is not a law of nature, the will of God, or a historical necessity; rather, a superstition, neither strong, nor terrible, but weak and contemptible." To free oneself from this superstition and destroy it, is as easy as to stamp on a spider. He determined to carry out the teaching of Christ; to leave all—home, children, lands, to give away his six hundred thousand kopecks and become a beggar—in order to win the right to do good. The question how far he succeeded in this undertaking, how far, as a matter of fact, he renounced personal possessions and crushed the feeble spider, forms the subject of our further inquiry.

IV

"Many people think," remarks the Countess's brother, in his *Reminiscences*, "that I have concealed all things not to the credit of Leo. But this supposition is unfounded, because there is simply nothing that needed hiding from strangers." This is a wide assertion, when we know that the greatest of saints and heroes have had moments of shame, weakness and shortcoming. The most faithful of Christ's disciples had on his soul a betrayal. But, however, Bers is first and foremost a maker of books, and what he writes is not life, but biography.

A yet more astonishing statement is one from the lips of Tolstoy himself, who, according to the testimony of one often with him, nowadays often says, "I have no secrets whatever from any one in the world. All are welcome to know what I do!"

The words are striking. Who is this that is bold enough to protest, "I have nothing to be ashamed of"? Is he a man who has a boundless contempt for his fellows, or in very truth a saint? There are in the life of every man dates of particular significance, which correlate and interpret the meanings of his existence, and decide once and for all who he is, and what he is worth; hours which give, as it were, an internal section of his whole personality to its inmost depths, betraying both his conscious and unconscious qualities; hours when all the future destiny of the man, to use a familiar phrase, is in the balance, swaying on the edge of the blade, ready to fall on one side or the other.

Precisely such a crisis in the life of Tolstoy was the decision to distribute his property. But strange to say, right up to that moment we have the most minute records of his doings, confessions, repentances, and admissions which enable one to follow every movement of his volition and conscience. But at this point they suddenly fail us and break off short! The garrulous self-revealer suddenly becomes silent, and for ever. True, we should have had no need of any confessions, if only his deeds, let alone his words, had spoken for him with sufficient clearness. But it is just Tolstoy's outward life, the life of his actions still more than that of his words which leaves us perplexed. As regards the inward part of his life, we learn about it only from a few hints that seem to break from him involuntarily, hints eagerly caught up, though scarcely intelligible even to the hearers; or from his own superficial accounts, in which we learn something so unexpected and contradictory as only to increase our mystification.

"With regard to his fortune," Bers informs us, "Leo told me that he wanted to get rid of it as an evil which burdened him, his convictions being what they were: but at first he acted wrongly in wanting to transfer this evil to another, or, in so many words, to distribute it without fail, and thus cause another evil, namely, energetic protest and serious discontent on the part of his wife. In consequence of this protest he proposed to her to transfer it all to her name, and when she declined he made the same offer, but without success, to his children."

"On one occasion," we are told by another witness, M. Sergyéenko, in *How Count Tolstoy Lives and Works*, "he met in the street a stranger, and had a talk with him. It turned out that this man was a bachelor, dining where the fancy took him, and able at all times, if he willed, to be as solitary in Moscow as on a desert island." In relating this encounter, Leo added, with a smile, "And I envied him so much that I am quite ashamed to own it. Just think that man can live *just as he pleases*, without doing harm to a soul! That, indeed, is happiness!" What is this? What was there to smile at? What was the smile like? And what a curious hidden bitterness there seems to me to have been in it!

And here is something still stranger, even what we may call a painful admission.

"I shall look for my friends among the peasants. No woman can stand to me in the place of a friend. Why do we deceive our wives by pretending to consider them our best friends? For it certainly is not true."[1]

Did he say that, too, with a smile? Is that, too, a joke? The happiest father of a family, the modern representative of the Old Testament patriarchs, Abraham, Isaac and Jacob, who had lived with his wife thirty-seven years, soul to soul, suddenly at the end of his life envies the freedom of a bachelor, as if this family life were a secret slavery, and gives an almost total stranger to understand that he does not consider his wife worthy the name of a friend. And the very same witness, who, just before, had glorified the domestic felicity of Tolstoy, in the same work, over and over again, with a light heart and imperturbable clearness, tells us, "However, in their theories of life, they (Leo and Sophia) are at

---

1. Tolstoy also said to M. Jules Huret, "You ask me whether I consider woman man's equal. I reply that I *know* she is, in all respects, morally his inferior."

variance." Well, "theories of life" are the thing that is most sacred to him. And if they are at variance in that point, in what are they at one? Can you evade such a variance by a joke? Yet what Bers tells about the sentiments of the "new-born" Tolstoy is still more startling. "Nowadays, Leo behaves to his wife with a touch of exactingness, reproachfulness, and even displeasure, accusing her of preventing him giving away his property, and going on bringing up the children in the old way. His wife, for her part, thinks herself in the right, and complains of such conduct on her husband's side. In her there has involuntarily sprung up a hatred and loathing of his teaching and its consequences. Between them there has even grown up a tone of mutual contradiction, the voicing of their complaints against one another. Giving away one's property to strangers and leaving one's children on the world, when no one else is disposed to do the same, she not only looks on as out of the question, but thinks it her duty as a mother to prevent." Having said as much to me, she added with tears in her eyes, "I have hard work now; I must do everything myself, whereas formerly I was only a helper. The property and the education of the children are entirely in my hands: yet people find fault with me for doing this, and not going about begging! Should I not have gone with him if I had not had young children? But he has forgotten everything in his doctrines."

And at last came the final, and scarcely credible admission, "Leo's wife, in order to preserve the property for her children, was prepared to ask the authorities to appoint a committee to manage the property."

Fancy Tolstoy declared incapable of managing his affairs by his wife! This is indeed a tragedy, perhaps the greatest in Russian life today, and in any case, in his life. This is that edge of the sword on which the whole destiny of the man, when in the balance, is poised, and we learn all this from casual observers, from people idly curious. And this terrible fact is born deaf and dumb, in the darkest and most secret corner of his life. There is not a word from himself, though his invariable habit has hitherto been to write confessions, and he even now declares that he has nothing to hide from the public.

But how did he come out of this tragic affair? Did he come to feel that he had again overestimated his real powers, that what seemed easy and simple was in reality difficult and complex, and that the "superstition of property" was not a "feeble spider," but the heaviest of the fetters of life, the last link of which is in the heart, the very flesh and blood of a man, so that to pluck it from his bosom means a fearful wound? Or did he realize that great and terrible saying of the Master, "A man's foes shall be those of his own household"?

We know how, in exactly similar circumstances, the Christian heroes of the past ages acted. When Pietro Bernardini, the father of St. Francis of Assisi, presented a complaint to the Bishop, accusing his son of wasting the property and wanting to give it to the poor, Francis, stripping himself of his clothing to his last shirt, laid the garments and his money at his father's feet, and said, "Till now I have called Pietro Bernardini father. But now, being desirous of serving God, I return to you, O man, all that I have had from you, and henceforth shall say, 'My father is not Pietro Bernardini, but the Lord, my Heavenly Father!' And wholly naked, as he came from his mother's womb, adds the legend, Francis threw himeslf into the arms of Christ."

So, too, acted the favourite saint of the Russian people, Alexei, a man of God who had secretly fled from his parents' house. And so, to the present hour, all Russian martyrs have acted, wishing to fulfill the saying of Christ, "Whose leaveth not house and lands and children for my sake, is not worthy of Me."

> *Vlas gave away the last he had,*
> *Till he stood barefoot, naked;*
> *He went to gather alms and gold*
> *To build a house unto the Lord.*
> *And consecrated to God's grace*
> *The exceeding strength of his own soul.*
> *And since that day he is beheld*
> *A beggar, close on thirty years.*
> *He lives upon the alms of scorn,*
> *To keep the vow he made.*

That is what should have come to pass. The great writer of our country should have made himself the champion of the Russian people, a manifestation yet unknown and unique in our civilization, and the religious path once more found across the gulf, opened by Peter's reforms, between us and the people. It is not for nothing that the eyes of men are bent with such eagerness on him, not only on all he writes, but far more on all he does, on his most private and personal concerns, his family and home life. No, it is not mere idle curiosity. There is too much under that roof of moment to us all, to the whole future of

Russian culture. No fear of being too prying ought to hold us back. Has he not said himself, "I have no secrets from any one in the world. Let them all know what I do"?

And what *does* he do? "Not wishing to oppose his wife by force," says Bers, "he began to assume towards his property an attitude of ignoring its existence; renounced his income, proceeded to shut his eyes to what became of it, and ceased to make use of it, except in so far as to go on living under the roof of the house at Yasnaia Poliana." But what does "except in so far" mean? He carried out the word of the Lord, and left house and lands and children, "except in so far" as he still clung to them. He made himself a beggar and homeless, and gave away what he had, "except in so far" as he consented, for fear of grieving his wife, to keep what he had. And what "evil," what "violence to his wife" were in question? Certainly Christ did not advocate violence. He did not demand that a man should take away their living from his wife and children in order to give it to the poor, but He did demand, and most emphatically and clearly, that if a man cannot get rid of his possessions in any other way he should leave, together with his lands, house and property, his wife and children, and take up His cross and follow Him, that, at any rate, he should learn to the utmost the meaning of that saying, "A man's foes shall be those of his household."

But then, that is beyond a man's strength! It is a revolt against his own flesh and blood! And is not the whole teaching of Christ, at any rate taken from one point of view, as Tolstoy takes it, a revolt against our own flesh and blood? Nor did the Lord say that this was easy, or say that to renounce our possessions was as "crushing a feeble spider." He foresaw that this would be man's most binding chain, the last link of which could be torn from the bosom only with agony, that there was no other way he could free himself from it than by trampling on the most vital, dear, and implicit of human ties, by leaving, not only his property, but father and mother, wife and children. And that is why He said with such unutterable, mournful and compassionate irony, "Verily, verily, I say unto you, it is easier for a camel to pass through the eye of a needle than for a rich man to enter the Kingdom of Heaven."

So spoke He, but what says Tolstoy? He is silent, as if his acts spoke for him, or there were no contradiction in the matter, no tragedy—as if everything was as before, easy, clear and simple to him. It is only the strange legend, the biography of this latter-day saint, that answers for him: "*He tries to shut his eyes*, and is wholly absorbed in carrying out the programme of his life. He does not wish to see money, and, as far as possible, avoids taking it in his hands, and never carries it about him."[2]

And he has so far succeeded in making his wife's will accord with the will of God, that of late, Bers tells us, "the Countess has begun to look more calmly on the doctrines of her husband; she has got used to them." So this is the new way of remaining a camel, and of yet passing through the eye of the needle, "not to handle money," "not to carry it about with you," and to "shut your eyes"!

Can it be so? Is not this irony, is it not the worst kind of mockery of himself, of us, and of the teaching of Christ? And if this has any meaning as before a human court, then before God's judgment-seat the question will be at the last, "Has he, or has he not, fulfilled the injunction of Christ; has he given away his possessions?" There will be no evasion: there can be no ambiguity, only one answer—yes or no. We do not know what he himself thinks or feels about it, cannot see the inward side of his life, but the outward we know to the last detail. Thanks to the busy eyes of countless journalistic spies, the walls of his house have become as transparent as glass. We see how he eats, drinks, sleeps, dresses, works, cobbles boots and reads books. Perhaps these trifles, once so important, may give us the clue to the secret places of his conscience. But the more we watch, the further we penetrate, the greater our wonder. It is with special exactitude that the witnesses describe the plenty and abundance, the cup of hospitality full to the brim. One of them puts it, "There is the profusion and solidity of the old-fashioned gentlefolk in the town-house of the Tolstoys." We see this small two-storied private house in the Dolgo-Khamovincheski Pereülok (cross-street), which, of a winter's night, sends the light of its windows far amongst the white frost-spangled trees of the old-world garden. Within there is an atmosphere of cordial warmth, gaiety, and "undefinable, high-born simplicity," the broad staircase, the high, well-lit, rather empty drawing-rooms, devoid of any unnecessary ornament, the antique polished mahogany furniture, the "respectful footman" in dress coat and white tie, ushering in visitors, though it is to be noted that Leo makes no use of his services, for he keeps his own room in order and fetches the water in a cask, not on horseback but on his own back. The study "reminds one, in its simplicity, of Pascal's." It is a small, low room, with an iron pipe stretching across the ceiling. "When, early in

---

2. Anna Seyron.

DMITRY MEREZHKOVSKY

the eighties," says Sergyéenko, "the whole house was rebuilt, Leo would not sacrifice his study on the altar of luxury, assuring the Countess that many most useful workers lived and worked in incomparably worse surroundings than his." But he might have said with much truth that few workers live and work in better rooms than he. Therein is nothing superfluous, neither pictures, nor rugs nor nick-nacks. But experienced workers know that everything unnecessary is mere distraction, and prevents fixed and concentrated thoughts. The iron pipe across the ceiling seems unlovely, but it was specially constructed for Tolstoy on principles of hygiene. Its lamp induces excellent ventilation, and partly heats the worker's study. It insures a constant, gentle current of fresh air and a uniform temperature. What could be better? But the great merit of this room is its quiet. After the house was remodelled, this study, which had remained undisturbed, seemed perched between heaven and earth. It spoiled the side view of the house. "But in the matter of noiselessness and retirement the study had gained greatly." The windows look on the garden and not a sound reaches it from the street. This retreat, far removed from the living-rooms, always inclines to contemplation. Only those who pass all their lives in thought can appreciate at its full value this greatest virtue of a study, the felicity, the deep luxury of seclusion and silence—sole and indispensable luxury of brain-workers. And how rare it is, how hard to obtain in the large towns of today! In comparison with this kind of comfort how barbarous seem the bourgeois contrivances of our degenerate taste, coarse in its very effeminacy, and brutalized to the American level.

Still more pleasant, still more quiet is his workroom at Yasnaia Poliana, in the hush of the old park, with its avenues of immemorial birches and limes, in the noble and patriarchal retreat, one of the most charming nooks in central Russia. This room, with its plain floor, arched ceiling and thick walls, was formerly a store-room. In the hottest days of summer it was "as cool there as in a cellar." Various utensils, a shovel, a scythe, a saw, tongs, and a file give the furniture an idyllic and fresh charm, as of the days of childhood and Robinson Crusoe's abode. These two working-rooms, winter and summer, are two regular cells, quiet and luxuriously simple cells, for this latter-day disciple of Epicurus, who knows better than any how to extract from physical and spiritual existence the purest, most innocent and never-failing pleasure.

And everything in the house, as far as may be, matches the noble, subtle taste of the master—his love for refined simplicity. The Countess does her best to prevent the details of life vexing or alarming him. "All the complicated and laborious work of house-keeping and business is in her charge. She has no helpers."

Meanwhile the household order reigns complete. The Tolstoys' coachman had good reason for saying to Sergyéenko that the Countess was passionately fond of order. "She is untiring, and carries into everything her vital energy, domesticity and good management. She has only to leave the place for a day or two on business for the complicated machine, called a household, to begin at once to creak and jar. She is an excellent housewife, full of foresight, bustling and hospitable. You eat and drink as well at Yasnaia as anywhere."

At the table, always plentiful, moderate, simple and tasteful, special vegetarian dishes are served. This *régime* gives the Countess much solicitude. She is much averse to it, and only allows it in the house as a new kind of cross or thorn in the flesh, so troublesome and complicated is it. But she does not complain, and herself sometimes sees to the getting ready of new dishes in the kitchen. She has arrived at last at making the vegetarian table there so appetizing and varied that the carnivorous Leo, perhaps, never realizes how much it has cost her. Those vegetarian dishes, for all their simplicity, are really more choice than those of meat, because requiring more inventiveness, skill and patience on the part of the housekeeper. And it is certain that if, like Uncle Vlas, he frequented the highways, or, as he advised his eldest son, hired himself out as a journeyman labourer to some farmer, he would be forced to eat forbidden butcher's meat, some herring or Smolensk liver. Instead of that the thin mutton broth which he loves is, of course, scarcely less tasty than the most expensive and complicated soups, compounded by cooks with a salary of a thousand roubles a year, and the barley coffee with almond milk, if not as fragrant as pure Mocha, is all the more wholesome. Add to this the physical weariness, hunger and thirst, best of all sauces, and we think of the bilberry-water with which the old peasant once entertained Levine after mowing.

"'Well, this is my kvass! Good, eh?' said the peasant, winking; and, sure enough Levine had never drunk such liquor as this warm water, with leaves floating in it and the acrid taste of the bilberries. The old man crumbled bread into a cup, kneaded it with the handle of a spoon, poured in water from the bilberry jar, cut the bread up smaller and sprinkling salt on it began to pray, with his face to the east.

"'There now, squire, try my sopped bread' (bread steeped in kvass).

"The sopped bread was so appetizing that Levine changed his mind about going home to dinner."

You see, Tolstoy is a man who knows how to eat and drink better than the spoiled guests of Trimalchio, or the *gourmets* of today.

His dress is just as simple as his food, and far more comfortable and convenient than our own ugly, gloomy and ascetic garb, which confines the body miserably, is not national, and is despised by the people. Leo wears in winter grey flannel, very soft and warm, and in summer loose cool blouses of a peculiar cut. No one knows how to make them sit on him comfortably and easy, except old Barbara from the neighbouring village and perhaps also the Countess. His upper clothes, caftans, touloups (short pelisses), sheep-skin hat, high leather boots, are all carefully planned apparel, suited to drenching rain and dirty weather. Guests, and the members of the family, are often tempted to use these garments. This is the true garb of your village artist in comfort, who happens to live within northern latitudes. There is in all this a certain curious foppery. In youth he lamented his visage was just like a common peasant's. Now he prides himself on the fact. He loves to tell how, in the streets or strange houses, he is taken for a real peasant or vagabond.

"That means," he winds up, "aristocracy is *not* written on the face!"

On one occasion, in *War and Peace*, Pierre Bezukhov, too, you remember, dressed up in peasant garb and felt childish pride in admiring his bare feet, "taking pleasure in putting them in various postures, and scuffling about in the dirt with his big toe. And every time he stared down at them a smile of infinite content and self-satisfaction passed over his face." In his youth Leo dreamed with eagerness of the St. George's Cross and the epaulettes of an A.D.C. Now he is the slave of other subtler, more modern, marks of distinction. But in the long run does it really matter much whether we wear orders, ragged puttees or glittering epaulettes? And he need not distress himself, for aristocracy *is*, after all, written on his face in unmistakable characters, and under the peasant's short pelisse is visible in him the old unimpeachable man of the world. Under this rough external travesty the high breeding is, if possible, more marked and attractive. So, sometimes in the most magnificent Eastern fabrics, the woven foundation is extremely coarse and rough, the more richly to serve as foil to the delicate-sparkling traceries of gold and silken embroidery.

Soft beds, down pillows, he abhors as wearying and stifling. He prefers ventilated leather bolsters. But the Sybarite, tossing sleepless on an uneasy couch, tortured by a crumpled roseleaf, could not but envy the hard yet easy bed of Leo Tolstoy.

The idyllic perfume of manure moved almost to tears one of the most sensitive and sentimental of the spoiled fops of the eighteenth century, Jean Jacques Rousseau. Leo, too, loves its savour. "One morning," says Anna Seyron, "he came in to breakfast straight from a newly-manured field. At that time several strangers were staying in the house at Yasnaia. They had volunteered to improve the yield of the land, in company with the Count. All their boots stank of manure, the doors and the windows of the room were wide open, else it would have been impossible to breathe. The Count looked at us half-stifled women with a quizzical smile." He also likes all fragrances. When leaving the meadow, after mowing, Bers tells he always pulls hay from the hay-cock, and smells at it vigorously. "In summer he always keeps about him a flower, a single flower, but that of the sweetest. He keeps it on the table or in his hand or thrust into his leather belt. You should see with what delight he puts it to his nostrils, and in doing so looks at those about him with a wonderfully dreamy, tender expression. He is also very fond of French perfumes and scented linen. The Countess takes care that there is always a *sachet* of petal-dust in the drawer with his underclothes." You see the method of this enjoyment. After manure, the perfume of flowers and essences. Here is the symbol, here the point of union. Under the peasant Christian's pelisse we get, not a hair-shirt, no; linen, lavendered and voluptuous with eau de Chypre and Parma violets.

That cheerful philosopher in ancient Attica who tilled little garden with his own hands, who taught men to be easily content, to believe in nothing, either in heaven or earth, but simple enjoyment in the sunlight, flowers, a little brushwood on the hearth in winter, and in summer a little spring water out of an earthen cup, would have recognized in Tolstoy his true and, it would seem, his sole disciple in this barbaric age, when in the midst of senseless luxury, coarse, sordid, and barbaric American "comfort," we have all, long ago, forgotten the finer part of pleasure.

The Countess, who has, at last, ceased to quarrel about the giving up of the property, and with a sly motherly smile slips among her husband's linen a *sachet* with his favourite scents, is a faithful and trusty collaborator in this refinement of life. "She learns his wants from his eyes," an observer says; "she cares for him like an untiring nurse," says another, "and only leaves him for a little while at a time. As, for many years, she has studied minutely the habits of her husband, she can see, directly Leo leaves his study, from his mere look, how he has got on with his work and what humour he is in. And if he wants anything copied she at once lays aside all the work of which her hands are always full, and though the sun should fall from the sky yet, by a certain time, the copy will have been carefully written out by her hand and laid on her husband's writing-table."

Even if he seems ungrateful, says that his wife is "no friend of his," and heeds her love no more than the air he breathes, yet she wants no other reward than the consciousness that he could not get on without her for a day, and that she has made him what he is. "The untiring nurse" rocks, pampers and lulls, with care and caresses, like the invisible soft strength in the web of a "feeble spider," the self-willed, refractory and helpless child of seventy.

Does the worm gnaw at his heart? Is he pursued and harassed by the consciousness that he has not done the bidding of Christ, that, while the body is gratified the soul is mortally troubled? His wife says, in the very letter where she speaks of his conversion to Christianity, that he has grown grey and fallen into weak health; has become quieter, more languid. Bers also declares that when he saw Tolstoy again after some years, he at once felt "that the cheerful bearing, which had always been conspicuous in Tolstoy, was now wholly gone. The affectionate and grave tone of his greeting seemed to give me to understand that my present delight was great but that all such delights were illusory."

But no particular importance can be attached to this jadedness. No doubt it was connected with a temporary indisposition, one of those periodical fluctuations to which he is subject, those ebbings and flowings of physical vigour concomitant with his periodical spiritual upheavals. At any rate, Bers says that on the very day of his arrival his host did not maintain the grave mood, the new-found and monastic quietude: "Probably he guessed my sadness at the impression he had made on me, and to the general delight began to joke with me and suddenly jumped on my back as I was walking about the drawing-room." And in this playfulness, which certainly could hardly be expected of a man who wished to show by his demeanour that "these were not real pleasures," his visitor at once recognized the old Tolstoy. No, the delight in life is not yet dead in him, but perhaps bubbling and pulsating with even greater force than when he was a boy.

"It is impossible to depict with adequate completeness the joyous and infectious frame of mind which reigns at Yasnaia Poliana," says an eyewitness, "the source of which is always the host himself. I remember our games of croquet, in which all took part, children and grown-ups. We began generally after dinner and ended with the arrival of candles. I am still ready to look on the game as one of pure chance, because I played it with Tolstoy. The children are particularly fond of his society, and always want to be his partners, and are always glad when he devises some exercise for them. To amuse me he mowed, winnowed, did gymnastics, ran races and played at leap-frog and touch-last." This was some years ago. But Sergyéenko, who describes his life in recent years, says that even now he plays as he used to for whole days at lawn tennis and runs races with the children. It is a constant holiday, like some new Golden Age. "At the Tolstoys'," he goes on, "you always get the impression that the day is one fixed for amateur theatricals and a whole parterre of young people is getting ready for the event, filling the house with noisy merriment, in which, at times, the host joins. Especially if some amusement is got up that requires activity, endurance and skill he will look on for some time at the players and sympathize in their success or failure, and often can stand it no longer, and joins in the game, displaying so much youthful ardour and muscular flexibility that often people grow quite jealous as they watch him." Yes, it is a constant holiday, a constant game, now in the fields behind the plough, now at lawn-tennis, now in the meadows with the mowers, now in sweeping up the snow for tobogganing, now in making a stove for a poor old woman. And his wife vainly plagues herself with speculations as to whether trips of twenty miles on a bicycle can be good for him at his age. Whatever the doctors may say, he feels that this constant and seemingly excessive exertion of sinews and muscles, these constant gymnastics and games, which are still more delightful and pleasant when they can be called "work," are indispensable to his health and existence.

Bers tells us of one game invented by Leo which aroused in the children very lively and noisy enthusiasm. It is called "Numidian Cavalry," and consists in "Tolstoy's quite unexpectedly springing up, and raising an arm above his head, but leaving one wrist free play, while he prances about the rooms. All the children, and sometimes the adults, follow his example, just as unexpectedly." In this old man, who, like a young boy, suddenly runs briskly about and draws even grown people into the game, I recognize him who says of himself, with a bright boyish smile, "I am a merry fellow; I love everybody; I am an Uncle Yeroshka."

In picturing the first dream-like remembrance, bewitching and dark, of his far-off childhood, at the age of three or four, he gives us one of his happiest and most forcible impressions, of bathing in a tub. "I was, for the first time, conscious of and admired my young body, with the ribs that I could trace with my finger, and the smooth, dark tub, the withered hands of the nurse and the warm, steaming, circling water, its plashing, and above all the smooth feeling of the wet ends of the tub when I passed my hands over them." We may say that, from that moment, when as a child of three he first noticed and admired his own young naked body, he has never ceased to worship it. The deepest element in all his feelings and thoughts is just that first innocent, unalloyed consciousness of fleshly life—love of the body. This feeling he gave expression to in picturing the joyful consciousness of animal vigour, which, on one occasion, came over Vronski before a certain meeting with Anna Karénina. "This feeling was so powerful, that he laughed in spite of himself. He stretched out his legs, crossing one over the knee of the other, and taking it in his hand felt the well-developed calf, which had been hurt the day before in a fall, and leaning, breathed deeply several times: 'Good, very good!' he said to himself. He had before often felt a pleasant consciousness of his body, but never had he so loved himself and his own frame."

I fancy that nowhere is this sheer animal delight in physical vigour, familiar to the ancients but now chiefly found in children, expressed with such frank primitive innocence as by Tolstoy. And with the lapse of years it has not only not diminished but actually increased, seemingly set free and refined from all external admixtures. Like wine, it is with him stronger the older it gets. The springtime of his life seems dark and stormy in comparison with this golden radiantly calm autumn. As an Italian diplomatist of the fifteenth century has it about another great lover of life, Pope Alexander Borgia, Leo "is growing young in his old age." When he fancies he is preparing for death in reality he is, as it were, merely preparing for earthly immortality.

> *And if, with this earthly life,*
> *The Creator has bounded our fleeting span,*
> *If beyond grave and coffin*

And visible world nought awaits us—
Still the death of man finds the Creator justified.

"Who has not been in that small wooden house, painted in dark ochre?" says Sergyéenko, lovingly. "Learned men and authors, artists and actors, statesmen and financiers, governors, secretaries, county councillors, senators, students, soldiers, manufacturers, artisans, peasants, representatives of all parties and nations, not a day passes in winter that there does not appear in the Dolgo-Khamovnicheski Pereülok some new personage in search of an interview with the famous Russian author. Who is there that he does not greet, sometimes warmly and sympathetically, sometimes with perplexing questions and accusations? Young Russians and French folk, Americans, Dutchmen, Poles, English, Baroness Bertha Suttner, and devout Brahmins from India, the dying Turgeniev; even the brigand Churkin, rolling about like a wounded beast on his death-bed."

"It is delightful to know," the master said one day, "of one's influence on others, for then one has proof that the fire within is real, else it would not kindle other hearts."

These words remind us of his own confession to another confidant some years ago, "I did not rise to be general of artillery, but for all that I have become a general in literature." Now he could say that he has become general, not only in literature, but in the new social-democratic creed that is spreading through the world. And the second distinction is more honourable than the first. Thus he has managed to combine the most subtle refinement and indulgence of the flesh with glory, the last luxury and gratification of the spirit.

But where is the commandment of Christ as to renouncing all possessions, as to complete resignation, complete poverty, the only path to the Kingdom of God? Where is that bridge thrown over the gulf that has yawned between our creed and that of the Russian folk ever since the days of Peter's reforms? Where is the voice of Russia in the guise of a great martyr? And what has become, alas! of our hope of the possibility of a miracle in the history of Russian culture, of a man, the richest among his fellows not only in material but spiritual treasure, really earning his bread in the sweat of his brow, or, like Uncle Vlas, "bareheaded, in a rough smock-frock," holding out his hand for donations towards the building of a Temple for Russia and the Universe?

This jolly old pagan "sportsman," like Uncle Yeroshka, this rejuvenated Epicurean squire, luxurious in his very moderation and simplicity, with his admiring retinue of American Quakers, representatives of all political parties, "of all nations," Baroness Bertha Suttners, Paul Deroulèdes, governors, students, senators, financiers, *et hoc genus omne*, has lost his way. The man whom, according to his own conscience, he should have followed, was one of whom it was said, in no mere figure of speech, "The whole might of his soul, To God's own cause was consecrate"; the man whom, not only in words, gave away all he had,—

> *Himself remaining ragged, naked,*
> *Throughout the length and breadth of his own land;*
> *Treading in footprints of the King of Heaven,*
> *A peasant, penniless.*
>
> *Full of immedicable grief,*
> *Swarthy, straight-limbed, erect,*
> *Walks he with stately stride and slow,*
> *Through towns and villages.*
>
> *With Image and with Book he goes;*
> *Aye communing with his own soul.*
> *And still his iron-pointed staff*
> *Rings gently on the road.*

It is astonishing with what unanimous sympathy all the biographers dwell on the comfort, warmth and plenty of the family nest that the pair have made for themselves. It may be that some one of them has harboured for an instant some notion of the contradiction between the words and acts of the man who accuses all human culture of inconsistency. But, apparently, it has never dawned on them that the spectacle must be handled warily and delicately, that this plenty which they celebrate, and this lordly, this almost Philistine fulness of bread, this respectable and virtuous household, may have an unexpected effect on those who happen to recollect these words, "One refined life, led in moderation and within the bounds of decency, of what is commonly called a virtuous household, one family life, absorbing as many working days as would suffice to maintain thousands of the poor that live in misery hard by, does more to corrupt people than thousands of wild orgies by coarse tradesmen, officers or artisans given to drunkenness and debauchery, who smash mirrors and crockery for sheer fun."

Was it not his own well regulated and comfortable life at Yasnaia that Leo had in mind when he wrote these words? Must we not gather from them that he feels in his own house as in a den of robbers? Or are these "brave words" only and nothing more?

One of the guileless compilers of the Tolstoy legend, after telling us that the Count, although he has not distributed his fortune yet has ceased to make use of it, "except for the fact that he remains under the roof of Yasnaia," adds, apparently with a view to silencing at once all possible doubts and misgivings in the reader's mind, "They (the Tolstoys) give away every year from two to three thousand roubles to the poor." According to the calculation which in the eighties had such an effect on the conscience of the Count, these two or three thousand roubles would have been equivalent fifteen years ago to the two or three kopecks of Semyon the carpenter, and at present only to one or perhaps half a kopeck, for his fortune has increased considerably of late years; and goes on increasing, thanks to the business capacity of his wife, who, "on the advice of a friend," as Anna Seyron tells us, "has begun to make a profit out of the Count's writings." Things go so well with her that his former publishers, out of jealousy, are trying to stand in her way, but she fights them vigorously. This makes the Count's position really interesting. His religious conviction is "that money is harmful, and the root of all evil. Who gives money, gives a bad thing." And now, suddenly, a new gold mine has been discovered in his own publications. At first he refused to listen when there was talk of money in connexion with his books. He assumed a look of consternation and suffering. But the Countess firmly stood her ground in order to secure the future of the children. The former state of things could not go on when the family increased and the expenses with it.

It was just at this juncture that Leo "tried to shut his eyes," and "devoted himself wholly to carry out his plan of life," his "four stages." But the more pitilessly he laid bare the contradictions of the bourgeois life of today, the more fervently he preached the fulfilment of the law of Christ, renunciation of all one's possessions, the better Sophia's publications spread, and the more income poured in. Thus the doctrine that seemed a danger has happily only furthered the financial prosperity of the family.

Sergyéenko tells us that on one occasion Leo's father, being sent in 1813, after the blockade of Erfurt, to St. Petersburg with despatches, was on the return journey taken prisoner at the hamlet of St. Obi, with his orderly, a serf. The latter succeeded in hiding all his master's gold in his boot, and during the several months for which they remained prisoners, never once betrayed his trust, or was found out. The money made his leg so sore on the march as to cause a severe wound, but he never let his pain be seen. And so, when they got to Paris, his master was able to live in perfect comfort, and always remembered his faithful orderly with gratitude.

On the fidelity of such men as this the entire fabric of patriarchal felicity, the "soberly conducted life of what is called a virtuous family" is based, as on a granite foundation. Does the centenarian housekeeper at Yasnaia, Agafia, remember the occurrence? At any rate she must certainly remember how the old master, Nicolai Tolstoy, otherwise Rostov of the novel, clenching his beef-eating fist, said: "That is the way to keep the peasant whelps in order." This is the same Agafia who, touching the childhood of the young master, relates that he was "a good child, only of weak character," and when she heard of his new eccentricities, only laughed a strange laugh. It was a slyer and subtler smile that I saw on the face of Vasili Sintaev, the peasant of Tver, also an advocate of the gospel of poverty, and one of the cleverest men in Russia, with whom I chanced to discuss Tolstoy, not long after the latter had paid Sintaev a visit. I venture to imagine that some such smile must, at times, flit over the face of the Countess, though long since resigned and grown used to the doctrines of her husband.

Yes, you grandfathers and great-grandfathers, grandmothers and great-grandmothers, whose ancient portraits look down from the walls of the pleasant country house at Yasnaia, with that gaze of solicitude peculiar to ancestors,—"If only all is well at home!" You may set your minds at rest; all *is* well at home, all as it was of old, as it was in your own day, is now, and shall evermore be. The famous "four stages" have not proved so terrible as might at first have been thought. While Leo is resting from a bicycle ride or peasant work in the fields, or lawn-tennis, or fixing up a stove for a poor old woman, the Countess sits up all night over the proof-sheets of a new edition, "a new goldmine," part of which was kept to some purpose for the master in that faithful orderly's boot, and the faces of the ancestors retain their benignant condescension in their faded frames.

"On one occasion, in my presence there came to see him," relates Bers, "a sick and weather-beaten peasant to ask for wood to build a shed. At his invitation we took our axes and in a few minutes had felled several trees in the wood on the estate, lopped the branches, and tied the beams to the peasant's cart tail. I confess that I took great pleasure in doing this. I felt a new thrill, perhaps due to Leo's influence, perhaps partly because it was a small service to a really sick, exhausted and needy fellow-creature. The peasant, with his humble look, stood apart meantime. Leo certainly noticed my delight and purposely left much of the work to me, and I felled almost all the trees, as if wanting in that way to conceal my novel sensations. When we had sent the man away, Leo said: 'Is it possible to doubt the need for, and satisfaction in doing, such acts?' And in fact, can one doubt it? But why did the man stand there all the same, looking humble and distressed, while the gentlemen were rejoicing in their own well-doing? What did he want more? What did he expect? Was it the usual charity in money? He must have been well aware that Tolstoy does not carry money on his person. Or was the sick man simply cold and sick and tired of waiting till the gentlemen had done their work? How surmise what mocking and ungrateful thoughts are streaming through the mind of a peasant while gentlemen are taking a particular pleasure in helping him? Men in general, and the tenants at Yasnaia in particular, are given to mockery and ingratitude."

"The most of them," he himself admits, "look on me as a horn of plenty, and nothing else. Can one expect any other attitude? Their life and ideas were framed ages ago under the stress of circumstances. Can one man change all this singlehanded?"

This argument is, however, identical with the Countess's retort when the property was to be distributed. "I cannot throw the children penniless on the world, when no one else wants to follow your example." This is the main and irrefutable argument of "the Prince of this World," that weighty logician who lulls us in heathen indifference, to whom it is due that Christianity, in the course of nearly twenty centuries, never advances: "If one man cannot change all this, why not let things go on as they are?" This is that paltry neutrality in which our democratic and Philistine world comes to a standstill, drags its feet, and finds the web of "the feeble spider of property" an iron chain. To our "safely" Christian feelings speaks the angel as to the church of Laodicea: "Would thou wert either hot or cold; but since thou art but lukewarm, I will spue thee out of my mouth."

"I have given you what I could, and can do no more," says Tolstoy, the apostle, with a touch of bitterness to the applicants that surround him.

We were making our way through the garden, when a peasant with a scrofulous child stopped us. Leo halted. "What is it?"

The man pushed forward the boy who, after various confused pretexts, drawling out the words, begged of him, "Gi-ive me the fo-o-oal."

I felt awkward, and did not know which way to look.

Leo shrugged his shoulders. "What foal?" What nonsense! I have got no foal."

"Yes, there is!" declares the peasant, pushing quickly forward.

"Well, I know nothing about it. Be off, in God's name!" answers Leo, and after going a few steps, jumps briskly over a ditch.

But is Tolstoy absolutely certain that he has no foal?

In *Childhood and Boyhood* he tells us how, on one occasion, having forgotten to confess one of his sins to the priest, he went to make a fresh confession. Going home from the monastery in a cab he felt an agreeable self-satisfaction and pride in his own piety. And he felt he must talk and share the feeling with somebody. But as no one was at hand except the cabman, he clambered to the box seat, and described to him these fine emotions.

"Really!" said the man incredulously, and for a long while after he sat stock still. I thought he was thinking of me, what the priest thought, "What an incomparably good young man!" But suddenly he turned round and said, "And what, sir, may be your honour's occupation?"

"What?" asked I.

"Your occupation, your honour's occupation?" he repeated, mumbling his toothless lips.

"Well, he evidently doesn't understand me," I thought, and talked to him no more till we arrived at the house.

"I blush even now," he adds, "when I remember the occurrence."

It strikes one that the sick serf who looked on in humiliation and vexation at the good gentlemen felling trees for him with their own hands, and the unabashed peasant who asked Tolstoy for the non-existent foal, might have inquired, like the cabman, "And what, sir, is your honour's occupation?"

But Tolstoy fulfils the commandment of Christ by retorting to this inquiry about property—that spider so easily crushed—"What? I know nothing about it; be off, in God's name! Be off!"

An eye-witness declares that whatever Tolstoy may do he never appears ridiculous. We remember the moment when, to evade that unfortunate peasant, with an agility wonderful in an old man of seventy, he jumped the ditch, and we have our doubts. I am only too well aware that in such an act there is, not only a ridiculous, but a pitiful element, and one terrible, both to himself and to us all. As is almost always the case in the life of today, the piteously ridiculous is also the dreadful.

Is it not dreadful that even this man, who has utterly thirsted for truth, who has so remorsefully found fault with himself and others, should have admitted such a crying deception to soul and conscience—such a monstrous anomaly? Despite all appearances, the smallest and the strongest of the devils, the latter-day Devil of Property, of Philistine self-content and neutral pettiness, has won in this man his last and greatest victory.

If the Tolstoy legend had been concocted in the twilight of the Middle Ages, we might have taken that importunate peasant who demanded an impossible foal, for some shape assumed by the Fiend. And when the Count ran away from him, the Tempter must have grinned and muttered one of his favourite remarks, "Don't you know that I, too, am a logician?"

V

"You are a king, live alone!" soliloquized Pushkin; but in spite of spiritual solitude, he always lived in a larger circle of friends than belonged to any other writer. His capacity for sudden and incautious friendship was astonishing, as was his simple and easy intercourse with all men, great and small: with Gogol and Arina Rodionovna, the Emperor Nicholas, Baratynski, Delvig, Yazykov, and Lord knows who else—almost any one who came to hand.

> *Thou lovedst to come stooping from thy zenith,*
> *To hide thee in the shadows on our plains;*
> *Thou lovedst sky-thunder, and yet lovedst too*
> *The murmur of the bees in the red rose.*

How much he had of unaffected forgiveness and condescension towards smaller men! And there is towards rich and great no shade of envy, self-interest, or malice. With what frankness he shows us his heart! With what regal generosity, nay, prodigality! He seems, in all his nature, like others, a good little Pushkin. He seems like others to the core; "that dear, good fellow, Pushkin." Scarcely one of his friends suspects his awful greatness, his hopeless solitariness. It was suddenly manifested only just before his death, when he could say to himself with quiet bitterness, "You are a king, *die* alone!"

And Goethe, yet more lonely than Pushkin, knew how to "drop to the shadow of the low plain" from the icy summits where the Eternal Mothers dwell, to make friends with Schiller, the fiery and the earthly.

In Tolstoy's life we are struck by a peculiar loneliness, not that proper to genius, but another—social, terrestrial, and human. He has won for himself almost all that a man can win, except a friend. His relations with Fet cannot be called friendship, for he contemplates him too much from above. And how could Fet be a friend to him? Their intercourse is rather the intercourse of the chiefs of two gently-born and landed families, no more. All his life Tolstoy has had about him mere relatives, admirers, observers, or observants, and latterly, disciples, these last being really farther away from his soul than any. As the years go on this reasoned and calculated aloofness, this cautiousness in affection, this complete incapacity for friendship, increase. Only once did Fate, as if putting it to the touch, send him a worthy and illustrious friend, and Tolstoy himself repelled, or at least failed to retain him. That friend was Turgeniev.

Their relations form one of the strangest psychological riddles in the history of Russian literature. Some mysterious force attracted them, time after time, towards one another, but when within a certain distance impelled them apart, only to draw them together again later. They were mutually disagreeable, almost intolerable, and at the same time most closely akin. They were more necessary to each other than other men, yet could never meet in peace. Turgeniev was the first to recognize and welcome in Tolstoy a great national writer. "When this new wine settles, we shall get a vintage fit for the gods," he wrote as early as 1856 to Drujinin. And upwards of twenty years later he wrote to Fet: "The name of Tolstoy is beginning to acquire European celebrity; we in Russia have long since known that he was peerless." "The opinion of a man whom I do not love," owns Tolstoy, "is dear to me, and that the more, the more I grow in stature; I mean the opinion of Turgeniev." "When we are apart, although this sounds strange enough," he writes to Turgeniev himself, "my heart flies to you as to a brother. In a word, I love you; of that there is no doubt." Grigorovich tells us of the soirées of the *Contemporary* in Nekrasov's rooms in the fifties, "Tolstoy lies full length on a morocco sofa in the central reception room, and snorts himself into a rage, while Turgeniev, parting the tails of his short cutaway and sticking his hands in his pockets, keeps striding to and fro through the three rooms." To prevent a catastrophe, Grigorovich goes up to Tolstoy.

"My dear fellow, don't excite yourself, you know how he appreciates and loves you."

"I will not let him insult me," says Tolstoy, with dilating nostrils. "There he is now, parading up and down past me on purpose, and kicking his democratic heels."

At last the catastrophe which Grigorovich had reason to fear came to pass at Stepanovka, Fet's place, in 1861, a quarrel about some trifle[1] which nevertheless nearly led to a duel. Turgeniev was to blame, for he lost his temper and spoke too strongly. Tolstoy was right, as

---

1. Another account says: "This furious quarrel arose out of a cynical remark made by Tolstoy when he heard that Turgeniev had engaged an English governess to teach his natural daughter. Turgeniev challenged him, and Tolstoy avoided a duel by apologizing."—ED.

DMITRY MEREZHKOVSKY

unexceptionable in attitude as in most of his social relationships, and in spite of apparent heat, inwardly cool, reserved and self-controlled. For all that, strange as it may seem, the culpable Turgeniev makes a better figure in the dispute than the correct Tolstoy; for he at once came to himself, and in a manly, simple and magnanimous way retracted his words. Tolstoy took, or wanted to take, this retraction for cowardice.

"I despise this man," he wrote to Fet, knowing that his words would be repeated to his opponent.

"I felt," owned Turgeniev, "that he hated me, and cannot understand why he is always appealing to me. I should have kept away from him as before; but I tried to make advances, and this almost brought us to a duel. I never liked him, and don't know why I was blind to all this before."

It seemed as if all was finally at an end between them. But lo, seventeen years after, Tolstoy is again making the first advance to the other, again "appealing" to him, and offering to make it up. Turgeniev at once responded with joyful alacrity, as if he had himself desired, and been waiting for the reconciliation. He met Tolstoy like one of his nearest and dearest, after a long and enforced separation, and his last thought was given to this "friend."

"Dear and beloved Leo Nikolaievitch," wrote Turgeniev, "I have not written to you for a long time, for I lay and lie (in two words) on my death-bed. I cannot get well; that is not to be thought of. But I write in order to tell you how glad I am to have been your contemporary, and to make my last earnest request. My friend, return to literary work. This talent of yours has come down from whence all else comes. Oh! how happy should I be could I believe that my entreaty would prevail with you. My friend, our great national writer, grant my request!"

In these words there is a tacit fear for Tolstoy, a silent disbelief in his conversion to Christianity. The public action of Tolstoy did not respond to the appeal of Turgeniev. And who knows, this letter may have wounded him, full as it was of that sincerity with which men speak on the verge of the grave. It may well have been more painful than any of their former encounters. Did he not repeat in his heart, with revived dislike and the vain desire to be contemptuous, "I despise this man"? For it has always so happened in those crises, when we might expect frank, high-minded and decisive utterance. He shut his ears to the last prayer of his friend and adversary.

Turgeniev once passed a profound and penetrating judgment on Tolstoy: "His chief fault consists in the absence of *spiritual freedom*."

Of the character Levine, who, as he clearly saw, is the double of Tolstoy, Turgeniev wrote to a friend, "Could you for a moment entertain the idea that *Levine is at all capable of caring for any one?* No; affection is a passion eliminating 'self.' But Levine, when he learns that he is beloved and happy, does not cease his devotion to himself. *Levine is an egotist to the marrow of his bones.*"

"You have one characteristic in a rare, an astonishing degree—candour," remarks Nekhliudov to Irteniev.

"Yes," agreed Irteniev, not without secret satisfaction; "I always say precisely the things I am ashamed to say."

But it is a strange effect that the "candour" of Tolstoy produces, if you penetrate into it a little deeper. This candour enables him the better to conceal the inmost recesses of his soul, so that the more frank he appears the more secretive he is. He always confesses the things that he is ashamed of, with the exception of the chiefest and most dread secret of all. That he never mentions to anybody, not even himself. Turgeniev was the only man with whom he could not, as with others, be either silent or guardedly outspoken. Turgeniev saw too clearly that he could never care for any one but himself, and that in this lay the last shame, the last dread which he nowhere dares confess. In this too great perspicacity of Turgeniev's lies the cause of that enigmatical force, now attractive, now repellent, which played such strange tricks with the pair. Like two mirrors set opposite each other, reflecting and fathoming each other to infinity, both feared the too clear view of their own latencies.

Not less noticeable are the relations between Tolstoy and Dostoevsky. They never met, but the former was for many years meaning to make the other's acquaintance. "I considered Dostoevsky my friend, and never thought but that we should meet, and as that never happened it must be my fault."

He was always intending, but he never carried out his intention—never found time; and it was only after poor Dostoevsky's imposing funeral, when everybody was talking about him and making as much fuss as if they had just discovered him, that Tolstoy at last joined in the general acclamation, remembered his deferred affection, and "suddenly" realized that this was his "nearest, dearest and most-valued fellow-creature." "It was as if a prop had been taken from me. I was thunderstruck, wept, and am still weeping. A few days ago, just before his death, I read *The Humiliated and Oppressed*, and was greatly moved by it."

It is curious that Tolstoy's emotion did not choose something more worthy of it, say *Crime and Punishment*, or *The Idiot*, or *The Brothers Karamazov*, but he got no further than one of the few mediocre and immature productions of Dostoevsky. Possibly, again, he had not found time.

But there is a more curious passage in the letter of condolence. "It never occurred to me to compare myself with him, never," he declared. "All his work was such that the more he did the better I found it. Art excites in me envy, and so does intellect; but the work of the heart only pleasure."

How are we to understand this? Is Tolstoy too secretive here, or too candid? He owns to envy in general terms, but by no means to envy towards his greatest rival; and in the works of Dostoevsky, the author of *Crime and Punishment*, there is, forsooth, the "work of the heart" and no more. Is there really no more? Is there in Dostoevsky neither the "intelligence" nor the "art" which even Tolstoy might occasionally envy? Or are these in his case insignificant and slight, as compared with "feeling"? Such praise as this is hardly a thing to be proud of. The Count wept, and no doubt sincerely, but those words make one feel unaccountably chilly and ill at ease.

What did Dostoevsky think of the ethical teaching of the master and his Christian regeneration? What did this man, "most near, essential and dear" to him, this inward prop of Tolstoy's spiritual life, think about Tolstoy's holy of holies?

Dostoevsky was the first to point out the coming world-wide importance of the artistic creations of Tolstoy, at that time realized by no one else, and even now not fully understood And he saw Tolstoy's weakness as clearly as his strength. Of Levine he said much the same as Turgeniev did, "Levine is an egotist to the marrow of his bones," only in different words. He asks himself, "What caused Levine to be so gloomy and alone, and to stand aside so surlily?" And he returns more than once to this question, meditating *inter alia* on the so-called "democratization" of Levine and Tolstoy, and their attempts "to return to the soil." Dostoevsky felt that, more than any one else in Russia, he had the right to express an opinion on this point: "I have seen our common folk and known them, have lived years enough with them, eaten with them, slept with them, have myself been 'numbered with the transgressors,' worked with them at real hard labour. Do not tell me that I don't know the people! I know them well."[2]

And he considered that the gulf separating such men as Levine and Tolstoy from the people was more impassable than they supposed. "There is nothing more dreadful than to live in a 'world' which is not your own. A peasant transported from Taganrog to Port Petropavlovsk at once finds there a familiar Russian peasantry, at once falls in with them and gets on with them. It is not so with the man of family. He is utterly parted from the common people, and this is only fully apparent when the gentleman is suddenly deprived of his former privilege, and becomes part of the commonalty. It is not enough that all your life you have been in daily contact with the people, as a friend, as a benefactor and protector; you never learn their real inwardness. Your knowledge is an illusion and no more."

"You must simply do what your heart bids you," continues Dostoevsky; "if it bids you give away your property, give it; if it bids you go work for the common good, do so; but even then, do not do as other dreamers, who must take straightway to the wheelbarrow, saying, 'I will be a peasant.' The wheelbarrow also may be a mere uniform, a convention. It is not essential to give away your substance or put on a smock-frock, that is only the letter and a form; what is essential and of consequence is simply *your determination to do anything as a practical demonstration of your love.* You may candidly admit your own class limitations. All attempts to 'join the people' are merely a travesty, uncivil to the people and humiliating to yourself."

"My doubts have ended," declared Levine, "and in what? He has not yet precisely defined the object of his faith. *Is* it faith? There can hardly be final belief in such men as Levine. He loves to call himself of the people, but he is a gentleman, an average Moscow fop of the upper class, of which the historian is undoubtedly Tolstoy. Such men as this Levine, however long they may live with the people, never become merged in the people; nay more, in many respects never understand them. An impetuous whim, an angry act of will, however fantastic, will not transform him into a common man. You may be a squire, and a working squire, and know a labourer's work, and reap yourself, and know how to harness a cart, yet still in your soul, however you may struggle, there

---

2. Dostoevsky writes on Tolstoy's religious ideas in his *Diary of an Author* (or *Author's Note-book*), which was published periodically from 1873 to 1881.—Ed.

DMITRY MEREZHKOVSKY

will remain a touch of what I think may be called idleness, that physical and spiritual idleness which, despite hard effort, clings to the class by inheritance, and which, in any case, the people see in every gentleman. And so Levine feels now and again some flaw in his faith, and all at once it topples down. In a word, this simple soul is empty and chaotic. Otherwise he would not be a perfect and cultured Russian gentleman, still less an ordinary member of the noble class."

The coinciding judgment on Levine and Tolstoy formed by minds so original and opposite as Turgeniev the Westernizer and Dostïoevski the Slavophil, seems worthy of remark. "He never loved any one but himself"; "an egotist to the marrow of his bones"; "an ordinary Moscow fop of the upper class"; an "empty and chaotic soul," "*fainéantise*," and so on. This seems final condemnation.

It appears that Turgeniev and Dostoevsky are right, but the truth seen by them is limited. Combatants like him themselves, they have not expressed, perhaps have not discerned, the seeker after a new religion in Levine and Tolstoy. For us, farther off and calmer, it is easier to see into this human soul, which is still great as no others are—possibly because we can be more compassionate. And only in utmost compassion lies perfect justice.

Epicurean qualities—qualities of the hunter Yeroshka, of the lounging Moscow fop, yes; but he is profounder than the Epicureans. The basis of his soul, as with all the true men of today, is deep, tragic, and terrible. Look in his face, powerful in ruggedness, the face of a blind subterranean Titan, and you will feel that this is no mere Russian squire of the eighteenth century. Through the radiant joy of living on that face I trace the mark of Cain, or of our age, the mark of secret immedicable anguish and dark pride. And those whom Baratynski called

> *The mighty and gloom-stricken children*
> *Of Poetry's mystical pain*

might at times welcome in him one of their own:

> *"Thou didst drink of the same cup as we—*
> *Of greatness poisoned."*

He has not reached what lies before us, but knows that to what is behind there is no return. He has not made the further shore, nor winged his flight to the further brink of the abyss, but his greatness is seen even in failure.

He has never loved any man, even himself. He has never adventured on that greatest love which is passionless and fearless. But who has thirsted for love with more avidity than he? He has never believed in anything, but who has thirsted for belief more insatiably? It is not everything; but is it not enough? "What though," he says in the *Confession*, "I, a fallen fledgling, am lying on my back and crying in the high grass? I cry because I know that my mother bore me within her, covered me, warmed, fed, loved me. Where is she, that mother? If she deserted me, then why did she do so? I cannot disguise from myself that some one begot me and tended me with feelings of love. Who is that some one?"

I simply do not believe Tolstoy when he declares that he has found the truth, and is for ever set at rest; that now "all is clear" to him. It seems to me that when he says this he is further than ever from God and the truth. But I cannot refuse to believe him when he speaks of himself as a pitiful fledgling fallen from the nest. Yes, however terrible, it is true. This Titan, with all his vigour, is lying on his back and wailing in the high grass, as you and I and all the rest of us. No, he has found nothing, no faith, no God. And his whole justification is solely in this hopeless prayer, this piercing and plaintive cry of boundless solitude and dread. Yes, he too, and all of us, can only dimly feel without as yet knowing how truly pitiful is our plight, deprived of that vast natural and maternal Church, I mean not the Church of the past or the present, but of the future, that which keeps saying, under her breath, to mankind, "How often would I have gathered you as a hen gathers her chickens under her wings, and ye would not!"

How near he was to what he sought! Another moment, another effort, and all would have been revealed to him. Why did he not take that step? What obstacle kept him from the goal of the future? What endless weakness in his endless strength kept him from bursting the last veil, transparent and thin as a "weak spider's web," and having sight of the Light? And now, has he accomplished all that he was destined to accomplish? Has the wheel of his spiritual evolution come full circle? Has he come to a standstill, turned to stone, or will he revive again to undergo the last, really the last, regeneration? Who can forecast the future of this man? Yet more momentous words and actions we probably must not look for from him now.

Goethe says, "Well it is for that man who can make the end of his life tally with the beginning," that is, the old man's "wisdom of the serpent," tally with the "simplicity of the dove" in the child. Will Tolstoy succeed in making them tally? Will the last bandage fall from the eyes of the blind Titan?

In his first book there is a picture of vernal nature after a storm, as it appears to the eyes of a child. "I spring from the britchka[3] and eagerly drink in the freshened fragrant air. Everything is moist and sparkles in the sun, as if covered with varnish. On one side of the road is a fallow field, stretching out of view, here and there traversed by shallow hollows, shining with moist soil and green leaves, and spreading in a shadowy carpet to the very horizon. On the other, a pine-wood, overgrown with nut and rock-cherry underwood, stands still, as if in excess of happiness, and slowly lets fall from its newly washed boughs the bright raindrops on the fallen brown foliage. On all hands crested larks rise, singing gaily, or drop swiftly down: amongst the moist bushes are heard young birds pattering, and from the middle of the copse comes the clear note of a cuckoo. So bewitching is this wondrous perfume of the woods after the spring storm, the savour of birch, of violets, dried leaves and rock-cherries that, springing from the step of the britchka, I rush to the bushes, and in spite of a shower of raindrops, tear down one of the wet boughs of the cherry, beat the blossoms in my face, and revel in their delicate perfume. My boots are drowned in mire, and stockings long since wet through, I wade through the dirt and run to the carriage window."

"'Liubochka! Katenka!' I cry, handing in several boughs of cherry, 'Look, how nice!'

"The girls scream in dismay at the drops and sigh, and Nini calls to me to come away, or I shall certainly get a whipping.

"'Just smell how sweet it is!' I cry."

Will this recollection of his childhood flash before him in his last hours? Will he drink once more that intoxicating perfume, and feel the fresh touch, like a child's kiss, of the boughs against his face? Will he at last become aware that in this endless earthly delight and love for the things of earth lay, for him, the germ of the more than earthly? Will he understand that his indomitable inhumanity—his animal and yet divine love for the body, which he has struggled vainly all his life to

---

3. Carriage.

suppress, was in truth for him all his life as wholly innocent as when he rolled in self-admiration in his tub as a naked child?

Tolstoy's love for himself alone would have been religious, even sublime, if it had continued to the end, had he loved himself, not for his own sake, but the God in him, just as he says he loves the commandments of the Lord, not for themselves, but because they are God's. Will he at last realize that here there is nothing high nor low, that paths diverse, yet equally true, lead to one and the same goal; that, in reality, all paths are one; that it is not against and not away from things earthly, but only *through* things earthly, that we attain the more than earthly, not in conflict with, or divested of, but only through the bodily that we attain the spiritual? Shall we fear the flesh—we inheritors of Him who said, "My blood is drink indeed, and my flesh is meat indeed," we, whose God's "Word was made Flesh"?

Momentous may well be the effect on the world that Tolstoy, (at present, after all, the greatest and most influential of Russians) should, before his death, realize this fact that we have dimly come to understand; that he should find time, if not to write, at least to tell us about it. Ah! we should listen thirstily to his words; should treasure them, though uttered in the last delirium, however weakly and indistinctly they might fall on the ears of others! For to us the spoken word is more pregnant, more essential than the written. What is *said* is, and shall be; that only is written which *has* been, and is no more. Our final truth cannot yet be written down, it can only be spoken and carried out. Will Tolstoy find time? God grant him and us that he may!

VI

Unlike Tolstoy, Dostoevsky does not care to talk about himself. This man, apparently so bold, even cruel and cynical, an exposer of others' hearts, is full of modesty and "lofty shamefastness" about his own. The sufferings he had been through never embittered or hardened, or made him pose as a martyr. He bore himself as if there had been nothing exceptional about his past, and looked gay and brisk when health would let him. A gushing young lady at one of his brother's editorial evenings at length said, "Gazing at you I can trace your suffering."

Visibly vexed, he cried, "What suffering," and began to joke about indifferent matters.

He drew little on his personal experiences, had little self-consciousness, complained of no one, but tried to excuse and ennoble in his imagination the environment from which he sprang, as if to persuade himself and others that his life had been happier than it really was.

"I was one of those to whom the return to the national, the knowledge of the Russian people's heart, was easy. I came of an honest Russian stock. As far back as I remember, I remember loving my parents. The children in our house knew the Gospel from earliest childhood. At ten years old I knew all the chief episodes of Russian history, read aloud to us of evenings by our father. Every visit to the Kremlin and the Moscow cathedrals was for me a red-letter day."

He used to say fervently of his dear parents, "Ah! brother, they were people ahead of their age, and they would still be so if living now. We shall not make such fathers or such home-folk, you and I!"

May we trust these rosy recollections? The father appears to have been exceptionally touchy, impatient, and vehement; "a surly, highly-strung suspicious sort of man."

"I am sorry for my poor father," writes the sixteen-year-old Dostoevsky himself, in 1838, "he is a strange character and endlessly unfortunate! I can't help bitter tears when I think I can do nothing to comfort him."

We get vague hints of the enigmatical and tragic nature of the strange father. The wearisome nature of this father, his surliness, irascibility and suspiciousness, certainly had an effect on the character of his son. Only one of his biographers raises the veil from this family secret, and instantly drops it again. Speaking of the cause of the falling sickness from which Dostoevsky suffered, he writes, "It dates back to his earliest youth, and is connected with a *tragic event* in their family life."

No doubt this incident in the life of a "truly Russian and honourable family," as Dostoevsky has it, must have been truly terrible if, as the family biographer hints, it could cause epilepsy in the child. All was not, probably, as bright and comforting in this boyhood as it seemed to Dostoevsky through the mists of memory. It is his own life that he refers to when he calls the hero of the story "The Hobbledehoy," *a member of a chance family*, in contrast, perhaps, to Tolstoy's, who had such a splendid "Childhood and Boyhood." And it is surely of himself that he speaks when he puts these yet sadder words into his hero's mouth, "The consciousness that in me and with me, however ridiculous and abject I may seem, lies somewhere that jewel of power which makes them all, sooner or later, change their opinion of me, this consciousness, I say, almost from my earliest and most humble years formed the only source of my vitality, my guiding star and solace; otherwise, I might have killed myself while still a child."

Compare his beginnings, merely worldly "chances," with Tolstoy's, the descendant on his mother's side of the Grand Duke St. Michael of Chernigov; and on his father's of Peter Andreïvich Tolstoy, favourite of Peter the Great, Chief of the Secret Chancery and Tutor to the Tzarevich Alexei. Dostoevsky was the son of a staff-surgeon and a tradesman's daughter, born in a charity-hospital at Moscow, the Maison Dieu, near the Maria Grove; sure enough, member of a "chance family." His first impressions were of penury. His father, who had five children, rented an apartment consisting of two rooms and a kitchen. A dark nursery corner for the two elder boys, Michael and Fedor, was carved out of the small entrance-hall by a match-board partition. "Our father," says one of them, Andreï, "used to say he was a poor man, and his boys must be prepared to fend for themselves, for at his death they would be left beggars." In 1838 Dostoevsky wrote from school, "My dear, kind, good father, can you suppose that your son, when he asks you for help in money, asks for more than is necessary? Because of your poverty," he concludes "I shall not drink tea." "You complain of pennilessness," he tells one of his brothers about the same time; "well, we must make the best shift we can. I am not over rich either. Believe me, on leaving the camps I hadn't a farthing, and fell sick of a chill in the rains on the road, as well as of hunger, for I hadn't a *sou* to moisten my throat with a mouthful of tea."

Thus the life of Dostoevsky begins in poverty, which was not fated to come to an end till near on his death, and which depended, not so much on external accidents, as on his own nature. There are people who cannot spend and are foredoomed to hoard; there are others who cannot save, and are congenitally damned to thriftlessness. Dostoevsky, like Goldsmith, "never knew how much he had," either in money, clothes, or linen. A German doctor, who endeavoured to teach his house-mate German carefulness, "found him without a farthing, living on bread and milk, and even for that he was in debt at the little milk-shop."

Fedor belonged to those characters, to live with whom is good for everybody, but who themselves are always in want. He was robbed unmercifully, but was himself so confiding and kindhearted that he would not look into the matter or blame the servants or their hangers-on, who took advantage of his trustfulness. "The very fact of living with the doctor," adds one biographer, "went near to becoming for him a cause for fresh expense. For every poor creature that came to the doctor for advice the doctor's companion was ready to receive as an honoured guest."

Tolstoy relates that in the Liapino Night Refuge he himself sought for folk sufficiently needy to deserve help in money, to whom he could distribute thirty-seven roubles, entrusted to him by wealthy and charitable men in Moscow. This money remained in his hands. He sought, and could not find, such poor. We may say with confidence, Dostoevsky would have had no difficulty in finding them. The innate generosity of Dostoevsky, his proneness to throw money to the winds, is in queer contrast to Tolstoy's equally innate disinclination to the smallest extravagance. The one careful and domestic, the other a profuse and houseless vagabond. Dostoevsky, you see, has no difficulty in believing that money is an evil, and that we ought to renounce property. This victim of poverty dealt with money as if he held it not an evil, but utter rubbish. Dostoevsky thinks he loves money; but money flees him. Tolstoy thinks he hates money but money loves him, and accumulates about him. The one, dreaming all his life of wealth, lived, and but for his wife's business qualities would have died, a beggar. The other, all his life preaching and dreaming of poverty, not only has not given away, but has greatly multiplied his very substantial possessions.

All worldly advantages in Tolstoy are so to speak centripetal, in Dostoevsky centrifugal. The latter felt the presence in his nature of some fateful force, inviting misfortune. He ascribed the cause of his sufferings to himself and his so-called "viciousness." "I have a dreadful vice," he owns to his brother, "boundless vanity and ambition." "I am as sensitive as if I had been flayed, and the very air hurts me," says the hero of *Notes from a Cellar,* who, in many respects, resembles Dostoevsky himself. "A few days ago Turgeniev and Bielinski found fault with me for my irregular life." "I am wrong in the nerves, and suffer from a nervous fever of some kind; I cannot live regularly, so Bohemian am I." There is scarcely real penitence in such admissions. But we find some sad and surprising self-criticisms. "The devil knows," he say in one place, "that if what is good is given to me, I infallibly spoil it by my vile disposition." And again, many years later, referring to a loss at roulette at Baden, "In all places and things I have crossed the last limits." Our age, which is afraid of "last limits," could not forgive Dostoevsky and punished him contemptuously and pitilessly. In this respect, as in many others, he is a man of another age, and born out of due time. As for Tolstoy, is it not noticeable that in spite of all the apparent passionateness of his impulses in the field of speculation, never in real life or in his actions did he "take the last plunge, or "overstep the mark"?

Dostoevsky led off with a success, the novel *Poor Folk.* "Am I really so remarkable?" he thought in a sort of timid enthusiasm, with regard to the impression made by this book (by a youth of twenty) on the critics Nekrasov and Grigorovich. "I will be worthy of these men's praise! For what men, what men they are! I will deserve it, and even to become as fine a fellow as they."

His next story, *The Double,* came to grief. Friends turned away from him, feeling that they had made a mistake in taking him for a different man. Fate's irony sent him a momentary success in order to aggravate subsequent disaster.

From that time his literary career was a life-long and desperate struggle with what is called "Russian public opinion," and with the critics. And how petty and disproportionate, how accidental to us (who are beginning to realize the true merits of this writer) seems the fame which came to him not long before his death, especially as compared with the life-long fame of Tolstoy!

"Give me the good, aud I shall infallibly turn it into bad by my disposition." The truth of this self-criticism was seemingly proved with special palpableness in the Petrachevski affair, for which he paid so dearly. The Petrachevski circle or club, was a group of young men whose aims were not so much revolutionary or political as socialistic. They held the doctrines of Fourier.

The following account of the incident is given by M. Waliszewski in his excellent *History of Russian Literature:* "Dostoevsky's special function in connection with it (that is, the club), was to preach the *Slavophil doctrine,* according to which, Russia, sociologically speaking, needed no Western models, because in her *artels* (workman's guilds) and her system of mutual responsibility for the payment of taxes (*Krougovaia Porouka*), she already possessed the means of realizing a superior form of social arrangement. One evening he, Dostoevsky, had gone so far as to declaim Pushkin's *Ode on the Abolition of Serfdom,* and when, amid the enthusiasm stirred by the poet's lines, some one present expressed a doubt of the possibility of obtaining the desired reform except by insurrectionary means, he is said to have replied, "Then insurrection let it be!" No further accusation was brought against him, but this sufficed. On December 22, after eight months' imprisonment, he was conducted, with twenty-one others to a public square where a scaffold had been erected. The prisoners were all stripped to their shirts (there were twenty-one degrees of frost) and their sentence was read out: they were condemned to death. Dostoevsky thought it must be a horrible dream. He had only just calmly communicated a plan of some fresh literary composition to one of his fellow-prisoners. "Is it possible that we are going to be executed?" he asked. The friend to whom he had addressed the inquiry pointed to a cart laden with objects which, even under the tarpaulin which covered them, looked like coffins. The registrar descended from the scaffold, and the priest ascended it, cross in hand, and exhorted the condemned men to make their last confession. One only, a man of the shop-keeping class, obeyed the summons,—the others were content with kissing the cross. In a letter addressed to his brother Michael Dostoevsky has thus related the close of the tragic scene. "They snapped swords over our heads, and they made us put on the white shirts worn by persons condemned to death. Thereupon we were bound in threes to stakes, to suffer execution. Being the third in the row, I concluded I had only a few minutes to live before me. I thought of you, and of your dear ones, and I contrived to kiss Plétchéeiv and Dourov, who were next to me; and to bid them farewell. Suddenly the troops beat a tattoo, we were unbound, brought back upon the scaffold, and informed that his Majesty had spared our lives." The Tzar had reversed the judgment of the military tribunal, and commuted the penalty of death to that of hard labour. The cart really contained convict uniforms, which the prisoners had at once to put on. One of them, Grigoriev, had lost his reason.

Dostoevsky was more fortunate. He was always convinced that, but for this experience, he would have gone mad. "By a singular process of reaction," (continues M. Waliszewski) "the convict prison strengthened him, both physically and morally. The Muscovite nature, full of obscure atavism, the inheritance of centuries of suffering, has an incalculable power of resistance. At the end of four years, the horrible 'House of the Dead' opened its gates, and the novelist returned to ordinary life, stronger in body, calmer in nerve, better balanced in mind. He had still three years to serve in a regiment as a private soldier. When these were over, he was promoted to the rank of officer, and allowed to reside, first at Tver, and then at St. Petersburg."

It is difficult to imagine what exactly led him to mix himself up with socialism. The dreams of the Socialists were not only absent, but alien to his nature. He said that "life in a Fourieristic Commune or *phalanstère*, seemed to him more dreadful and repulsive than any convict prison." If we compare his evidence on the trial with what he afterwards gave to the world voluntarily, it will be scarcely possible to suspect the sincerity of his contention that he belonged to no socialistic organization, being convinced that their establishment, whether in Russia or France, would entail inevitable ruin.

What chiefly turned him against Socialism, although obstinately endeavouring, like his contemporaries, to manage things on earth without God, and without religion, was the moral materialism of socialistic doctrine. From the evidence of an eyewitness, Petrachevski must have repelled him by the fact that he was "an atheist, and laughed at all belief." Precisely in the same way, the frivolous attitude of Bielinski towards religion awoke in him that unbridled blinding hatred, which during many years blazed up in him every time with renewed violence, when he thought of Bielinski as what he called "the most putrid and shameful manifestation of Russian life" (Letter to Strakhov, from Dresden, May 30, 1871). In his *Diary* for 1873 he very maliciously and subtly reproduces Bielinski's story, apparently sarcastic, but in reality in the highest degree simple-minded; to say no more about their philosophical discussions, in which the Russian critic endeavoured to convert the future author of *The Idiot* to atheism. "Every time," says Bielinski, "that I speak of Christ in that way his whole face changes, as if he wanted to cry. 'Why, believe me, you simple-minded man,' he again attacked me," records Dostoevsky—"believe that your Christ, if he had been born today, would have been the most unremarkable and ordinary of men, so utterly would he have broken down before modern science and the present movers of humanity." "That man spoiled my Christ for me," he suddenly breaks out thirty years later, as if the talk had taken place only the day before, and full of vehement reproach. "That man spoiled my Christ for me, though he never was capable of placing himself and the leaders of the world side by side with Christ for comparison. He was never conscious how much there was in him and them of selfishness, wickedness, impatience, irritability, of paltriness, but most of all self-seeking. He did not say to himself at any time, 'But what are we to put in his place? Shall it be ourselves, when we are so contemptible?' No, he never thought of the fact that he was contemptible, he was self-satisfied to the last degree, and it was a personal, abominable, and shameful insensibility" (Letter to N. Strakhov, May 18, 1871, *v.* his collected works, vol. i. p. 312. St. Petersburg, 1883).

And so, if anybody ever was guiltless of the atheistic socialism of that period, it certainly was Dostoevsky. He became a martyr, and almost perished for what he never for a moment believed in, but hated with all the force of his nature. But what attracted him to these men? Was it not what all his life made him seek out what mas most difficult, disastrous, hard, and terrible, as if he felt suffering necessary to the full growth of his powers? He broke bounds among these political conspirators, playing with danger as he always and everywhere did—as afterwards at cards, at sensual enjoyment, at mystical terrors. During the eight months in the Fortress of Peter and Paul he read two *Journeys to the Holy Places* and the works of Demetrius of Rostov. "The latter," he writes, "took up much of my time."

When the condemned men were brought on to the Semienovski Square and tied by threes to posts Dostoevsky kept his self-command. He was pale, but walked quickly on to the scaffold, "more in a hurry than as if overcome." It only remained for the words "Let go" to be given, and all would have been at an end. But when the handkerchief was waved and the execution stopped, in the words of one of the condemned, "To many of them the news of their reprieve came by no means as a matter for rejoicing: it was an insult," or—as Dostoevsky afterwards put it—"a monstrous and uncalled-for defamation."

The moments passed by Dostoevsky in the expectation not of probable, but of certain death "within five minutes," had on his whole after life an ineffaceable effect. They shifted his angle of vision with regard to the whole world, and he knew something which no man could know who had not been through such moments. Fate sent him, in a certain rare experience, a new standard, as it were, of all that is. It was a knowledge not thrown away. He used it later on to make startling revelations.

"Fancy," he says, through the mouth of his *Idiot*, "fancy torture for instance, and add wounds and physical agony; and be sure all this will turn your thoughts from mental suffering, so that your wounds alone are enough to rack you till you die. And yet the greatest pain is not in the wounds, but lies in this—that you know for a certainty that in an hour, in ten minutes, in half a minute, then directly, then that instant, the soul will leave your body and you will no longer be a living being, and that to a certainty: the great thing is the certainty. So you put your head right under the knife, and hear it coming down on your head, and that quarter of a second is the most fearful of all. Who has said that human nature was capable of bearing this without going mad? Why such shame, so monstrous, unnecessary, useless? It may be there lives a man who has had the sentence read to him, and gone through the agony, and then been told, 'Listen, you are pardoned!' Such a man as that could, perhaps, tell us about it. It was of this torture and this terror that Christ has spoken."

But he accepted his imprisonment with submission, not complaining, not liking others to pity him. He endeavoured to elevate and refine his recollections of his punishment, just as he did those of his childhood, and saw in it a stern but salutary lesson of Fate. "I do not murmur," he writes to his brother from Siberia; "this is my cross, and I have deserved it." But if it was true that he did not murmur, it must not be forgotten how much resignation cost him.

"I am almost in despair. It is difficult to express how much I have suffered. Those four years I look upon as a time of living burial. I was put in a coffin. The suffering was inexpressible and incessant, because every hour, every minute weighed down my spirits like a millstone. In all the four years there was not a minute in which I forgot I was a convict. But why talk about it? If I wrote you one hundred pages you would never have an idea of that time. You must at least have seen it—I will not say gone through it—yourself."

And so if on the whole we may console ourselves with the thought that his sentence was beneficial to him, it was only beneficial in a transcendental sense. Again we encounter mysterious forces, which seem to watch over all the fortunes of Dostoevsky and lead him to a certain goal. His imprisonment was one of the pains of fate which he courted, moulding a soul needed to create what he created—

As a spark-shedding sledge-hammer moulds the steel.

All that Tolstoy dreamed of and aimed at, serious in plan, but play in practice—forswearing property for manual labour, becoming one with the people, all this Dostoevsky had to experience under the crushing vigour of the hardest fact.

The prisoner's short pelisse and fetters were for him by no means merely a symbol. They were his own living death, his own expulsion from the community. How many trees soever Tolstoy felled for poor villagers, it was, as I have said before, less work than pleasure, ascetic exercise, gymnastics. The essence of the poor man's work, physical and mental alike, consists in the feeling not only of moral but of physical compulsion, in actual danger, fear, humiliation and helplessness, of want: "If I do not work, then, in a day, in a month, or in a year, I shall be without a mouthful of bread." This, commonplace in practice, is not at all easily understood by people with such a bringing up as the Count. You, the comfortable, have no means of arriving at a conception of the ache of penury.

Fortunate Dostoevsky! When fresh from the scaffold, in the summer of his first year in prison, some two months were spent in carrying bricks from the banks of the Irtysh to a barrack that was being built, some seventy toises distance, across the rampart of the fort. "This work," he tells us, "actually grew to be pleasant to me, though the rope by which the bricks had to be carried constantly galled my shoulders. But what I liked was that the work visibly developed my strength."

If the consciousness of his growing strength was pleasant to him, yet it was no symbolical toil—not one of the "four stages," or Epicurean sport, or mere exercise. He knew that on his bodily strength life and safety depended, and whether he should or should not live through his sentence. Refusal to carry bricks meant reprimand and the lash; so the seriousness and necessity of the work gave him a love of life.

No need to speculate on casting off property. He was himself an outcast. Tolstoy, on the other hand—you remember his correct but subsequently fruitless calculation—that he ought to have given the old beggar-man two thousand roubles, in order to equal in charity the two kopecks of the carpenter Semyon—was led to doubt whether he had any right to help the poor—a doubt up to now apparently undispelled. For Dostoevsky the convict such doubts could not exist. It was for him not to give, but to receive alms. "It was soon after my arrival at the prison," he says, "and I was coming back from the morning work alone with a sentry. A mother and daughter came towards me—the girl some ten years old and pretty as an angel. I had seen them once before. The mother was a soldier's widow. Her young husband had died in the hospital of the prison at the time when I myself was lying there ill. They came to take leave of him; and both wept terribly. On catching sight of me the child flushed, whispered something to her mother, who instantly stopped, hunted a quarter-kopeck out of her bundle, and gave it to the child. She ran after me. 'There, poor man, take this for Christ's sake!' she cried, stopping in front of me and pushing the coin into my hand. I took it, and the child, quite contented, went back to her mother. That coin I kept by me for a long time."

Tolstoy may indeed have "ceased to make use of his property"; nevertheless we feel that the shame and pride, the pain and pleasure experienced by Dostoevsky when he accepted the charity of that little girl have never fallen to the lot of Tolstoy to experience. Therein lies the vast difference in the thought and intention, the action and feeling of these two great writers.

"At the first service in the chapel," Dostoevsky tells us, "we stood in a dense group right round the doors, in the hindermost place of all. I remember how, when a child at church, I used to look at the common people crowding thickly round the entrance, humbly drawing back before the officer's thick epaulet, the stout gentleman, the lady, gaily dressed but most devout, who always went forward to the best places, and were ready at any instant to fight for them. Yonder, at the entrance, it used to seem to me then they did not even pray as we did. They prayed humbly, zealously, like clods, and as if with full consciousness of their humble station. Now it was my turn to stand in the same place, or not even the same, for we were fettered and in caps, and all avoided us—even seemed to be afraid of us—and always gave us alms. I remember that I actually liked this: a kind of subtle, strange feeling of gratification rose in me. 'Let it be so, since it must!' I thought. The prisoners prayed very fervently, and each of them every time brought his beggar's mite for a taper or put it in the alms-box. 'I, too, am a man,' was perhaps his thought, or he felt as he gave it, 'Before God all are equal.' We communicated at the early service. When the priest, with the cup in his hands, read the words, 'Are ye come out as against a thief?' almost all rolled on the ground, clattering their fetters, and seeming to think that the words were literally meant for them."

Such a trial gave him the right to declare that he had lived with the people and knew them. When, in company with the other convicts, he repeated inwardly, "Are ye come out as against a thief?" he did not contemplate an abstraction, but actually *was* in the gulf, while Tolstoy's moral theorizing was always peeping over its edge.

Dostoevsky's epilepsy was ascribed by him to his imprisonment. We know from another witness that in fact this complaint began in his childhood. In his exceptionally high and refined sensibility lay the chief cause of the complaint. But it developed during the period of his sentence. In the letter to Alexander II, from "a former State prisoner," he writes: "My complaint is increasing. Every attack makes me lose memory, imagination, mental and bodily strength. The outcome of it will be enervation, death, or madness." He went through periods when the epilepsy threatened complete obfuscation of his mental faculties. The attacks usually came upon him about once a month, but sometimes, though very seldom, they were more frequent. He once had two in a single week.

His friend Strakhov adds in his remarkable account: "I once saw one of his ordinary attacks. It was, I fancy, in 1863, just before Easter. Late in the evening, about eleven o'clock, he came to see me, and we had a very animated conversation. I cannot remember the subject of it, but I know that it was important and abstruse. He got very excited, and walked about the room, while I sat at the table. He said something lofty and jubilant, and when I confirmed his opinion by some remark he turned to me a face which positively glowed with the most transcendent inspiration. He paused for a moment, as if looking for words, and had already opened his mouth to speak; I looked at him, all expectant of fresh revelation. Suddenly from his open mouth there issued a strange, prolonged, and inarticulate moan. He sank senseless on the floor in the middle of the room."

"At that moment the face—especially the eyes—suddenly became extraordinarily distorted," begins his own description in *The Idiot*. "Convulsions and tremors came over the whole face and body. An inconceivable sound, like no other sound, broke from his throat. All that was human vanished. A bystander could scarcely imagine but that some one else was crying out from within the man. There was something mystical in the terror caused by that sight."

The ancients called this the "sacred sickness." The nations of the East saw in it also "something mystical"—the gift of prophecy, second-sight, divine or demoniacal. In the history of the great religious movements also we meet with this little-explained malady, especially at the first inception of those religions, at their darkest subterranean sources. In one of his most meaningful works, *The Possessed*, Dostoevsky himself often recurs with obstinate fancifulness to the famous fallen pitcher of the epileptic Mahomet, which had no time to empty itself, while the prophet, on Allah's steed, was girdling the Heavens and Hell. He, too, had felt that "something lofty and jubilant"—a sort of religious revelation for which Dostoevsky sought and could not find words in the moment of his swoon.

In any case "the sacred sickness" had a startling effect on the writer's life. It influenced his whole artistic creation, his spirit, his philosophical speculations. He speaks of it with a peculiar suppressed excitement, a kind of mystic fear. The most conspicuous and opposite of his heroes, the outcast Smerdiakov, the "holy" prince Myshkin, the prophet of the "Man-god," the Nihilist Kirillov are epilepts. The attacks of the disease were in his eyes dreadful interludes, cessations of light, but also suddenly-opened windows, through which he looked into the light beyond. "Then suddenly it was as if something had been rent asunder before him, an unwonted *inward light* dawned on his soul," he says in one of his descriptions. "Dostoevsky many a time told me," records Strakhov, "that before an attack there are moments of an exalted state of mind. 'For some instants,' he would say, 'I experience such bliss as would be impossible in an ordinary condition, and of which other people have no conception. I feel a perfect harmony in myself and the whole world, and this feeling is so strong and delightful that for some seconds of this rapture you might give ten years of your life, or even the whole of it.'" But "after the attack his condition was very dreadful, and he could hardly sustain the state of low-spirited dreariness and sensitiveness. He then felt

DMITRY MEREZHKOVSKY

himself a criminal of some kind, and fancied there hung over him a vast, invisible guilt, a great transgression."

Great sanctity, great criminality, supernal jubilation, supernal dejection, both feelings suddenly combined and blended in a flash, blinding as lightning in the last "quarter of a second," before the fallen pitcher of Mahomet has had time to empty itself, while from the breast of the possessed the awe-inspiring voice is already breaking.

Here we are trenching on what is deepest, most elemental, and unexplained in the nature of the man. All the threads of the skein are tangled in this knot. It seems as if these sudden outbursts of a force inaccessible to our inquiries, but perhaps silently stored in all of us, dormant but expectant, made the bodily integument of Dostoevsky— the veil of flesh and blood (dividing the soul from that which is behind all things)—finer and more transparent than in other men. Through this very ailment he may have been able to discern what is invisible to others.

Here again is forced on us the involuntary contrast with Tolstoy. The sacred and demoniacal sickness of the one is by no means necessarily a mere weakness or poverty, but on the contrary an electric and accumulating superfluity of vitality, a carrying over to the utmost limit of the refinement, acuteness, and concentration of spirituality. Contrast it with the not less divine and demonic superflux of bodily carnality, strength, and health in Tolstoy: with the excess of a vital force, electric and original, as in the other, only differently manifested, differently expressed. In the sequel we shall see that Tolstoy draws his religiousness—not imaginary or falsely Christian, but really pagan— from its depth in the recesses of this carnality, this divine animalism; I say "divine," meaning that from a certain religious point of view the animal in man is sacred as the spiritual. Flesh and spirit are merely opposed in their provinces and manifestations. Finally, they are a unity. The bad old habit of pseudo-Christianity—or more properly, Paulinism—make most men of the present day, even those who have renounced religiosity, depreciate the carnal in favour of the spiritual, the abstract, the rational, the unfleshly, as something lower and sinful, or, at any rate, coarse, shameful, and bestial. There is, however, a profounder stage of religious theory, which is uniting because *symbolical*—for, as I said before, symbol, σύμβολον means unification—to which the flesh is transcendent as the spirit, a theory in which the world of the animal, which appeared dark and base, becomes on a par with the world of the spiritual, deemed so glorious and ethereal, the nocturnal hemisphere of the heavens tallies with the diurnal. Tolstoy, as a thinker and artist, having plunged into the exploration of this world of animality at its farthest boundaries, finds another principle, eternally opposed to it, and *seemingly* contradictory to it—the consciousness of the threatening destruction of the animal entity, or the consciousness of death. And it is here that his tragedy begins; here that first dawns that "cold, white light," to him the light of a new Christian revival, which struck Prince Andrei on the night before the battle of Austerlitz.

"And from the height of this conception—that is, the conception of death—all that before had tortured and busied him suddenly was flooded with a cold white light, without shadows, without perspective, without distinction of outlines. All life appeared to him as a magic lantern, into which he had long looked through glass and by artificial illumination. Now he suddenly saw without the glass, in the bright light of day, these ill-painted pictures. 'Yes, yes, there they are—these lying shapes that have moved and delighted and tortured me,' said he to himself, sorting in his imagination the chief scenes of his life's magic lantern; but now, looking at them by this cold white daylight, the well-defined thought of death, he exclaimed, 'All this is terribly simple and sordid!'"

Thus for Tolstoy the light of death is thrown on life from without, separating and dulling the colours and shapes of life.

To Dostoevsky the revealing light comes from within. The light of death and that of life are in his eyes a single fire, lit within the magic lantern of phenomena. To Tolstoy the religious meaning of life is comprised in the passing from life to death, to the other world. Dostoevsky regards this trivial passage as if it did not exist: he is dying all the while he is alive. Constantly yawning declivities, glimpses of life, the attacks of the "sacred distemper," have refined and made transparent the fabric of his animal life. His soul's dark cottage gives forth rays of inward light. To the first the secret of death lies beyond life; to the second life itself is just the same secret. To him the cold light of an every-day St. Petersburg morning is also the terrible "white light" that Tolstoy saw before battle. For Tolstoy there exists only the eternal antagonism of life and death; for Dostoevsky only their eternal oneness. The former looks at death from within the house of life with the eyes of this world; the latter, with the eyes of the spirit world, looks on life from a footing which, to those who live, seems death. Which of these two views is the truer? Which of these two lives is the finer?

I own that from the first chapter of my inquiry the reader has cause to suspect me of a prejudice against Tolstoy and in favour of his contemporary. As a matter of fact, I only wished to pull back and fairly adjust the rope, too far strained in the opposite direction by the popular Christianity of Tolstoy and of Europe today. This kind of Christianity seems to me one-sided—conceived solely in the ascetic sense and by prejudiced men. But if I have been partial, or even apparently unjust, what has been written is only a prelude: I am going further than this stage of the inquiry, and shall endeavour to penetrate further into the artistic, philosophical, and religious work of the two writers. Hitherto I have compared them as men, from the so-called Christian point of view. But if I had also compared them from the opposite standpoint—the so-called pagan, or what is deemed heathen—then I should have been led to conclude that the life of Tolstoy, with all its inexhaustible freshness, strength, and unfailing earthly exhilaration, is more perfect or fairer than that of Dostoevsky. And lastly, from the third standpoint, the symbolical, reconciling, uniting the two opposite religious poles, do not the two men's lives seem equally, though diversely admirable? They are not completely admirable, because neither the one nor the other has that degree of culture that even Pushkin postulated—the one because of the preponderance of the flesh over the spirit, and the other because of that of the spirit over the flesh. Yet none the less both these lives, equally grand, equally typical of our nation, complete and amplify each other. Each is the other's complement, as if expressly created for prophetic juxtaposition and comparison.

They are like two lines running in opposite directions from a single point and that at an opposite point will meet, completing a circle. They are two prophecies, seemingly contradictory, but really in accord, of some unseen yet foreseen Russian genius who shall be elemental and national, as was the poet Pushkin, from whom both Tolstoy and Dostoevsky derive. He was, it is true, more conscious of himself, and therefore more universal. What we need is a genius like his, all-embracing and symbolic.

Tolstoy and Dostoevsky are the two great columns, standing apart in the propylaeum of the temple—parts facing each other, set over against each other in the edifice, incomplete and still obscured by scaffolding, that temple of Russian religion which will be, I believe, the future religion of the whole world.

VII

When Pushkin[1] died Dostoevsky was sixteen years old. His brother records how "the news of the death of Pushkin never reached our family till after our mother's funeral. Probably our own grief and confusion and the fact that just then the family went out little into the world was the cause. But I remember that my brothers almost went out of their senses when they heard of the death and of all the accompanying circumstances. My brother Fedor himself repeated several times that if it had not been for our family mourning he would have asked his father's leave to wear black for Pushkin."

The death even of his mother did not stifle in Dostoevsky his grief for the loss of Pushkin. Even at sixteen he had an instinct of how living was his bond of kinship with Pushkin, whom he not only worshipped as a great teacher, but loved as a man.

At the same age, Tolstoy, as he owns in *Youth*, looked on Pushkin as on any other Russian writer—merely as "a little book in a yellow binding, which he read and studied as a child." He compares, with shame, his then bad taste with the taste of his companions at the Moscow University. "Pushkin and Jukovski[2] were literature to them. They despised Dumas, Sue, and Fevalle, and judged far more correctly and decidedly of literature than I. At that time *Monte Cristo* and various 'Mysteries' had just begun to appear, and I was reading through the stories of Sue, Dumas, and Paul de Kock. All the most improbable characters and events were to me as vivid as reality. I did not venture to suspect the author of romancing. On the basis of these stories I had even formed new ideals of moral excellence, to which I wished to attain. I must live in all respects and actions as much *comme il faut* as possible. In appearance and habits I tried to resemble the gay heroes of these stories."[3]

---

1. Pushkin (born 1799, died 1837), half a romanticist in Byron's manner, half a realist, was the author of *Eugéne Oniegine*, perhaps the greatest of Russian poems. He wrote it during nine years of a stormy career, ended by a duel. His fame is now at its height.

2. Jukovski was a romantic poet, born in 1786. He died in 1852. He was the natural son of a Russian boyar and a Turkish slave; fought at Borodino. After it wrote a great poem, *The Bard in the Russian Camp*, in imitation of Gray.

3. Tolstoy's *Youth*.

DMITRY MEREZHKOVSKY

Such, respectively, was the artistic bringing-up of Tolstoy and Dostoevsky. No doubt, even at sixteen, the latter realized the coarseness and paltriness of Dumas and Paul de Kock. His literary tastes and judgments were, for a lad, strikingly subtle, mature, and independent. To him national and Western European literature were equally accessible. In one of his somewhat pompous youthful letters from the Engineering Institute he tells his brother: "We have talked over Homer, Shakespeare, Schiller, and Hoffmann. I have got Schiller by heart, spoken his language, raved about him. The name of Schiller has become a household word to me." But he cannot only appreciate Shakespeare and Schiller. These were comparatively accessible to the comprehension of our young people at that day, attracted as they were by romanticism and the Gothic. He also highly values the great French Classics of the seventeenth century, Corneille and Racine, on whom Bielinski afterwards passed sentence so glibly. The boy Dostoevsky does not share the attitude, then fashionable amongst us and inspired by German critics, of pedantic contempt for what is called "pseudo-classical literature." Deep feeling for the most far-off and alien culture is shown by the fact that, while acknowledging the inward artificiality and imitativeness of the French classics, this Russian lad of a "decent Moscow family," the son of a pauper hospital surgeon, is able to revel in the completeness and rounded harmony of form of the Court poets of Louis XIV. "But, Phèdre, brother! You will be Lord knows what if you say that this is not the highest and purest nature and poetry. Why, it is an outline by Shakespeare, a statue in plaster, if not in marble!" Perhaps in all Russian literature there is no criticism of "Phèdre" more compact and exact.

In another letter he defends Corneille against the attacks of his brother. "Have you read *The Cid*? Read it, you wretch, read it, and go down in the dust before Corneille"!

If you take into consideration the deep natural religiousness of Dostoevsky, then the following comparison of Christ and Homer, in spite of its naïve enthusiasm, is striking: "Homer—he may be a legendary personage like Christ, made flesh by God and sent upon earth—may afford a parallel only to Christ Himself, and not to Goethe. Fathom him, brother; really understand the *Iliad*; read it carefully; for confess, you have not read it. Why, in it Homer gave the whole ancient world its organization, its spiritual and earthly frame, in the same measure as Christ framed the modern world. *Now* do you understand?"

And throughout life Dostoevsky kept this feeling for universal, or in his phrase "omni-human" culture, this capacity for feeling at home everywhere and falling in with the vital ideas of all ages and peoples—a capacity which, as he told the world in his last *Oration*, he considered to be the chief characteristic of Pushkin; and he believed the Russian genius in general to be more *universal* in its assimilative capacity, and therefore superior to the geniuses of other European nations. He writes thus to Strakhov in the summer of 1863, at the time of his first trip abroad: "Strange! I am writing from Rome, and yet am saying not a word about it. But what could I say to you? My Lord! is it possible to describe it in letters? I came here at night two days ago. Yesterday morning I saw over St. Peter's. The impression was a powerful one, Nicolai, making a cold thrill run down my back. Today I saw the Forum and all its ruins; then the Colosseum. Well, what *am* I to say to you?"

He had the right to say afterwards that Europe to him was "something sacred and strange—that he had two countries, Russia and Europe. Venice, Rome, Paris, and the treasures of their knowledge, arts, and history were once dearer to him than Russia." And in this sense he, being next to Pushkin *the most Russian of Russian authors, was at the same time the greatest of our cosmopolitans.* He showed by his example that to be a Russian means being in the highest degree European, that is, cosmopolitan.

Tolstoy, although himself an artist of European celebrity, and himself deeply characteristic of Russian nature, is wholly devoid of that capacity for fully absorbing universal culture, which seemed to his rival a distinguishing feature of the Russian. In spite of all his calculated and supposedly Christian cosmopolitanism, among the great Russian authors there is not, I think, another so hampered as he, in his creative power, by conditions of place and time and the limits of his own nationality. All that is not Russian and contemporary is, I will not say inimical, but simply alien to him, incomprehensible and uninteresting. The creator of *Peace and War* (a work meant to be historical) may perhaps on his intellectual side acknowledge history, and even be to some extent acquainted with it. But the imagination of his heart has never felt it; he never penetrated, or tried, or thought it worth while to penetrate into the spiritual life of other ages and nations. The "enthusiasm for the distant" for him does not exist—that inspired realization of history— nor grief for, nor living delight in, the past. Every fibre and root in him is fixed in the present. His only interests are contemporary national activity—the Russian working class and the Russian gentleman. We know that in his youth he was in Italy, but he brought thence no impressions. If we did not know for certain, excluding his biographers, there would be room to doubt that he had ever crossed the Alps. "The fragments of sacred wonders" awoke in him no tremor. "The old stones of wonder" remained dead to him. If on one occasion, *en passant* and with a light heart, he speaks of Michelangelo's *Last Judgment* as an "absurd production," it is not from his own recollection, but from having seen some casual copy.

What seems artificial culture may in reality be just as natural as nature itself. But to Tolstoy culture is always fictitious, and therefore false. This exaggerated fear of the artificial becomes in him at last a fear of all cultivation. Therefore prose seems to him more natural than verse. And forgetting that metrical speech is really more primitive, and that people in their most passionate, their most natural moods are prone, like children and young races, to express themselves in rhythm, he lays it down that all poetical works, being artificial, are therefore meretricious. "Even in his youth he laughed at the greatest creations of Russian literature, merely because they were written in verse," a German biographer of his notes. "Delicacy of form had, in his eyes, no importance; because in his opinion (to which, it may be remarked, he has always since adhered) such a form fetters thought." Nowhere is this absence of sympathy with general culture so clearly expressed as in one of his latest productions, in which he sums up the artistic judgments of a lifetime in the book *What is Art?*

With regard to the new "decadent" tendency, as it is called, he makes a promise of reserve which he does not keep. "To blame modern art because I, a man brought up in the first half of the century, do not understand it, is what I have no right to, and cannot do. I can simply say that I do not understand it. The sole superiority of the art which I acknowledge (as against the decadent school) lies in this, that the art which I acknowledge is intelligible to a greater number of people than that of the present day." But not contenting himself with admitting his failure to understand this art, he judges and condemns at haphazard and pellmell; and tars with one brush alike Böcklin and Klinger, Ibsen and Baudelaire, Nietzsche and Wagner. On the "Mysteries" of Maeterlinck and Hauptmann he expresses himself thus: "They are blind men who sit on the seashore and, for some unintelligible reason, keep repeating the same phrase; they are as real as Hauptmann's Bell, which flies into a lake, sinks, and goes on sounding there." Nietzsche seems to him (as to the most careless of our journalists) a half-witted idiot.

It might seem that to a "man of the earliest half of the century" the artists and poets of former generations who are *not* "decadents" ought to be particularly dear and intelligible. As a matter of fact, Tolstoy dashes down fames undisputed and ancient with even greater remorselessness than the modern and doubtful. Thus he declares that "a work founded on plagiarism, such as, for instance, Goethe's *Faust*, may be very well executed and full of mind and all manner of beauty, but it cannot produce on us a real artistic effect, because it is devoid of the chief characteristic of a work of art—organic unity. To say of such a work that it is good because it is poetical is like saying of a false coin that it is good because it is like a genuine one." *Faust* is to him false coin, because it is too artistic and artificial. The love-tales of Boccaccio he regards from an ascetically Christian standpoint as "a mass of sexual nastiness." The creations of Æschylus, Sophocles, Euripides, Dante, Milton, and Shakespeare, the music of Wagner and Beethoven's later period, he first calls "calculated and un-spontaneous," and later "coarse, savage, and often senseless." During a performance of *Hamlet* he experienced "that particular *malaise* which meretricious works produce, and at the same time, from the mere description of a drama of the chase, acted by a remote tribe of savages, concludes that "the latter is a work of true Art" (vol. xv. pp. 167–168).

To the man of Western European culture such childish blasphemies (which may seem "Russian barbarity," but which, in fact, are the barbarity resulting from the present democratic and pseudo-Christian brutalization of taste in Europe generally) must appear the mere fury of some savage Caliban, shattering Egina marbles or slashing to pieces the portrait of Monna Lisa. But the devil is not as black as he is painted. This Herostratus,[4] who raises his hand against Æschylus and Dante, to whom Pushkin is still if not "a school-book in a yellow cover" yet a dissipated man who wrote improper love verses, bows down in simplicity before Berthold Auerbach, George Eliot, and *Uncle Tom's Cabin*. In the long run, not so much from what he denies as from what he admits, you become convinced that in his *conscious* judgments on branches of art that are strange to him Tolstoy, at the closing of his days,

---

4. Herostratus was an Ephesian, who burnt the famous temple of Diana merely to win notoriety.

has not gone far from his first youth, when he studied Fevalle, Dumas, and Paul de Kock. And, more deplorable still, from under the dread mask of Caliban peeps out the familiar and by no means awe-inspiring physiognomy of the obstinate Russian democrat squire, the gentleman Positivist of the sixties.

Still more startling is the expression by him of this helplessness of self-knowledge in relation to his own creations. "I began to write out of vanity, love of gain and pride," he assures us in his *Confession*. "I, the artist, the poet, wrote and taught, I myself knew not what. They paid me money for doing this; I had excellent food, lodging and society, and I had fame. Apparently what I taught was very good. The candid opinion of the 'set' in which I lived was that we wanted to get as much money and applause as possible. For the attainment of this object we had nothing to do but write little books and papers. And so we did." "That activity," he records, after the religious transformation of the eighties, "which is called creative and artistic, and to which I formerly devoted my whole powers, has not only lost in my eyes its former importance, but has become positively distasteful to me for the unfitting position which it occupied in my life and usually occupies in the minds of people of the well-to-do classes." The testimony of his biographer Bers on the point that from his present "Christian" standpoint Tolstoy regards all his former work as harmful because it describes love in the sense of sexual attraction and violence, deserves all the more credence that this opinion follows perfectly logically from other judgments of Tolstoy on Art. Does he not himself, at the end of his life, when summing up his work as an artist, lay down with the mixture of deliberate candour and unconscious pretension peculiar to him—"I must further remark that my own literary productions I assign to the category of bad art, with the exception of the story *God sees the Truth*, and *The Prisoner of the Caucasus*," that is, with the deliberate exception of two of the weakest of his didactic tales?

Even at the height of his productive period he wished to convince himself and others that he thought much the same about his works as now. "I am entering," he writes to Fet in 1875, "on the tedious and petty *Anna Karénina* with only one wish, to clear the ground for myself as soon as possible, to have time for other occupations." Was this saying sincere? Tolstoy loved *Anna Karénina* when he wrote that sentence, although his love must have been less conscious than Goethe's love for *Faust* or Pushkin's for *Eugène Oniegine*.

In this kind of unconsciousness lies one of the main differences between him and Dostoevsky. Though a great writer, he was never a great *man of letters* in the sense that Pushkin, Goethe, and Dostoevsky were men of letters. They considered themselves not merely the vicegerents but the journeymen of Language. To them it was not only their spiritual, but their daily bread. I mean by "literature" not something more artificial and factitious, but merely more deliberate than the spontaneous "making" of the early poets. Literature to man, however deliberate, is as natural as singing to birds. Culture is not necessarily something at variance with, but educative of human nature. From an abstract point of view culture and nature are one, and he who quarrels with the artificiality of culture quarrels with the nature of man, and with the most divine and permanent force in it.[5]

In Tolstoy's contempt for his own artistic performance there is something dark and complex—something he has never made clear, even to himself. At any rate, in his literary self-appraisement there are queer fluctuations and incongruities. "Never was there a writer so indifferent to success as I," he assures Fet on one occasion. Nevertheless on the appearance of *Peace and War* he asks this very Fet with touching outspokenness, "Write and tell me what will be said in various quarters that you wot of, but above all tell me the effect on the masses. I feel sure it will pass unnoticed. I expect and wish it, so long as they do not curse me, for curses upset me." But in his own words one of the most simple-minded and veracious biographers declares there was always in him "a pleasant consciousness of the fact that he was both a writer and an aristocrat"—a writer indeed, or, in the ancient phrase, a "free artist," but not a man of letters in the same sense as Pushkin and Goethe. All his life he has been ashamed of literature; and, both from the conscious, popular, and democratic point of view, and from the unconscious and aristocratic point of view has despised it, either as something mediocre and *bourgeois*, or something artificial, unholy, and ignoble. In this contempt we have an ill-concealed pride of birth, more deeply seated than might appear at the first glance—a "gentility" self-repudiating, self-ashamed, but frequently visible.

Dostoevsky, on the other hand, loved Literature. He took her as she is with all her conditions, never stood aloof or cast supercilious slurs on her. This absence of the slightest intellectual pride was in him

---

5. "The art itself is nature."—Shakspeare.

a fine and even touching trait. Our literature was the soil on which he grew, from which he never tore himself. He cherished it with a kinsman's love and gratitude. He knew well that when he came before the public and into a literary sphere he was coming out into the square of the market place, and never dreamed of being ashamed of his craft or of his fellow workers. He was proud of his calling, and counted it high and sacred.

As men with the old pride of gentry thought it degrading to earn their bread by manual labour, so Tolstoy, from a tyrannical, lofty, and contemptuous theory of the world, considers it derogatory to take pay for intellectual labour. From youth up, ignorant of want and work, he only shrugs his shoulders scornfully when he hears that the true artist can work for money.

Dostoevsky writes: "I have never sold any of my books without getting the price down beforehand. I am a literary proletarian, and if anybody wants my work he must insure me by prepayment." This man—who has such pride, such sensitiveness that, as he puts it, "the very air hurt him," who valued the "free artistry" not less than Tolstoy himself—was never ashamed to work for money, like a plain journeyman. He speaks of himself as a "post-hack." He writes against time three and a half printed newspaper pages in two days and two nights. "Many a time," he confesses, "the beginning of a chapter of a novel was already at the printer's and being set up while the end was still in my brain and had to be ready without fail next day. Work out of sheer want has crushed and eaten me up. Will my miseries ever come to an end? Oh! for money, and independence!" Such is the never ceasing cry of his life. Sometimes, when exhausted with the struggle with penury he curses it; but he is never ashamed of it. In him there is a peculiar inward pride in the midst of outward humiliation inseparable from the position of a brain worker amidst the commercial society of today.

Immediately after quitting prison, and after a right Christian chastening, he falls into the sin of ordinary and cynical hatred: "I know very well that I write worse than Turgeniev, but not, after all, very much worse; and in the end I hope to write not at all worse. Why should I, when I am so needy, get only thirty-eight pounds, and Turgeniev, who has two thousand serfs, get more than one hundred and fifty pounds? Poverty forces me to hurry, and so, of course, spoil my work." In the postscript he says that he "sends Katkov, the great Moscow editor, fifteen sheets at one hundred roubles (thirty-eight pounds) a sheet—

one thousand and five hundred roubles in all. I have had five hundred roubles from him; and besides, when I had sent three-quarters of the novel I asked for two hundred to help me along—or seven hundred altogether. I shall reach Tver without a stiver, but on the other hand I shall very shortly receive from Katkov seven or eight hundred roubles. That is something and I shall have room to turn round in." The tale is always the same. Endless rows of figures and accounts, interspersed with desperate entreaties for help ("For God's sake, save me!" he writes on one occasion to his brother) fill all the letters of Dostoevsky. It is one long martyrology.

Especially hard for him were the four years from 1865 to 1869, perhaps equivalent to another four years' penal seritude. As before his first misfortune, Fate began with a caress. The paper he edited, the *Vremya*, had some success, and promised a regular income; so that he was dreaming of respite from want, when an unexpected and wholly undeserved punishment fell on him. The *Vremya* was prohibited by the censorship for an article—harmless, but misunderstood—on the question of Polish affairs. This blow, like his condemnation to death, was due to official stupidity. But the misunderstanding almost ruined him. He was now forbidden his profession. The authorities could not see that he was really their ally. Yet perhaps they were right. Perhaps the future creator of *The Grand Inquisitor* was not to them such a valuable ally as he desired to seem. Dostoevsky did not lose heart, but almost directly after the catastrophe of the *Vremya* took to publishing a new paper, the *Epocha*, though without his former success. The opportune moment had been let slip irretrievably. The *Epocha* incurred the wrath not of the Government Censorship, but of the so-called "Liberals," whose opinion had always been, and probably always will be, the inseparable companion and the most exact and faithful opposite, like a reflection reversed, as in water, of the opinion of the Government. But Dostoevsky was the horizon at which these two censures united. Dostoevsky, the idealist logician, the extremist, found himself between two fires—a position from which he was not to escape as long as he dived. He was not only the enemy of the Government, but the enemy of its enemies. The *Epocha* was weaker than its opponents, who were not held accountable. They permitted themselves not only every form of vulgar abuse—calling Dostoevsky "a rapscallion," "mendicant," "a guttersnipe," and so on—but even ventured to hint that the *Epocha* and its staff were dishonourable Government spies. "I remember," he writes, "poor Michael[6] was greatly vexed when his account with the subscribers" was somehow unearthed, and it was made to appear that the editor had overreached them. "They"—his "Liberal rivals"—he recorded afterwards in his diary, "declared me a scribbler that the police ought to deal with."

At this same time his brother Michael, the critic Grigoriev (his dearest friend and collaborator on *The Times*), and his first wife, Maria, all died one after another. "And here am I left all alone," he writes to Wrangel, "and I feel simply broken. My whole life is broken in two. I have, literally, nothing left to live for. Shall I make new ties, plan a new life? The very thought of it is abhorrent to me. My brother's family is left without resources of any kind. They are thrown on the world. I am the only hope left them. They all, widow and children, come crowding round me, expecting me to save them. I loved my brother boundlessly, and I cannot possibly desert them. By carrying on the publication of the *Epocha* I could feed them and myself, of course, by working from morning to night for the rest of my life. There are my brother's debts to pay. I do not wish his name to be held in evil remembrance." And again: "I have begun to print" (the last few numbers of the *Epocha*) "at three printers at once, and have spared neither money nor my own health. I am sole editor, read all proofs, manage things with authors and with the Censorship, revise articles, procure money, sit up till six in the morning, and sleep only five hours out of the twenty-four. The paper has been got into order, but it is too late."

Finally the second paper came to grief. Dostoevsky was forced to own himself, in his own phrase, "temporarily insolvent." Beside his debt to the subscribers, he proved to have a debt of some one thousand four hundred pounds in bills and seven hundred pounds debts of honour. "O my friend!" he writes to Wrangel, "I would gladly go back to prison again for so many years only to pay off my debts and feel myself once more free. Now I am beginning to write a novel under the rod, that is, from necessity and in haste. Of all my store of strength and energy there is only left in my soul an unquiet and turbid wreck akin to despair. With alarms, humiliations, a new habit of coolest calculation, I am also alone. Of old friendships and my former forty-year-old self nothing is left." The most relentless of his creditors, the publishing bookseller Stellovski, a notorious rascal, threatened to put him in prison. "The

---

6. Michael was Dostoevsky's brother and the editor of the review entitled *The Times*.

broker's assistant," he writes, "has already come for an execution." Other creditors threatened the same fate and presented a petition. He had to choose between the debtor's prison and flight. He chose the latter, and escaped abroad.

There he spent four years in inexpressible misery. Of his almost incredible extremes of want—seeing that even then he was the author of *Crime and Punishment*, one of the great Russian writers, and, to more acute appreciators, one of the great writers of the world—we get some idea from his letters to a friend from Dresden during 1869. They merely relate to the most humdrum details, but these are necessary to our judgment of the man. If one does not hear the groans, or see the face of a man in pain, it is impossible to realize his suffering. "During the last half year I and my wife have been in such poverty that our last linen is now at the pawnshop. Don't tell any one this," he adds in a parenthesis, full of reserve and wretchedness. "I shall be obliged directly to sell the last and most indispensable article, and for a thing worth one hundred thalers to take twenty; and this I shall be forced to do to save the life of three human beings, if he delays his answer, even though unsatisfactory." This he—the last hope, the straw at which he catches—is a certain Mr. Kashpiriev, publisher of the *Dawn*, a person quite unknown to Dostoevsky, but whom, nevertheless, he asks for Christ's sake to rescue them by sending two hundred roubles. "But as this, perhaps, is difficult to do at the moment, I ask him to send *immediately* only seventy-five roubles (this to save me from going under at once). Being quite unacquainted personally with Kashpiriev, I have written in an exaggeratedly respectful though somewhat insistent tone. (I am afraid of his getting annoyed, for the respect is overdone, and the letter, I fancy, written in a very foolish style)."

Almost a month later he writes: "From Kashpiriev, so far, I *have received no money*, only promises. If you only knew in what position we now are. You see, there are three of us—I, my wife (his second, Anna), who is nursing a child and must eat well, and the child (a new-born daughter, Liuba), who may get ill through our poverty and die. We must christen Liuba, but have not yet been able to do this for want of money."

The rest consists wholly of details, the tragic significance of which can be understood only by those who have themselves known want. For instance, in the second letter to his brother in April, 1864, he says: "I am not going to buy any summer shoes: I go about in the winter ones."

"Does he" (Kashpiriev), he goes on, "think that I wrote to him about my necessities simply for the beauty of the style? How can I write the novel when aching with hunger—when, in order to get two thalers for a telegram, I have had to pawn a pair of trousers! The devil take me and my hunger! But then she (his wife) is nursing the child. What if she goes out by herself to pawn her last warm woollen petticoat? And this is the second day we have had snow (I am not romancing, look at the papers), and she might catch cold. Can he (Kashpiriev) not understand that *it shames me* to explain all this to him? But that is not all: there is something still more painful. So far we have not paid the nurse or the landlady, and that all in the first month after her confinement. Does he not realize that it is not only me but my wife that he has injured in treating me so carelessly after I myself wrote to him of the needs *of my wife*? Injured, injured! he has *branded* me with his words. Therefore he has not the right to say that he 'spits at my hunger, and that I dare not hurry him.'" And so on—monotonous groans of senseless pain. The business letter becomes a delirium of despair, and moreover unjust to Kashpiriev, who was not responsible, as it afterwards proved, for the delay was due to the stupidity of an assistant at the bank on which the order was made. Dostoevsky's voice bursts forth in shrill, unrestrained excitement, as before an attack of epilepsy.

"And they expect literature of me now!" he concludes in a fury. "Why, how can I write at all? I walk about and tear my hair, and cannot sleep of nights. I am always thinking, raging, and waiting. Oh, my God! Lord, Lord, I *cannot* describe all the particulars of my necessities, for I am ashamed to do so. And after this they expect of me artistic feelings, pure poetry, without bombast. They point to Turgeniev and Goncharov! Let them see the state in which I have to work!"

And such was his whole life, almost to the end.

"I, an artist, a poet, have myself taught I know not what," says Tolstoy. "They have paid me money for it; I have had good food, quarters, women's society; I have had Fame. Literature, just like exemption from service, is an artificial exploitation, advantageous only to those who write and publish—useless to the people." "No work costs the worker so little as literary work."

Well, what if he had seen Dostoevsky, whom he considered a true artist—"the man I most need, the most akin to me"—going to pawn his clothes to get two thalers for a telegram; would Tolstoy's shrug of the shoulders still have been contemptuous? Does not a true artist sometimes crave for money? And how about that narrow-minded division of mental from manual labour? Tolstoy's supercilious feelings and notions on literature, labour and want, are not due to coarseness or callousness of heart, but simply inexperience, total ignorance of real life from a point of view essential to moral judgments.

The striving after perfection, the satisfaction of artistic conscience, are to Dostoevsky a matter of life and death. "Do not think," he writes in the same terrible year, 1869, "that I am baking sweet cakes. However badly and poorly what I write turns out, yet the idea of the novel and the work on it are to poor me, the author, dearer than anything in the world! Of course I am spoiling the idea, but what am I to do? Will you believe it, in spite of its having been written three years I am rewriting that cherished chapter again and again?" After finishing one of the best and most profound of his books, *The Idiot*, he complains: "I am dissatisfied to repulsion with the story. Now I am making a last effort over the third part. If I put things right I shall get right myself; if not I am done for." And before going abroad, when working at *Crime and Punishment*, he says: "At the end of November much was written and ready, but I burned it all and began afresh."

"As a rule I work nervously, with difficulty and much thought," he says; "but I am now working harder than usual, and it upsets me, even physically." In another letter from Geneva: "I must work hard, very hard. Meanwhile my attacks are decidedly increasing, and after each one I can get no judgment out of myself for four days. My attacks now began to recur every week," he records of his last days in St. Petersburg, "and to *be clearly conscious* of this nerve and brain disturbance was unbearable. The plain truth is that my judgment was going. This fact sometimes caused me moments of fury. Some inward fever is burning me up. I have fever, in fact, every night, and every ten days an epileptic attack; I am dying."

"Yet am I only preparing to live," he owns in one of his most desperate letters. "Laughable, isn't it? Fluctuating vitality!" A critic says: "I saw him in the thick of his troubles, after the suppression of his paper, after his brother's death, and while being hunted for debt he never lost heart. It is impossible to imagine circumstances which would have crushed him. His terrible susceptibility made self-control difficult, and he generally gave full play to his feelings. Perhaps this made life possible." "My fluctuating vitality seems exhaustless," he says in an early letter, and on the eve of death he might have repeated, in the words of one of his characters: "I can bear everything, any suffering, if I can only keep on saying to myself 'I live; I am in a thousand torments, but I live. I am on the pillar, but I exist. I see the sun, or I do not see the sun, but I know that it is. And to know that there *is* a sun, that is life enough.'"

And in these same four years, overwhelmed by the deaths of his friend, brother, and wife, harassed by creditors, the authorities, and the "Liberals," misunderstood by his readers, in solitude, poverty, and sickness, he composes one after the other his greatest productions—in 1866 *Crime and Punishment,* in 1868 *The Idiot,* in 1870 *The Possessed*—and plans *The Brothers Karamazov.* From all that he created, however large in scope, it is evident that it is nothing to what he could have created under different social conditions. "Assuredly," says Strakhov, who was intimately acquainted with his inner history, "he wrote only a tenth part of the stories which he for years had planned. Some of them he told orally in detail, and with great *verve*, and of subjects which he had not had time to work out he had no end."

He was not a mere man of letters, but a true hero of the literary calling. Yes, in that life, whatever mistakes and weaknesses there may have been, were moments crowned with heroic achievement and sanctity. "I am convinced," says Tolstoy, in speaking of the men of letters with whom he was brought in contact in his youth"—(Dostoevsky was not, although he might have been, among them)—"I am convinced that almost all these authors were immoral men, worthless in character, self-confident and self-satisfied, as only men can be who are wholly pious, or ignorant of what piety is. When I remember the time and my then frame of mind, and that of those people, I feel sick, sorry: just the feeling which one experiences in a madhouse."

Throughout life Tolstoy has remained faithful to this "madhouse" view of literature. All his life he has sought justification and sanctity in renouncing cultured society, in recourse to the people, in the mortification of the flesh, in manual labour, in everything save that to which he appeared called of God. Dostoevsky has shown by his life a man of letters may be heroic as any warrior, martyr, or lawgiver of the past. Among the heroes of language, among the heroes of art and knowledge, it may be that those will yet appear who are to have chief dominion over men in the third and last dispensation, the kingdom of the soul.

VIII

In the eyes of a man acknowledging only Christian sanctity and the forcible mastery of spirit over flesh, mortifying both flesh and spirit, the sentence passed by Tolstoy on his own career will seem just. "I devoured the produce of the labour of my peasants; punished, misled, deceived them. Falsehood, theft, debauchery of all kinds, drunkenness, violence, murder, there was not a crime which I did not commit." But if, apart from the sanctity of the spirit, we admit also a sanctity of the body outside the Christian law—the ancient heathen or Old Testament standard of righteousness, not abolished, but only remodelled by Christ—then the life of Tolstoy will be one of the most consistent, uniform, and admirable of lives. It may even be called magnificent. From what has been written above it will have been seen that his self-condemnation will not stand. The careful master and manager, the affectionate father of a family, like one of the Old Testament patriarchs, his whole life breathes purity and freshness, like some old but lusty tree, some cool and transparent subterranean spring.

There are no morbid contrasts or deceits in the life itself, in acts or even in feelings. These begin to appear only when we proceed to compare his perfect pagan conduct with his imperfect Christian intentions. His acts are not put to shame by acts, but only by words and thoughts. In order that the life of Tolstoy may seem stainlessly fair, we must forget not what he does and feels, but merely what he says and thinks about his acts and feelings. He has fulfilled the old law; and the tragedy of his life lies in the fact that he has not justified the acts of his law by his Faith and his Consciousness. It is the old tragedy of the Old Testament men, of all spiritual Israel. When the Law has been fulfilled to the utmost they cease to be satisfied with the Law and expect a Deliverer. But when the Messiah comes, being over-weighted with the yoke of the Law, they have not the strength to acknowledge Him and His new and terrible liberty, they reject Him, and again expect Him for ever. And in this expectation lies their righteousness—a virtue which is perennial, and perhaps included in Christianity itself. Judging by that ethical standard alone Leo Tolstoy had the right to say of himself, "I have nothing to hide from people; let them know all that I do." This old man's life really stands the test: the last coverings have been stripped from it, laid bare before the eyes of the world. There

DMITRY MEREZHKOVSKY

is nothing for him to be ashamed of—all is pure, all innocent as the nakedness of a child. Few other lives of the great today would stand such an ordeal; certainly not the life of Dostoevsky. It is easy to fall into error and be unjust when comparing the lives of the two men, because we know all about the first, while about the second (Dostoevsky) we do not know all. From hints in his letters, from oral traditions, but chiefly from the way in which his personality is reflected in his writings, we can surmise much that is hidden. We must do justice, too, to the nearest friends of Dostoevsky, who have endeavoured to give us his biography. His intimate friends and biographers are men in the highest degree courteous, respectful—even too respectful—to the memory of the dead. They have not portrayed what the Apocalypse calls "the depths of Satan" inherent in the man. Even such a subtle and penetrating mind as that of the critic Strakhov, I will not say whitewashes, but greatly simplifies the personality of his friend, softens, modifies, and smooths, and brings it down to the average level.

Examining the character of Dostoevsky as a man, we must remember his insuperable need as an artist to fathom dangerous and criminal depths of the human heart, especially the depths of the passion of love in all its manifestations. At one end of his gamut he touches the highest, most spiritual passion, bordering on religious enthusiasm, of the "angel" Alesha Karamazov;[1] at the other that of the evil insect, "the she-spider who devours her own mate." We see the whole spectrum of love in all its blended shades and transformations, in its most mysterious, acute, and morbid sinuosities. Remarkable is the inevitable blood-bond between the monster Smerdiakov, Ivan, "who fought with God," the cruel sensualist Dmitri, who seemed as if stung by a gadfly, the stainless cherub Alesha, and their father according to the flesh, the outcast Fedor Karamazov. Equally remarkable is the bond between them and their father in the spirit, Dostoevsky himself. He would have disowned this family, perhaps, before men, but not before his own conscience or before God.

There exists in manuscript a posthumously printed chapter of *The Possessed*, the confession of Stavrogine, where, amongst other things, he relates the seduction of a girl. This is one of the most powerful creations

---

1. The reference is to Dostoevsky's great unfinished novel in four volumes, *The Brothers Karamazov*. "A most invaluable treasury of information concerning the contemporary life of Russia, moral, intellectual, and social."—Waliszewski.

of Dostoevsky, in which we hear a note of such alarming sincerity that we understand those who hesitated to print it, even after the writer's death. It is *too* lifelike. But in the misdeeds of Stavrogine, even in the last depths of his fall, there is at least an unfading demoniacal reflection of what once was beauty; there is the dignity of evil. But Dostoevsky does not hesitate to depict even the most vulgar and commonplace immorality. The hero of his *Notes from Underground* stands on the mental height of his greatest heroes, those that were nearest to his heart. He expresses the very essence of the religious struggles and doubts of the artist. In this confession we feel self-incrimination, self-castigation, not less unsparing and more austere than that of the *Confession* of Tolstoy. And this is what this "hero" confesses: "At times I suddenly plunged into a sombre, subterranean, despicable debauchery, or semi-debauchery. My squalid passions were keen, glowing with morbid irritability. The outbursts were hysterical, accompanied by tears[2] and convulsions of remorse. Bitterness boiled in me. I felt an unwholesome thirst for violent moral contrasts, and so I demeaned myself to animality. I indulged in it by night, secretly, fearfully, foully, with a shame that never left me, even at the most degrading moments. I carried in my soul the love of secretiveness; I was terribly afraid that I should be seen, met, recognized."

In delineations of this kind Dostoevsky has so much strength and daring, such novelty of discovery and revelation, that we ask, "Could he have learnt all this merely from objective experience of others, from observation? Is it the curiosity *only* of the artist?" Assuredly it was not necessary that he himself should kill an old woman in order to experience the feelings of Raskolnikov, the leading character in *Crime and Punishment*. Much must be laid to the account of the insight of genius—much, but not all. Even if in the acts of the writer there was nothing corresponding to the curiosity of the artist, yet it is worthy of notice that such images could rise before his fancy. The fancy of Tolstoy would never have been capable of these figures, though it penetrates into recesses of sensuousness not less deep. The interest of Dostoevsky in "the stings of the gadfly," the seduction of girls, or the love adventure of Fedor Karamazov with Lizaveta the Fetid, Tolstoy would certainly have considered senseless or revolting. Sexual passion appears with him at times a cruel, coarse, even animal force, but never unnatural

2. Compare Dr. Johnson's similar outbursts.

or perverted. The greatest of human sins, punished unmercifully by divine justice in the spirit of the Mosaic Law, is, to the creator of *Anna Karénina* and the *Kreuzer Sonata*, the infringement of conjugal fidelity. The measure with which he metes out all the phenomena of sex is the simple, healthy, chaste passion of the patriarchs for their wives, under the law given to men by Jehovah, "*Increase and multiply.*" Levine owns that he could never picture to himself happiness with a woman otherwise than in the form of marriage; to tempt another man's wife seems to the possessor of Kitty as senseless as, after a costly and ample dinner, to steal a roll from a stall in the street. However repentant for his gallantries Tolstoy may be, we feel that in this respect, as compared with Dostoevsky, he is as innocent as Levine.

When the novelist Turgeniev and Bielinski, the famous critic, "reproved Dostoevsky for his disorderly life," he informs his brother: "I am ill in the nerves, and afraid of delirium or nervous fever. Live decently I cannot." His respectful and discreet biographer[3] hastens to suggest that he speaks here of merely monetary irregularities, but the reader is driven to doubt.

Here is another hint as to the extremes of which he was capable, not only in imagination, but in act. "My dear fellow," he writes to Maikov in 1867 from abroad, "I feel that I can look on you as my judge. You are a man with a heart, and it does not hurt me to repent before you. But I am writing for your eye alone. Do not hand me over to the tribunal of the world. Travelling not far from Baden, I took it into my head to turn aside thither. I was harassed by the temptation to sacrifice ten louis d'or and perhaps gain two thousand francs. I had before happened to win sometimes. But worse than this, my nature is wicked and too passionate. The devil straightway played me a trick, for in three days I won four thousand francs with unusual ease. The great thing is the play itself. You don't know how it weighs on me! No, I swear to you, it was not mere greed of gain. I went on risking and lost. I proceeded to stake my last money, excited to feverishness, and lost. Then I proceeded to pawn my clothes. Anna—(his wife)—pawned everything, save what she stood in, to the last shred. (What an angel she is! How, in our despair, she comforted me!)" Then follow prayers for money, humiliating even if the close friendship between him and Maikov is taken into account. "I know that you yourself have no money to spare. I should never apply to

---

3. O: Muller.

you for help, only I am sinking—have almost completely gone under. In two or three weeks I shall be without a farthing, and a drowning man will clutch at a straw. Except you I have *no one*, and if you do not help me I shall perish wholly! Dear fellow, save me. I will repay you for ever with friendship and attachment. If you have nothing, borrow of some one for me. Forgive me for thus writing. Do not leave me alone! God will repay you for this. Give a drop of water to a soul parching in the wilderness, for God's sake!" Notice the painfully abject language. It reminds one of the comic personages in his own stories, when they have lost the sense of self-respect, the drunken little Marmeladov and the adventurous Captain Lebedkine, recounting their poverty. Dostoevsky himself has lost self-control; does not care what Maikov thinks of him; has broken loose into feverish hysteria; is still drunk from enjoyment of the game.

We feel that if he had got the money at Baden he would have again lost control, again played it away.

On one occasion, when young, Tolstoy also lost heavily at play. But he did not "break loose"; he stopped in time with the self-command and soberness peculiar, not to his speculation, but to his action. He gave up playing, went to the Caucasus, quartered himself in a Cossack camp, and lived there with the greatest frugality on sixteen shillings a month, saved money, and paid his debt for cards. We see the true strength of the man, the sense of proportion, the power over himself, the tenacity, and consequently, from a certain standpoint, his moral superiority over Dostoevsky.

All these are trifles, but we know that even in more important respects the latter "broke loose." In a fit of youthful boasting he fancied that in his book *The Double*, or *Alter Ego*, he had surpassed *Dead Souls*. Thus, in blind anger against Bielinski, he accused that critic—who, if not sufficiently perspicacious, was in the highest degree well-intentioned— of "despicable malice and stupidity." In the very letter in which he tells Maikov of his losses at play he notably expounds himself. "Everywhere and in everything I go to extremes: all my life I have overshot the mark." It is necessary to add that he had been fated "to overshoot the mark" not only from strength, but from weakness.

"Do not hand me over to the judgment of men in general," he begs Maikov. This reminds one of the hero of *Notes from Underground*—"I was terribly afraid that I should be seen and recognized." Perhaps he does not sincerely repent of what he calls his "paltrily passionate nature."

Yet to purify it of his own set purpose, or to justify it before the tribunal of the world, are tasks beyond his strength. The evil is not in what he does, but in the fact that he is ashamed of what he does. His life will not, like Tolstoy's, stand complete exposure. He has hidden much, or is fain to hide, and we feel that this dark side of his life[4] is not edifying. If the life of Tolstoy is the pure and virgin water of a spring, that of Dostoevsky is the upgush of fire from elemental depths, mixed with lava, ashes, smoke, and sulphur.

It is impossible not to believe in the sincere endeavours of Tolstoy to love his neighbours, but we may doubt whether he has really loved any one of them as a Christian. But the fire of love, penetrating and purifying Dostoevsky, glows even in the most commonplace acts. In one letter he writes to his orphan stepson: "Pasha is a good boy, a sweet boy, with no one left to care for him. I will share my last crust and shirt with him, and my life as well!" This was no empty word: he was ready, and without abstract reasoning as to the right to help the poor or no.

"They tell me as a consolation," he writes, after the death of his daughter Sonia, "that I shall have other children. But where is my Sonia? Where is that little spirit for whom I boldly declare I would accept the pains of the Cross if only she might live? The more time goes on, the more bitter is memory—the more clearly do I see her face. There are moments which it is almost impossible to bear. She had regained consciousness and recognized me; and when on the day of her death I went out (curse me!) to read the papers, having no idea that in two hours she would die, she so followed and accompanied me with her eyes, so looked at me, that I still see those eyes more and more distinctly. How can I love another child? What I want is Sonia." Utterly self-forgetting, he loves the child of his flesh, not only according to the flesh, but Christianly, according to the spirit—as a separate, eternal, irreplaceable personality. Here is no patriarch Job consoled for his dead child by others. "But where is Sonia? I want Sonia." Has Tolstoy ever uttered such simple words of simple love? We remember again Tolstoy's words to a stranger about his own wife, Sophia: about her who has devoted her life to him and cared for him with a mother's tenderness for thirty years. "I choose myself friends among men. No woman can take the place of a friend to me. Why do we lie to our wives, assuring them that we can hold them friends? Flat untruth!" In this cold and cruel

---

4. It is that side of the planet Venus which is always turned from the sun.—ED.

speech is the chill of the whole life, the chill of the underground spring. But it is as God created it. I dread only his surface lukewarmness, which aspires to be Christian.

And so both Tolstoy and Dostoevsky remain imperfect in our sight. Neither one nor the other approaches that highest reconciling and fusing region of thought and inspiration where the eternal azure is transfused by the eternal sun, and opposites meet in the Absolute.

In any case the earth-glow of Dostoevsky is to me sacred as the chill of Tolstoy. Nothing I might learn of evil, of criminal, about Dostoevsky would darken his figure or dim the light of sanctity round him. The fire that burnt within him mastered and purified all. In the latter half of 1880, when he was finishing *The Brothers Karamazov*, as Strakhov records, "he was unusually thin and exhausted. He lived, it was plain, solely on his nerves. His body had become so frail that the first slight blow might destroy it. His mental labour was untiring, although work, as he himself told me, had grown very difficult to him. In the beginning of 1881 he fell ill of a severe attack of emphysema, the result of catarrh of the pulmonary passages. On January 26 he had hemorrhage in the throat. Feeling the approach of death he wished to confess and take the Sacrament. He gave the New Testament, used by him in prison, to his wife to read aloud. The first passage chanced to be Matthew iii. 14, 'But John held him back and said, It is I that should be baptized by Thee, and dost Thou come to me? But Jesus answered and said unto him, Detain Me not, for thus it behoves us to fulfil a great truth.' When his wife had read this he said, 'You hear? "Detain me not"; that means I am to die.' And he closed the book." A few hours later he did actually die instantaneously from the rupture of the pulmonary artery. He had lived for "the great truth," of which he thought in his last moments.

He loved to read out Pushkin's *Prophet* in the evenings. Those who heard him will never forget it. He began in a jerky, hollow, suppressed voice. But in the silence of the audience every syllable could be distinguished. And the voice grew ever louder, acquiring a power that seemed superhuman; and the last line he did not read, but shouted in tones that shook the room—

And with thy word inflame the heart of Man.

And the colourless, pitiable, "Liberal-Conservative" St. Petersburg crowd—perhaps the coldest and most commonplace crowd in the

DMITRY MEREZHKOVSKY

world, like the crowd in Maria del Fiore four centuries ago, when Fra Geronimo Savonarola was preaching—thrilled at that awe-inspiring cry. At that moment it was suddenly aware Dostoevsky was more than a great writer—that in him burned the seed of the religious fires of history.

On one occasion Strakhov read him his poems, which included the line, addressed to the Russians of the day—

Could ye but know the powers locked in yourselves!

"In some folks' brain," he says himself, "there always remains something not to be imparted to others, though one wrote volumes of explanations and explained his thought for five and thirty years. One thought will hover in his restless head which can never break out of it, and that perhaps the most important of all."

This presentiment has been fulfilled. He died without telling us his chief secret. Twenty years after his death, if he knew how he has been understood, would he not be justified in once more exclaiming, "They do not understand the main thing," and perhaps more especially *now*, when his fame is paling before the ever rising and dazzling fame of his great rival? But the "main thing," we feel, in Tolstoy's art is more realized and understood in Dostoevsky. Tolstoy is lord of the present; Dostoevsky's fame is of the future. I do not say this to belittle Tolstoy, for I think that the present is by no means less important than the future. Today is already tomorrow unrealized. I wish merely to say that we already are prescient of a third comer who is greater than these—he who shall reconcile both these men's spirits. To him shall be the victory; in him the revelation of the "main thing" that was in them both.

"The works of Pushkin, Gogol, Turgeniev, and Derjavine," says Tolstoy, "are unknown and useless to the people. Our literature is not suited to the people. These works, which we so cherish, remain to them a sealed book." Once, when talking to a coachman, who asked him for *Childhood and Youth*, Leo answered: "No, it is a hollow book. In my youth I wrote much nonsense. But I will give you *Come to the Light while there is Light*. That is much better than *Childhood and Youth*."

"I am like Paul," says Dostoevsky; "folk don't praise me, so I must praise myself!" And not long before his death, in a notebook under the heading *Myself*, he wrote: "I am certainly of the people, for my tendency issues from the depths of the Christian—that is, the popular spirit; although I am unknown to the Russian people of today I shall be known to them in the future."

Each of these views is right in its own way.

Of course Tolstoy and Dostoevsky are both popular in the sense that they aim at what really ought to become popular and part of the universal culture. They aim at it, but do they attain it? They have recognized the gulf that divides culture from the people, and wish to be of the people. Yet even Pushkin, though far less conscious of this gulf, is, I think, more of the people than they. Neither possesses the perfect simplicity which makes the Iliad of Homer, the Prometheus of Æschylus, and the Divine Comedy of Dante, expressions of the spirit of the nation, as of the world-spirit. Both are still too complicated, too artificial, too much in a hurry to escape from convention and "become simple." He who needs to become simple is not yet simple, and he who wishes to be of the people is not yet of the people. Pushkin, Tolstoy, and Dostoevsky will long remain "caviare to the general."

The living founder of a new sect, calling itself "the Church of the Orthodox Christians," a former convict, living in Sakhaline, named Tikhon Bielonojkin, said recently to a "cultured" Russian, who was inquiring into popular customs, "You collect oil, I understand. You have put a great deal of it into a lamp. Light that lamp, that there may be a light to serve men. If not, what is the good of your oil?"

We men of culture and reasoning are oil without fire. The people, full of strength and belief, are fire without oil. The oil is being wasted, the fire is sinking. Tolstoy and Dostoevsky, great precursors of him who will put the oil and fire together, are our typical Russians. Taken separately they can be judged and compared; we can ascribe to one superiority over the other. Seen together, I no longer know which of them is nearer to me, or which I most love.

"His was a peasant's face," says one, describing Tolstoy—"simple, rustic, with a broad nose, weather-beaten skin, thick beetling brows, from under which the small grey keen eyes looked brightly. Sometimes, when he flashes up and gets hot, these eyes are piercing and penetrating. And with all the 'peasant look,'" adds the writer, "you at once recognize the man of good society, the man of breeding, the Russian gentleman."

It is worthy of note how in the faces of great Russian writers, as that of Turgeniev when old, there is this mixture of plebeianism, the "peasant look," with the look of the noble—the look of European high breeding. The union seems splendid and natural, as if one did not interfere with the other.

Tolstoy's traits are those of a man who has lived life long and grandly, perhaps stormily, rarely happily. The face of Nimrod, mighty hunter before the Lord, in spite of the wrinkles of seventy, it is full of unfading youth, freshness, and somewhat haughty frigidity.

And here beside it is the face of Dostoevsky, never young even in youth, shadowed by suffering, and the cheeks sunken. The huge bare brow, bespeaking the clearness and majesty of reason; the piteous lips, twisted as if by the spasm of the "sacred sickness; the gaze dim and inexpressibly heavy, as if turned inwards; the slight cast in the eyes, as of one possessed. What is most painful in this face is a sort of immobility in the midst of movement, an endeavour arrested and turned to stone at the height of effort."

In spite of all contrasts, at times these faces are strangely alike. Dostoevsky too has the peasant look. "He looks quite the private soldier," says a friend.

If consummate genius has pre-eminently the face of the people, neither in Tolstoy nor in Dostoevsky have we as yet such a face. They are still too complex, passionate, and turbulent. There is not the final stillness and serenity, that "decorum" which our folk has been seeking for unconsciously for so many ages in its own Byzantine art, in the old Icons of its saints and martyrs. And neither of these faces is beautiful. Russia has never yet possessed a world-wide face, beautiful and national too, as that of Homer, the youthful Raphael, or old Leonardo. Even the outer semblance of Pushkin appears to us that of a St. Petersburg dandy of the thirties, in a Childe Harold cloak, arms folded on the chest like Napoleon's, with the conventional Byronic meditation in the eyes, curly hair and thick sensual lips. Yet this was the most national, the most truly Russian of the Russians. There were moments of sudden transfiguration, when he became unrecognizable. As Alcibiades says of Socrates, the mask of the Satyr betrayed the hidden God. In all Pushkin—in the outer man, as in his poetry—there is something over-light, transitory, evasive, unearthly, volatile. It was not for nothing that his friends called him "the Spark." For he was no planet, but a swift shooting star, a presage of harmony possible to Russia, but even by him never perfected. And his flight left us only the dim chrysalis, without its glowing inward nucleus. Nobody can give us now the true portrait of Pushkin. But the Russian people has not, so far, found its proper embodiment or type. Its typical man lies not in Pushkin, or even in Peter, but still in the Future. This future man, third and final, perfectly "symmetrical," who will be wholly Russian and yet cosmopolitan—a face, I fancy, splendidly symmetrical—is to be sought for in a balance between the two great natures—Tolstoy's and Dostoevsky's. Some day there will flash between them, as between two opposite poles, a spark of that lightning which means national conflagration.

In this Russian shall the "Man-god" be manifested to the Western world, and the "God-man," for the first time, to the Eastern, and he shall be, to those whose thinking already reconciles both hemispheres, the "One in Two."

PART SECOND

TOLSTOY AND DOSTOEVSKY AS ARTISTS

IX

The Princess Bolkonski, wife of Prince Andreï, as we learn from the first pages of Tolstoy's great novel *Peace and War*, was rather pretty, with a slight dark down on her upper lip, which was short to the teeth, but opened all the more sweetly, and still more sweetly lengthened at times and met the lower lip. For twenty chapters this lip keeps reappearing. Some months have passed since the opening of the story: "The little princess, who was *enceinte*, had meanwhile grown stout, but her eyes and the short downy lip and its smile, were curled up just as gaily and sweetly." And two pages later, "The princess talked incessantly: her short upper lip with its down constantly descended for a moment, touched at the right point the red lower one, and then again parted in a dazzling smile of eyes and teeth." The princess tells her sister-in-law, Prince Andreï's sister, Princess Maria, of the departure of her husband for the war. Princess Maria turns to her, with caressing eyes on her person. "Really?" The princess's face changed, and she sighed. "Yes, really!" she replied, "Ah, it is all very terrible!" and the lip of the little princess descended. In the course of one hundred and fifty pages we have already four times seen that upper lip with its distinguishing qualifications. Two hundred pages later we have again, "There was a general and brisk conversation, thanks to the voice and the smiling downy lip that rose above the white teeth of the little princess." In the second part of the novel she dies in a confinement. Prince Andreï entered his wife's room: she lay dead in the very attitude in which he had seen her five minutes before, and the same expression, in spite of the still eyes and the paleness of the cheeks, was on this charming child-like face with the lips covered with dark down. "I love you all, have harmed nobody. What have you done with me?" This takes place in the year 1805.

The war had broken out, and the scene of it was drawing near the Russian frontiers. In the midst of its dangers the author does not forget to tell us that over the grave of the little princess there had been placed a marble monument: an angel that had a slightly raised *upper lip*, and the expression which Prince Andreï had read on the face of his dead wife, "Why have you done this to me?"

Years pass. Napoleon has completed his conquests in Europe. He is already crossing the frontier of Russia. In the retirement of the Bare

Hills, the son of the dead princess "grew up, changed, grew rosy, grew a crop of curly dark hair, and without knowing, smiling and gay, raised the *upper lip* of his well-shaped mouth just like the little dead princess." Thanks to these underlinings of one physical feature first in the living, then in the dead, and then again on the face of her statue and in her son the upper lip of the little princess is engraved on our memory with ineffaceable distinctness. We cannot remember her without also recalling that feature.

Princess Maria Volkonski, Prince Andreï's sister, has a heavy footstep which can be heard from afar. "They were the heavy steps of the Princess Maria." She came into the room "with her heavy walk, going on her heels." Her face "grows red in patches" During a delicate conversation with her brother about his wife, she "turned red in patches." When they are preparing to dress her up upon the occasion of the coming betrothed, she feels herself insulted: "she flashed out, and her face became flushed in patches."

In the following volume, in a talk with Pierre about his old men and beggars, about his "bedesmen," she becomes confused and "grew red in patches." Between these two last reminders of the patches of the princess is the description of the battle of Austerlitz, the victory of Napoleon, the gigantic struggle of nations, events that decided the destiny of the world, yet the artist does not forget, and will not to the end, the physical trait he finds so interesting. We are forced to remember the glaring eyes, heavy footsteps, and red patches of the Princess Maria. True, these traits, unimportant as they may seem, are really bound up with deep-seated spiritual characteristics of the *dramatis personae*. The upper lip, now gaily tilted, now piteously dropped, expresses the childlike carelessness and helplessness of the little princess. The clumsy gait of the Princess Maria expresses an absence of external feminine charm; both the glaring eyes and the fact that she blushes in patches are connected with her inward womanly charm and spiritual modesty. Sometimes these stray characteristics light up a vast and complex picture, and give it startling clearness and relief.

At the time of the popular rising in deserted Moscow, before Napoleon's entry, when Count Rostopchin, wishing to allay the bestial fury of the crowd, points to the political criminal Verestchagin (who happened to be at hand and was totally innocent) as a spy, and the scoundrel who had ruined Moscow, the thin long neck and the general thinness, weakness and fragility of his frame of course express the defencelessness of the victim in face of the coarse mass of the crowd.

"Where is he?" said the Count, and instantly saw round the corner of a house a young man with a long thin neck coming out between two dragoons. He had "dirty, down at heel, thin boots. On his lean, weak legs the fetters clanked heavily. 'Bring him here,' said Rostopchin, pointing to the lower step of the *perron*. The young man, walking heavily to the step indicated, sighed with a humble gesture, crossed his thin hands, unused to work, before his body. 'Children,' said Rostopchin, in a metallic ringing voice, 'this man is Verestchagin, the very scoundrel that ruined Moscow.' Verestchagin raised his face and endeavoured to meet the Count's eyes, but he was not looking at him. On *the long thin neck* of the young man a vein behind the ear stood out like a blue cord. The people were silent, only pressed more closely together. 'Kill him! Let the traitor perish, and save from slur the Russian name,' cried Rostopchin. 'Count!' was heard saying amid the renewed stillness the timid yet theatrical voice of Verestchagin, 'Count, one God is above us.' And again the large vein in his *thin neck* was swollen with blood.' One of the soldiers struck him with the flat of the sword on the head. Verestchagin, with a cry of terror, with outstretched hands plunged forward towards the people. A tall youth against whom he struck clung with his hands to his *thin neck* and with a wild cry, fell with him under the feet of the onrushing roaring populace." After the crime, the very people who committed it with hang-dog and piteous looks gazed on the dead body with the purple blood-stained and dusty face and the mangled *long thin neck*. Scarce a word of the inward state of the victim, but in five pages the word *thin* eight times repeated in various connexions—and this outward sign fully depicts the inward condition of Verestchagin in relation to the crowd. Such is the ordinary artistic resource of Tolstoy, from the seen to the unseen, from the external to the internal, from the bodily to the spiritual, or at any rate to the emotional.

Sometimes in these recurrent traits are implicated deeper fundamental ideas, main motives of the book. For instance, the weight of the corpulent general Kutuzov, his leisurely old man's slowness and want of mobility, express the apathetic, meditative stolidity of his mind, his Christian or more truly Buddhistic renunciation of his own will, the submission to the will of Fate or the God of this primitive hero; in the eyes of Tolstoy, a hero pre-eminently Russian and national, the hero of inaction or inertia. He is in contrast with the fruitlessly energetic, light, active, and self-confident hero of Western culture, Napoleon.

Prince Andreï watches the commander in chief at the time of the review of the troops at Tsarevoe Jaimishche: "Since Andreï had last seen him Kutuzov had grown still stouter and unwieldy with fat." An air of weariness was on his face and in his figure. "*Snorting and tossing heavily* he sat his charger." When after finishing the inspection he entered the court, on his face sat "the joy of a man set free, purposing to take his ease after acting a part. He drew his left leg out of the stirrup, rolling his whole body and, frowning from the effort, with difficulty raised it over the horse's back. Then he gasped and sank into the arms of supporting Cossacks and aides-de-camp; stepped out with a plunging gait and heavily ascended the staircase creaking under his weight." When he learns from Prince Andreï of the death of his father, he sighs "profoundly, heaving his whole chest, and is silent for a time." Then he "embraced Prince Andreï, pressed him to his stout chest, and for long would not let him go. When he did so, the prince saw that the swollen lips of Kutuzov quivered, and tears were in his eyes." He sighs, and grasping the bench with both hands to rise, rises heavily and *the folds of his swollen neck disappear*.

Even more profound is the significance of *rotundity* in the frame of another Russian hero, Platon Karataev. This rotundity typifies the eternal completeness of all that is simple, natural and artificial, a self-sufficingness, which seems to the artist the primary element of the Russian national genius. Platon Karataev always remained in Pierre's mind as the strongest and dearest memory and personification of all that is Russian, good, and *rounded off*. When next day, at dawn, Pierre saw his neighbour, the first impression of something round was fully confirmed; the whole figure of Platon in his French cloak, with a cord girdle, a forage-cap and bast shoes, was *round*, the head was completely *round*, the back, the chest, the shoulders, even the arms, which he carried as if he was always going to lift something, all were *round*: the pleasant smile and the great brown tender eyes were *round*. Pierre felt something "*round*, if one might strain language, *in the whole savour of the man*." Here, by one physical trait, carried to the last degree of geometrical simplicity and obviousness, is expressed a huge abstract generalization. Tolstoy's religion and metaphysics enter into the delineation by this single trait.

Similar deep expressiveness is given by him to the hands of Napoleon and Speranski, the hands of men that wield power. At the time of the meeting of the Emperors in face of the assembled armies, the former gives a Russian soldier the Legion of Honour, he "draws off the glove from his *white small hand*, and tearing it, throws it away." A few lines later, "Napoleon reaches back *his small plump hand*." Nicolai Rostov remembers "that self-satisfied Bonaparte with *his little white hand*." And in the next volume, when talking with the Russian diplomat Balashiev, Napoleon makes "an energetic gesture of inquiry with *his little white, plump hand*."

He sketches, too, the whole body of the Emperor, stripping the studious demi-god, till he stands, like other men, food for cannon.

In the morning, just before the battle of Borodino, the Emperor, in his tent, is finishing his toilette. "Snorting and panting, he turned, now his plump back, now his overgrown fatty chest to the brush with which the valet was rubbing him down. Another valet, holding the mouth of the bottle with his finger, was sprinkling the pampered little body with eau-de-cologne, with an air that said he alone could know how much and where to sprinkle. Napoleon's short hair was damp and hanging over his forehead. But his face, though bloated and yellow, expressed physical well-being. 'More now, harder now!' he cried, stretching and puffing, to the valet who was rubbing him, then bending and presenting his fat shoulders."

This white hand denotes the upstart hero who exploits the masses.

Speranski[1] too, has white fat hands, in the description of which Tolstoy plainly somewhat abuses his favourite device of repetition and emphasis. "Prince Andreï watched all Speranski's movements; but lately he was an insignificant seminarist, and now in his hands, those white plump hands, he held the fate of Russia, as Volkonski reflected." "In no one had the Prince seen such delicate whiteness of the face, and still more the hands, which were rather large, but unusually plump, delicate and white. Such whiteness and delicacy of complexion he had only seen in soldiers who had been long in hospital." A little later he again "looks involuntarily at the white delicate hands of Speranski, as men look generally at the hands of people in power. The mirror-like glance and the delicate hand somehow irritated prince Andreï."

The detail is repeated with unwearying insistence till in the long run this white hand begins to haunt one like a spectral being.

---

1. A handsome guardsman in the great novel *Peace and War*.

In comparing himself with Pushkin as an artist, Tolstoy said to Bers that the difference between them, amongst other things, was this, "that Pushkin in depicting a characteristic detail does it lightly, not troubling whether it will be noticed or understood by the reader, while he himself, as it were, stood over the reader with this artistic detail, until he had set it forth distinctly." The comparison is acute. He *does* "stand over the reader," not afraid of sickening him, and flogs in the trait, repeats, lays on colours, layer after layer, thickening them more and more, where Pushkin, barely touching, slides his brush over in light and careless, but invariably sure and faithful strokes. It seems as if Pushkin, especially in prose harsh, and even niggardly, gave little, that we might want the more. But Tolstoy gives so much that there is nothing more for us to want; we are sated, if not glutted.

The descriptions of Pushkin remind one of the light watery tempera of the old Florentine masters or Pompeian frescoes, dim, airily translucent colours, like the veil of morning mist. Tolstoy paints in the more powerful oil colours of the great Northern Masters. And side by side with the dense black and living shadows we have sudden rays of the blinding all-penetrating light, drawing out of the dark some distinct feature, the nakedness of the body, a fold of drapery, a keen, quick movement, part of a face stamped with passion or suffering. We get a startling, almost repulsive and alarming vividness. The artist seeks through the natural, strongly emphasized, the supernatural; through the physical exaggerated the hyperphysical.

In all literature there is no writer equal to Tolstoy in depicting the human body. Through he misuses repetitions, he usually attains what he needs by them, and he never suffers from the *longueurs* so common to other vigorous masters. He is accurate, simple, and as short as possible, selecting only the few, small, unnoticed facial or personal features and producing them, not all at once, but gradually and one by one, distributing them over the whole course of the story, weaving them into the living web of the action. Thus at the first appearance of old Prince Bolkonski[2] we get only a fleeting sketch, in four or five lines, "the short figure of the old man with the powdered wig, small *dry hands* and grey, overhanging brows that sometimes, when he was roused, dimmed the flash of the clever youthful eyes." When he sits down to the lathe "by the movement of his small foot, the firm pressure of

---

2. In *Peace and War*.

DMITRY MEREZHKOVSKY

his thin veined hand" (we already know his hands are dry, but Tolstoy loves to go back to the hands of his heroes), "you could still see in the Prince the obstinate and long-enduring force of hale old age." When he talks to his daughter, Princess Maria, "he shows in a cold smile, his strong but yellowish teeth." When he sits at the table and bends over her, beginning the usual lesson in geometry, she "feels herself surrounded with the snuffy, old-age, acrid savour of her father," which had long been a sign to her. There he is all before us as if alive, height, build, hands, feet, eyes, gestures, brows, even the peculiar savour belonging to each man.

Or take the effect on Vronski when he first sees Anna Karénina. You could see at a glance she belonged to the well-born; that she was very beautiful, that she had red lips, flashing grey eyes, which looked dark from the thickness of the lashes, and that "an excess of life had so filled her being that in spite of herself it showed, now in the flash of her eyes, now in her smile." And again as the story progresses, gradually, imperceptibly, trait is added to trait, feature to feature: when she gives her hand to Vronski he is delighted "as by something exceptional with the vigorous clasp with which she boldly shook his own." When she is talking to her sister-in-law Dolly, Anna takes her hand in "her own vigorous little one." The wrist of this hand is "thin and tiny," we see the "slender tapering fingers," off which the rings slip easily.

In the hands of Karénina, as in those of other characters (it may be because the hands are the only part of the human body always bare and near elemental nature, and unconscious as the animal), there is yet greater expressiveness than in the face. In the hands of Anna lies the whole charm of her person, the union of strength and delicacy. We learn when she is standing in the crowd at the ball "that she always held herself exceptionally erect"; when she leaves the railway carriage or walks through the room she has "a quick, decisive gait, carrying with strange ease her full and perfectly proportioned body." When she dances she has "a distinguishing grace, sureness and lightness of movement"; when, having gone on a visit to Dolly, she takes off her hat, her black hair, that catches in everything, "ripples into waves all over," and on another occasion "the unruly short waves of her curly hair keep fluttering at the nape and on the temples."

In these unruly curls, so easily becoming unkempt, there is the same tension, "the excess of something" ever ready for passion, as in the too bright flash of the eyes, or the smile, breaking out involuntarily and "fluctuating between the eyes and the lips." And lastly, when she goes to the ball, we see her skin. "The black, low-cut velvet bodice showed her full shoulders and breast polished like old ivory, and *rounded* arms." This polishedness, firmness, and *roundness* of the body, as with Platon Karataev, is to Tolstoy very important and subtle, a mysterious trait. All these scattered, single features complete and tally with one another, as in beautiful statues the shape of one limb always corresponds to the shape of another. The traits are so harmonized that they naturally and involuntarily unite, in the fancy of the reader, into one living, personal whole: so that when we finish the book we cannot but recognize Anna Karénina.

This gift of *insight into the body* at times, though seldom, leads Tolstoy into excess. It is easy and pleasant to him to describe living bodies and their movements. He depicts exactly how a horse begins to start when touched by the spur: "Jarkov touched his horse with the spurs and it thrice in irritation shifted its legs, not knowing with which to begin, reared and leaped." In the first lines of *Anna Karénina* Tolstoy is in a hurry to tell us how Stepan Arcadievich Oblonski, of whom we as yet know nothing, "draws plenty of air into his broad pectoral structure," and how he walks with "his usual brisk step, turning out the feet which so lightly carry his full frame." This last feature is significant, because it records the family likeness of the brother Stepan with his sister Anna. Even if all this seems extravagant, yet extravagance in art is not excess, it is even in many cases the most needful of all things. But here is a character of third-rate importance, one of those which vanish almost as soon as they appear, some paltry regimental commander in *Peace and War*, who has no sooner flitted before us than we have already seen that he "is broader from the chest to the back than from one shoulder to the other," and he stalks before the front "with a gait that shakes at every step and his back slightly bent." This shaky walk is repeated four times in five pages. Perhaps the observation is both true and picturesque, but it is here an inappropriate touch and in excess Anna Karénina's fingers, "taper at the ends," are important; but we should not have lost much if he had not told us that the Tartar footmen who hand dinner to Levine and Oblonski were broad-hipped. Sometimes the distinguishing quality of an artist is shown, not so much by what he has in due proportion as by the gift which he has to excess.

The language of gesture, if less varied than words, is more direct, expressive and suggestive. It is easier to lie in words than by gesture or facial expression. One glance, one wrinkle, one quiver of a muscle in the face, may express the unutterable. Succeeding series of these unconscious, involuntary movements, impressing and stratifying themselves on the face and physique, form the expression of the face and the countenance of the body. Certain feelings impel us to corresponding movements, and, on the other hand, certain habitual movements impel to the corresponding *internal* states. The man who prays, folds his hands and bends his knees, and the man too who folds his hands and bends his knees is near to the praying frame of mind. Thus there exists an uninterrupted current, not only from the internal to the external, but from the external to the internal.

Tolstoy, with inimitable art, uses this convertible connexion between the external and the internal. By the same law of mechanical sympathy which makes a stationary tense chord vibrate in answer to a neighbouring chord, the sight of another crying or laughing awakes in us the desire to cry or laugh; we experience when we read similar descriptions in the nerves and muscles. And so by the motions of muscles or nerves we enter shortly and directly into the internal world of his characters, begin to live with them, and in them.

When we learn that Ivan Ilyich[3] cried out three days for pain "Ugh, U-ugh, Ugh!" because when he began to cry "I don't want to!" he prolonged the sound "o-o-o," it is easy for us, not only to picture to ourselves, but ourselves physically experience this terrible transition from human speech to a senseless animal howl. And what an endlessly complex, variegated sense at times a single movement, a single attitude of human limbs receives at his hands!

After the battle of Borodino, in the marquee for the wounded, the doctor, in his blood-stained apron with hands covered with blood "holds in one of them a cigar between the middle and fore-finger, so as not to mess it." This position of the fingers implies both the uninterruptedness of his terrible employment, and the absence of repugnance for it; indifference to wounds and blood, owing to long habit, weariness, and desire to forget. The complexity of these internal states is concentrated in one little physical detail, in the position of the two fingers, the description of which fills half a line.

When prince Andreï, learning that Kutuzov is sending Bagration's force to certain death, feels a doubt whether the commander-in-chief has

---

3. In *The Death of Ivan Ilyitch.*

the right to sacrifice, in this self-confident way, the lives of thousands of men, he "looks at Kutuzov, and what involuntarily strikes his eye at a yard's distance is the clean-washed sutures of the scar on Kutuzov's temple, where the bullet at Ismail penetrated his head, and his lost eye." "Yes, he has the right," thinks Volkonski.

More than anything which science tells Ivan Ilyich about his illness by the mouth of the doctors, more than all his own wonted conventional ideas about death, does a chance look reveal the actual horror of his state. "Ivan Ilyich began to brush his hair and looked in the mirror: he was horrified by the way that his hair clung closely to his long forehead." No words would suffice to express animal fear of death, as this state of the hair noticed in the mirror. The indifference of the healthy to the sick, or the living to the dying, is realized by Ivan Ilyich, not from the words people use, but only by "the brawny, full-veined neck, closely girt by its white collar, and the powerful limbs habited in tight black breeches, of Fedor Petrovich" (his daughter's betrothed).

Between Pierre and Prince Vasili[4] the relations are very strained and delicate. Prince Vasili wishes to give Pierre his daughter Ellen and is waiting impatiently for Pierre to make her an offer. The latter cannot make up his mind. One day, finding himself alone with the father and daughter, he rises and is for going away, saying it is late. "Prince Vasili looked at him with stern inquiry, as if the remark was so strange that it was impossible to believe his ears. But presently the look of sternness changed. He took Pierre by the arm, put him in a chair and smiled caressingly, 'Well, what of Lelia?' he said, turning at once to his daughter and then again to Pierre, reminding him, not at all to the point, of a stupid anecdote of a certain Sergyè Kuzmich. Pierre smiled, *but it was plain from his smile* that he knew that it was not the story of Sergyè Kuzmich that interested Prince Vasili at the moment: and Prince Vasili was aware that Pierre saw this. The former suddenly muttered something and left the room. It seemed to Pierre that Prince Vasili, too, felt confused. He looked at Ellen, and she too seemed embarrassed, and her eye said, 'Well you yourself are to blame.' What complex and many-sided significance evoked by a single smile! It is repeated and mirrored in the minds of those around, in a series of scarcely perceptible half-conscious thoughts and feelings, like a ray or a sound.

---

4. In *Peace and War*.

Pierre sees Natasha after a long separation, and the death of her first betrothed, Prince Andreï. She is so changed that he does not recognize her. "'But no, it cannot be,' he thinks. 'This stern, thin, pale, aged face? It cannot be she. It is only the memory of a face.' But at that moment Princess Maria says, 'Natasha.' And the face with the observant eyes, with difficulty, with an effort, as a stuck door is opened, smiled at him and from this opened door suddenly, startlingly, came the breath, floating round Pierre, of that long forgotten happiness. It came and took hold of and swallowed him whole. When she smiled, there could no longer be a doubt; it was Natasha, and he loved her." During this scene, one of the most important and decisive in the action of this novel, only four words are pronounced by Princess Maria, "Then don't you recognize her?" But the silent smile of Natasha is stronger than words; it decides the fate of Pierre.

Tolstoy depicts by gesture such intangible peculiarity of sensation as a bar of music, or of a song. "The drummer and choir leader looked sternly over the soldiers of his band and frowned. Then having convinced himself that all eyes were fixed on him, he appeared carefully to raise in both hands some unseen precious object above their heads, held it there some seconds and suddenly threw it away desperately. 'Ah! alackaday, my tent, my tent! my new tent!' took up twenty men's voices."

He has equally at command the primal elemental masses and the lightest molecules scattered, like dust, over our inward atmosphere, the very atoms of feeling. The same hand which moves mountains guides these atoms as well. And perhaps the second operation is more wonderful than the first. Putting aside all that is general, literary, conventional, and artificial, Tolstoy explores in sensation what is most private, personal, and particular; takes subtle shafts of feeling, and whets and sharpens these shafts to an almost excessive sharpness, so that they penetrate and pierce like ineradicable needles; the peculiarity of his sensation will become for ever our own peculiarity. We feel Tolstoy afterwards, when we return to real life. We may say that the nervous susceptibility of people who have read the books of Tolstoy becomes different from what it was before reading them.

The secret of his effects consists, amongst other things, in his noticing what others do not, as too commonplace and which, when illumined by consciousness, precisely in consequence of this commonplace character seems unusual. Thus he first made the discovery, apparently so simple and easy, but which for thousands of years had evaded all observers, that the smile is reflected, not only on the face, but in the sound of the voice, that the voice as well as the face can be smiling. Platon Karataev at night, when Pierre cannot see his face, says something to him, "in a voice changed by a smile." The living web of art consists in such small but striking observations and discoveries. He was the first to notice that the sound of horse-hoofs is, as it were, a "transparent sound."

His language, usually simple and measured, does not suffer from an excess of epithet. When the sensation to be described is so subtle and new that by no combination of words can it possibly be expressed, he uses concatenations of onomatopoeic sounds, which serve children and primitive people in the construction of language.

In his delirium, Prince Andreï heard a low, whispering voice, ceaselessly affirming in time "I piti piti piti," and then "i ti ti," and again "i piti piti piti," and once more "i ti ti." At the same time at the sound of this whispered music Prince Andreï felt that over his face, over the very middle of it, moved some strange airy edifice of fine needles or chips. He felt, although it was hard for him, that he must assiduously maintain his equilibrium in order that this delicate fabric might not fall down. But still it did fall down, and slowly rose again to the sounds of the rhythmically whispering music. "It rises, it rises! It falls to pieces and yet spreads," said he to himself. "I piti piti piti, i ti ti, i piti piti—bang, a fly has knocked against it."

Ivan Ilyich, remembering before his death the stewed plums "which they advise me to eat now," remembered also the "dry, crinkled French prunes when I was a child." It would seem the detail was sufficiently definite. But the artist enforces it still more. Ivan remembered the peculiar taste of plums and "the abundance of saliva when you got to the stones." With this sensation of saliva from plum stones is connected in his mind a whole series of memories, of his nurse, his brother, his toys, of his whole childhood, and these memories in their turn evoke in him a comparison of the then happiness of his life with his present despair and dread of death. "No need for that, too painful," he says to himself. Such are the generalizations to which, in us all, trifling details lead.

Sonia, when in love with Nicolai Rostov, kisses him. Pushkin would have stopped at recording the kiss. But Tolstoy, not content, looks for more exactness. The thing took place at Christmas, Sonia was disguised as a hussar, and moustaches had been marked on her lips with burnt cork. And so Nicolai remembers "the smell of cork, mixed with the feel of the kiss."

The most intangible gradations and peculiarities of sensation are distinguished by him to correspond with the character, sex, age, bringing up, and status of the person experiencing them. It seems that in this region there are no hidden ways for him. His sensual experience is inexhaustible, as if he had lived hundreds of lives in various shapes of men and animals. He fathoms the unusual sensation of her bared body to a young girl, before going to her first ball. So, too, the feelings of a woman growing old and worn out with child bearing, who "shudders as she remembers the pain of her quivering breasts, experienced with almost every child." Also of a nursing mother, who has not yet severed the mysterious connexion of her body with that of her child, and who "knows for a certainty, by the excess of milk in her, that the child is insufficiently fed." Lastly, the sensations and thoughts of animals, for instance the sporting dog of Levine, to whom the face of her master seems "familiar," but his eyes "always strange."

Not only the old Greeks and Romans, but in all probability the people of the eighteenth century, would not have understood the meaning of the "transparent" sound of horsehoofs, or how there can be "a savour of burnt cork mixed with the feel of a kiss," or dishes "reflect" an expression of the human countenance, a pleasant smile, or how there can be "a roundness" in the savour of a man. If our critics, the Draconian judges of the new so-called "decadence" of Art, were consistent throughout, should they not accuse even Tolstoy of "morbid obliquity"? But the truth is that to determine the fixed units of the healthy and the morbid in Art is much more difficult than it seems to the guardians of the Classical canons. Is not the "obliquity" they presuppose only an *intensifying*, the natural and inevitable development, refinement, and deepening of healthy sensuality? Perhaps our children, with their unimpaired susceptibility, will understand what is unintelligible to our critics and will justify Tolstoy. Children are well aware of what some fathers have forgotten, viz.: that the different branches of what are called "the five senses" are by no means so sharply divided from one another, but blend, interweave, cover and supplement one another, so that sounds may seem bright and coloured ("the bright voice of the nightingale," Pushkin has it) and concatenations of movements, colours, or even scents may have the effect of music (what is called "eurhythmia,") the harmony of movement, as of colours in painting. It is usually thought that the physical sensations, as opposed to mental, are a constant quantity throughout time in the historical development of mankind. In reality, the care of physical sensation changes with the development of intellect. We see and hear what our ancestors did not see or hear. However much the admirers of classical antiquity may complain of the physical degeneracy of the men of today, it is scarcely possible to doubt that we are creatures more keen-sighted, keen of hearing and physically acute, than the heroes of the *Iliad* and the *Odyssey*. Does not science, too, conjecture that certain sensations, for instance, the last colours of the spectrum, have become the general achievement of men, only at a comparatively recent and historical stage of their existence, and that perhaps even Homer confused green with dark blue in one epithet, for the hue of seawater? Does there not still go on a similar natural growth and *intensification* in other branches of human sentience? Will not our children's children see and hear what we as yet do not see and hear? Will not the unseen be seen to them, though undreamed of by our fathers, our critics, men of worn-out sensitiveness to impression, nay, even to the boldest and most advanced of ourselves? Will not our present "decadent" over-refinement, which so alarms the old believers of the day on Art, then seem in its turn obvious, primitive, Homeric healthiness and coarseness? In this unchecked development, movement and flow, where is the fixed standard for dividing the lawful from the unlawful, wholesome from morbid, natural from corrupt? Yesterday's exception becomes today's rule. And who shall dare to say to the living body, the living spirit, "Here shall you stop, no further may you go"? Why particularly here? Why not farther on?

However this may be, the special glory of Tolstoy lies exactly in the fact that he was the first to express (and with what fearless sincerity!), new branches, unexhausted and inexhaustible,—of over-subtilizing physical and mental consciousness. We may say that he gave us new bodily sensations, new vessels for new wine.

The Apostle Paul divides human existence into three branches, borrowing the division from the philosophers of the Alexandrian School, the physical man, the spiritual and the natural. The last is the connecting link between the first two, something intermediate, double, transitional, like twilight; neither Flesh nor Spirit, that in which the Flesh is completed and the Spirit begins, in the language of psycho-physiology the physico-spiritual phenomenon.

Tolstoy is the greatest depictor of this physico-spiritual region in the natural man; that side of the flesh which approaches the spirit, and that side of the spirit which approaches the flesh, the mysterious border-region where the struggle between the animal and the God in man takes place: Therein lies the struggle and the tragedy of his own life. He is a "man of the senses," half-heathen, half-Christian; neither to the full.

In proportion as he recedes from this neutral ground in either direction, it matters not whether towards the region of the cold "pre-animal" Nature, that region which *seems* inorganic, insentient, inanimate, "material" (the terrible and beatific calm of which Turgeniev and Pushkin have told so well); or as he essays the opposite region; human spirituality, almost set free from the body, released from animal nature, the region of pure thought (the passionate workings of which are so well embodied by Dostoevsky and Tiutchev) the power of artistic delineation in Tolstoy decreases, and in the end collapses, so that there are limits which are for him wholly unattainable. But within the limits of the purely natural man he is the supreme artist of the world.

In other provinces of Art, for instance the painting of the Italian Renaissance and the sculpture of the ancient Greeks, there have been artists who with greater completeness than Tolstoy depicted the bodily man. The music of the present day, and in part the literature, penetrate us more deeply. But nowhere, and at no time, has the "natural man" appeared with such startling truth and nakedness as he appears in the creations of Tolstoy.

X

Turgeniev wrote, with reference to *Peace and War*, "Tolstoy's novel is an extraordinary affair, but the weakest thing in it is just that over which the public is enthusiastic, the history and the psychology. His history is a puzzle, a deceiving of the eyes with thin details. Where is the characteristic feature of the epoch? *Where is the historical colouring?* The figure of Denison is drawn finely, but it would be good as an arabesque on a background, only there is no such background."

An unexpected judgment, and one that at first sight seems unfair. The vast and endlessly varied course of the Tolstoyan epic gives us so much *by the way* that the question of a goal does not occur to us. But in the long run it is impossible to evade the question, In what measure is the historical novel *Peace and War* true to history? The well-known historical personages depicted—Kutuzov, Alexander I, Napoleon, Speranski—pass before us, familiar historical events take place, the battles of Austerlitz and Borodino, the burning of Moscow, the retreat of the French. We see the whole moving, yet unmoved face of History, tossed by emotions and for ever turning to stone, like waves suddenly petrified. Is the living spirit of its epoch in the book? The spirit of history, the spirit of the time, that which Turgeniev calls "historical colouring," how difficult, how almost impossible is it to determine in what it consists! Of course every age has its own atmosphere, its peculiar *savour*, nowhere and never repeated. In the *Decameron* of Boccaccio we have the savour of the Italy of the early Renaissance, in Mickiewicz's *Pan Tadeüsz* that of the Lithuania of the opening of the nineteenth century; in *Eugène Oniegin*, that of Russia in the thirties. And this colouring, the peculiar reflection of the historical hour, is reproduced not only in the great, but in the trifling, as the glow of the morning or evening is reflected, not only on the hilltops, but in every blade of grass upon the mountains. Even the fashions of clothes, women's headgear, house-furniture, in this sense, never recur.

The more powerful, the more vital the civilization, the more clinging and distinctive is its historical savour. And as we plunge into the examination of a period, it breathes forth, takes hold of us like the penetrating, subtle and heavy aroma from a long-sealed casket, or like a strange low music that goes to the heart. The Napoleonic age is felt, not only in the majestic language of the proclamations to the army under the Pyramids, or in the articles of the Legislative Code, but in the pattern of embroidery, the white tunics of the Empress and her smooth white curule chairs.

In reading *Peace and War* it is very difficult to get rid of the astonishing impression that all the events depicted, in spite of their names and familiar historical guise, took place in our own day. The characters described, in spite of being portraits, are our own contemporaries. The air we breathe in *Peace and War* is the same so familiar to us in *Anna Karènina* and the second half of the nineteenth century.

Between the Masonic leanings of Pierre Bezukhov and the democratic tendencies of Levine, between the family life of the Rostovs and that of the Sherbatskis, there is just as listle difference in the historical colouring. People supposed to be born and brought up in the fifties and sixties of the eighteenth century on Derjavine, Sumarokov, Novikov, Voltaire, Diderot, and Helvetius, not only speak in *Peace and War* our present tongue, but think and feel the same new thoughts and feelings as we. It is almost impossible to conceive Prince Andreï, with his pitilessly keen, delicate and cold sensitiveness, so over-refined, and so morbid, so modern, as the contemporary of *Poor Lisa, Vadim, The Thunderers*, and the *Singer in the Camp of the Russian Warriors*. He seems to have read and felt Byron and Lermontov, but also Stendhal, Mérimée, and even Flaubert and Schopenhauer. Levine, in *Anna Karénina*, has not a single religious doubt which could seem strange or unintelligible to Pierre Bezukhov. They are not only spiritually akin, but of the same year, historical inseparables. To imagine Oniegin[1] without a Childe Harold cloak, or otherwise than in the fashionable clothes of a half-Russian, half-English dandy, the contemporary of Chateaubriand and Byron, or Tatiana, except in the dress of a country young lady of the twenties, is as difficult as to fancy Pierre Bezukhov in stockings and rosetted shoes and a coloured frock-coat with shiny buttons, or Natasha Rostov in the dress of our great-grandmothers. In Tolstoy's historical novel we lose the prismatic sense of distance between us and the characters; not because we are transplanted to their age, but, on the contrary, because they are transplanted to ours.

The author himself forgets this prism of distance. The occasional glimpse of a powdered peruke or breeches, or of an old-fashioned phrase, surprises the reader like an anachronism. Of the indoor home

---

1. Pushkin's hero.

surroundings of a Russian magnate of the Alexandrian age we meet in the whole course of *Peace and War* only one mention, occupying half a line; In the Moscow palace of the elder Count Bezukhov, there is "a plate-glass hall with two rows of statues in niches." Contrast Homer, with his endless descriptions of the chambers of King Alcinous, or depicting the exterior and interior of a human dwelling, the arrangement of the rooms, walls, beds, ceilings', pillars, beams, cross-beams, and all the details of household equipment. The work of men's hands, to the maker of the *Iliad*, is as sacred and worthy as the work of divine hands. He describes the every-day domestic surroundings of his heroes with the same lovingness as the earth, the sea, or the sky, and makes instinct with a life in sympathy with man the web of Penelope, the shield of Achilles, the raft of Odysseus, the amphoras with sweet perfumes and the baskets of washed clothes which Nausicaä is carrying to bleach by the river. In the whole superstructure of man's civilization over the world of elemental Nature, in all that men have invented, not only what is artistic, but in crafts and industries, in all that is the work of art, but never seems to him artificial, the writers of the Odyssey imagine something superhuman, divinely beautiful, the work and contrivance of the cunning worker Hephaestus, something burning with Promethean fire. And Pushkin, who so understood the charm of wild nature, at the same time rejoiced in the beauty of the city created by Peter the Tzar, "the most soulful of all towns" in the words of Dostoevsky; delighted in the ironwork in the rails of St. Petersburg gardens, the Admiralty spire, sparkling in the moonless glimmer of white nights, and even the fashionable luxuries of Oniegin, the tongs, combs and files in his dressing case; finds fault—in what sounding verse—with the defects of the Odessa aqueducts and admires the gay variegation of the Nijni Novgorod fair. All that is progressive, all that is human and tasteful is to Puskhin as important, and from a certain standpoint as natural as the primitive and elemental. And so Mickiewicz in *Pan Tadeüsz* makes the features of the comfortable old-world life of the Lithuanian squires blend with the features of nature in one living organism, in one animated image of Lithuania, his sacred country.

In face of the inexhaustible riches of Tolstoy in other quarters, the poverty of the historical, social and domestic colouring in his works is striking. So called "things," the humble and silent companions of man's life, inanimate but easily animated, reflecting man's image, in Tolstoy have no place. Only in *Childhood and Youth* is there a sympathetic

DMITRY MEREZHKOVSKY

description of the domestic surroundings of a Russian squire's family. In the end this sympathy with the life of the class from which he sprang is quenched in him and extinguished by his moral judgment, and the aim of contrasting that life with the life of the common people. Even the popular life throughout his books, from *Polikushka* to *The Power of Darkness*, is shown in darker and darker colours. It is shown, not massively or epically, as Pushkin drew it, but scattered, mutilated, and deformed by town civilization. Finally, the depiction of any kind of human life becomes a mere vehicle for abstract moralizing—for blame or justification.

His real and never-failing artistic power is concentrated for Tolstoy, as we have seen, in the physical frame, in the external movements and internal physical states and the sensations of his characters—in their "natural man." As he gets further from this borderland his light grows dim; so that we ever more faintly distinguish their garments, the details of their domestic life, the internal economy of their dwellings, the street life of the towns in which they live, and lastly, least of all that mental and moral atmosphere of ideas, that historical and social air which is formed not only of all that is true and eternal, but all the prejudices and conventions and artificialities that are peculiar to each age. Pierre Bezukhov as a Freemason is an unsuccessful attempt in this kind, and Tolstoy never afterwards made similar attempts. Pushkin's Tatiana listens to the stories of her nurse and meditates over the artless Martin Zadeka and the sentimental Marmontel. It is clear to us what effect Darwin and Moleshot had on Bazarov, the scientific hero of Turgeniev's *Fathers and Sons*; and what his attitude would have been towards Pushkin and the Sistine Madonna. We know well the books depicting sexual passions which Madame Bovary read, and exactly how they affected the birth and development of her own passion. But we should try in vain to conjecture whether Anna Karénina likes Lermontov or Pushkin the better, Tiutchev[2] or Baratynski.[3] Besides, she does not care for books. Those eyes, so apt to weep and laugh, to glow with love or hatred, care nothing for art.

The mind even of the practical man of today is the outcome of numberless influences, stratifications, aggregations of past ages and civilizations, i.e. culture. Which of us does not live two lives, the actual

---

2. A Pantheistic poet (born 1803, died 1876). He was a Slavophile, and his descriptions of Nature are excellent.

3. Baratynski lived from 1800 to 1844. A sentimental guardsman and Byronic poet.

and the reflected? The prober of the minds of the men of today cannot with impunity neglect this blending of two lives. Tolstoy does neglect it, and in this point, I think, is therefore inartistic. He extracts and lays bare the natural or animally human nucleus from its outward social and historical shell. All that man has built on to nature, all evolution, is to him merely conventional, false, and uninteresting. With a light heart he passes by, hastening away from this atmosphere, which seems to him infected and polluted by human breath, to the fresh air of all that is primitive and animal.

But even here, at the last stages of elementality, of pre-human and pre-animal nature—primal and apart from man, seemingly animated by another and not human form of life—there are bounds eternally inaccessible to Tolstoy. Pushkin first dissolved the antagonism of human consciousness and primitive unconscious nature into a perfect though unprofitable harmony:

> *And though at the grave's door*
> *Young life will ever play,*
> *And nature ever heedlessly*
> *Eternal bloom display.*

With Lermontov this antagonism becomes more painful and irreconcilable:

> *The skies wear majesty—*
> *The earth in the blue radiance sleeps.*
> *Why thus distressed, thus lorn am I?*
>
> *Amid the viewless field of space*
> *The ever-fleeing clouds,*
> *The filing herds, the transient crowds*
> *Pass over sky and leave no trace.*
>
> *In evil fortune's weary day*
> *Do thou of them alone take heed,*
> *The earthly to its earthly need*
> *Leave, and be careless even as they.*

As if he no longer hoped for complete unification with Nature, he says not "be with them," but "be *as they*."

In Tiutchev this contradiction becomes still more acute. There is unbearable discord:

> *Whence cometh this discord?*
> *And why in the universal choir*
> *Sings not the heart as sings the sea,*
> *Or murmurs as the brooding reed?*

Or, lastly, take Turgeniev. The very essence of his attitude to Nature lies in this sense of discord between the murmurs of the "thinking reed" and the meaningless clearness of Nature.

But Tolstoy's attitude towards Nature is twofold. To his consciousness, which would fain be Christian, Nature is something dark, evil, even fiendish. "It is that which the Christian should overcome in himself and transfigure into the kingdom of God." On the other hand, to Tolstoy's unreasoning pagan side man is made one with Nature, and disappears in her like a drop in the ocean. Olenine, steeped in the lore of Uncle Yeroshka, feels himself in the woods an insect among insects, a leaf among leaves, an animal among animals. He would have said, like Lermontov, "Be as they," because he *is* already of them. In Tolstoy's *Three Deaths* the dying young lady, in spite of her external conventional veneer of culture, is so little given to thinking that it clearly does not enter the writer's head to compare "the murmur of the brooding reed" with the unrepiningness of the dying tree.

Thus both in the Christian and the pagan Tolstoy we find no sense of opposition between Man and Nature. In the first case Nature disappears in Man; in the second Man is swallowed up in Nature.

Pushkin hears in the stillness of the night the mutter of the old wife, Destiny.

Tiutchev knows "a certain hour of universal silence" when gloom thickens—

> *As Chaos on the waters*
> *Forgetfulness like Atlas weights the land.*
> *Only the Muse's ever virgin soul*
> *By Gods in dreams is haunted and fore-awed.*

And in the breathless July nights he hears—

Only the flashing lightnings,
Like deaf and dumb daemonic souls,
Talk to each other.

In Turgeniev, too, the icy summits of the Finsteraarhorn and the Jungfrau in the deserted pale green sky, like the demons, hold converse on mankind, that pitiful human mildew on the surface of the globe.

Such visions of Nature have never disturbed the muse of Tolstoy. He has never heard in the stillness of the night "the mutter of the old wife, Destiny."

Does he love Nature? It may be his feeling for her is stronger and deeper than what people call "love of Nature." If he does love her, then it is not as an elemental being apart from and stranger to man, yet akin to man and full of divine and daemonic forces. Rather as an elemental *complement* of his own nature as "natural man." *He loves himself in her, and her in himself,* with enthusiasm, awe, or intoxication, with that great sober fondness with which the ancients loved her, and with which none of the men of today has yet learnt to love her. The strength and weakness of Tolstoy lies precisely in this—that he never can clearly distinguish the civilized from the elemental, or Man from Nature.

The gloom and mystery of the other world he, too, finds in Nature; but this gloom, this mystery, are full only of repellent terror. Sometimes he, too, finds the veil of phenomena lifted.

But behind this lifted veil Tolstoy sees not "the living chariot of the Universe, rolling in sight to Heaven's sanctuary," nor "the flight of angels," but a mere bottomless black void—the "bog" into which Ivan Ilyich, with his long inhuman cry, "I don't want to—o—o—o!" is slowly drawn. Even in the voice of the night wood Tolstoy only hears that dreary rustle of dry mugwort, in the snow-wrapped wilderness, which so frightens the dying master in *Master and Man.* But while the veil of day is down he clearly and dreamlessly sees Nature as she is, nor does her golden tent ever grow for him transparent, translucent, or luminous.

Either total darkness or perfect light, either sleep or waking. For him there is no twilight hour, blending sleep with waking; no morning or evening mist full of "prophetic dreams"; no spectral twilight, starry and glimmering, like the Pythian murmur of Pushkin's Fate—nothing fabulous, magical, or miraculous.

We shall see later that on only one occasion in his whole vast creation did he verge on these limits that seem unattainable to him, where the supernatural marches with the natural and is seen, not *within*, but behind and through the natural. Then he, as it were, overcame himself, went beyond himself. This is precisely that excessiveness, that final miracle of victory over his own nature, which marks the highest genius. However, when he verged on these boundaries he did not overstep them, but drew back.

XI

With regard to the earlier parts of *Peace and War* Flaubert writes to Turgeniev: "Thanks for enabling me to read Tolstoy's novel. It is a work of the highest order. What a painter! and what a psychologist! The first two volumes are excellent, but the third falls off terribly (*dégringole affreusement*). He repeats himself and philosophises; till at last you see the gentleman himself (*le monsieur*), the author, and the Russian; whereas up till then you had seen only Nature and Mankind."

The criticism is somewhat hasty and superficial. Flaubert is apparently still diffident, overcome with astonishment at this literary Leviathan from semibarbarous unknown Russia. "I cried out with enthusiasm while I was reading," he owns, "but it is long! Yet it is powerful, very powerful!"

It is true that there are startling inequalities in *Peace and War.* There are two reservoirs of language, two tongues.

Where he depicts reality, especially the primitive "natural" man, his language is distinguished by unequalled simplicity, strength, and accuracy. And if he seems at times to write with too much insistence and emphasis, in comparison with the winged ease of Pushkin's prose, it is the ponderousness and insistence of the Titan, who piles blocks upon blocks. Side by side with these Cyclopean masses how astonishing seem the acute, diamond-like particles and subtleties of his sensual observation!

But directly he enters on abstract psychology, not of the "natural" but the "spiritual" man—"philosophisings" in Flaubert's phrase, "lucubrations" to use his own words—as soon as we get to the moral transformations of Bezukhov, Nekhliudov, Pozdnyshev, or Levine, something strange happens, *il dégringole affreusement*, he goes off terribly: his language seems to dry up, wither, and become helpless, to cling convulsively to the object depicted, and yet to let it escape, like a man half paralyzed.

Out of a multitude of instances I will only quote a few at random. "What crime can there be," says Pierre, "in my having wished—to do good? Even though I did it badly, or only feebly, yet I did something for that end, and you will not only not persuade me *of this, that that which* I did was not good, but not even that you did not think so."

Touching the attitude towards Natasha's illness of her father, Count

Rostov, and her sister, Sonia, he says: "How would the Count have borne the illness of his beloved daughter if he had not known that if she did not get better he would not grudge thousands more to take her abroad? What would Sonia have done *if* she had not had the pleasant consciousness of *this that* she had not undressed for three nights, in order to be ready precisely to carry out all the directions of the doctor, and *that* she now did not get a night's sleep, *in order* not to let the time pass at which the pills ought to be given. And she was also pleased *at this that she*, by neglecting to carry out the instructions, could show *that she* did not believe in doctors."

Of the hypocritical solicitude of the sick Ivan Ilyich's wife we learn that "she had done everything for him only for her own sake; and she told him that she did what she had done simply for her own sake, as if it were such an improbable thing that he was bound to take it the other way about." What a strain of imagination is necessary in order to unravel this grammatical tangle in which the simple thought is involved!

Numerous instances of this mumbling of repetitions, and even violation of simple grammatical rules, might be given, but these are only found when Tolstoy is writing outside his limits.

Even the sensitiveness, usually so acute and ready in him, to the euphonious construction of language—what Nietzsche calls "the conscience of the ears"—deserts him in these cases.

It is as if his language, like a half-tamed savage animal longing for the woods, suddenly rebels. The artist struggles with it, vehemently trying to stretch it on the Procrustes' bed of Christian "meditations." There is no spectacle more pitiable and instructive. Sometimes he seems proud of carelessness in style, with that special pride peculiar to ascetics in the breach of outward decencies. He seems to say despotically: "So my style is not dainty enough? As if I cared for style! I speak what I think. My thoughts are their own recommendation." But owing to an excessive aiming at simplicity he sometimes falls into *simplesse*, and artificiality.

Turgeniev found the psychology in *Peace and War* weak. "What a psychologist!" cries Flaubert enthusiastically, in speaking of the same. These two judgments, however contradictory they may seem, may be reconciled.

The nearer Tolstoy is to the body, or that which connects body and soul—the animally primitive "natural" man—the more faithful and profound is his psychology, or more exactly his *psycho-physiology*.

But in proportion as, leaving this soil that is always firm and fruitful under him, he transfers his operations into the province of independent spirituality, unconnected with the body and bodily action, *leaving the passions of the heart for the passions of the mind* (for the mind *has* its passions, not less complex and strong, and Dostoevsky is their great delineator), the psychology of Tolstoy becomes doubtful.

It is impossible not to believe that the minute when Nicolai Rostov saw in the ravine dogs struggling with the hunted wolf, one of which had the quarry by the throat, was "the happiest moment in his life." But Christian sentiments, especially such Christian ideas as those of Irteniev,[1] Olenine, Bezukhov, Levine, and Nekhliudov,[2] excite a number of doubts. All these pictures of religious or moral revulsions—written, as it were, by a different man in another style—stand out on the ground-fabric of the work sharply and strangely, interrupting the clear current of the epic by abstract philosophisings in huge, spreading, misty patches. They do not spring or grow out of the living action, or add to it.

In these very passages the "psychology" of Tolstoy recalls the old Eastern fable of the youth who, wishing to learn what was inside an onion, began to take off layer after layer, skin after skin, but, when he had peeled off the last, nothing, or next to nothing, was left of the onion. Tolstoy, in his search for eternal truth, takes off layer after layer, convention after convention, illusion after illusion, stripping off the original and vital with the artificial; on his undoubtedly existing "onion" next to nothing finally remains.

We see Irteniev, the hero of *Childhood and Youth*, to the end. He is distinct, unforgettable, and humanly near to us; we see also, though less distinctly, Pierre Bezukhov, the vigorous Russian gentleman farmer, with his good-natured open face, his short-sighted, observant and thoughtful, but not clever eyes. Pierre, if he has not a vivid personality, yet has at least a vivid face, and is alive. With still less distinctness do we see Levine, the ungainly philosopher, though we are not quite convinced that he exists on his own account. With more and more frequency there looks out of him Tolstoy himself—*le monsieur et l'auteur*. But Pozdnyshev in the *Kreuzer Sonata* and Nekhliudov in *Resurrection* we certainly no longer discern at all. Pozdnyshev is a mere "plaintive

---

1. Characters in *Peace and War* and *Anna Karénina*.
2. In the novel *Resurrection*.

DMITRY MEREZHKOVSKY

voice and a pair of eyes, glowing with feverish half-crazy fire." In these eyes and the voice was centred all the life of his mind, soul, and body. But we do not even hear the voice of Nekhliudov, the hero of *Resurrection*. We get a crystallized lifeless abstraction, a moral and religious vehicle for a moral and religious deduction. Here is one who will never revolt against his Creator, or say or do anything unexpected.

He is a dreary megaphone, through which the "gentleman author" behind proclaims his theorems to the moral universe.

Tolstoy, a great creator of human bodies, is only to a modified extent a creator of human souls. He touches only the primitive roots of life. Is he the creator of what are called "characters"? Doubtless they are outlined by him, put together and moulded, but are they finished, perfected? do they become separate, individualised, unique and entire, living organisms?

The delineations of human individualities in Tolstoy recall half-rounded human bodies in bas-relief, which seem at times to be just going to issue and detach themselves from the flatness in which they are cast, but which never do detach themselves. We never see the other side of them.

In the figure of Platon Karataev the painter has, as it were, achieved the impossible, and succeeded in defining a living personality by the absence of all defined features and acute angles; in a special "roundness" the effect of which is startlingly evident, even geometrical, and proceeding not so much from the inward and spiritual as from the outward bodily presence. He is a molecule, the first and the last, the smallest and the greatest, the beginning and the end. He does not exist of himself: he is only a part of the whole, a drop in the ocean of the life of the nation. And this life he reproduces in his very impersonality, just as a drop of water in its *roundness* reproduces the world. Be that as it may, a miracle of art or a clever optical illusion almost takes place. Karataev, in spite of his want of personality, seems individual, apart, unique. Yet we should like to know the other side of him. He is good; but, maybe, just once in his life tyrannised over some one. He speaks in proverbs, but perhaps just once he added to these apothegms a word of his own. One word, one unexpected trait, and we might have believed him flesh and blood.

But, just at the moment of our most eager expectation, he dies, as if to baffle us; vanishes, is transformed like a bubble of water in the ocean. And when he becomes definite in death we are ready to admit that it would have been impossible for him to be definite in life. He has not lived, but has been "perfectly rounded," and by this alone fulfilled his destiny, so that it only remained for him to die. And in our memories, as in that of Pierre Bezukhov, he is for ever imprinted, not as a living *person*, but only as a living "*personification* of all that is national, good, and perfected." He is a moral generalisation.

The individuality of Prince Andrei from the first we see or conjecture. He becomes to us ever more intelligible in his living contradictions, combinations of cold reason with fiery dreaminess, contempt for men with unquenchable thirst for fame; "love for men," and outward aristocratic harshness; secret tenderness, and a sort of childishly defenceless impressionability of heart.

But here again, at the very moment when it seems only a few more strokes of the chisel are needed and his humanity would be complete, Prince Andreï proceeds to die. Unlike Karataev, he dies slowly and painfully. Death needs a good deal of time to smooth down his marked traits, prominent angles, and excrescences into the perfect "smoothness" of the original molecule, the bubble of water ready to mingle with the ocean. So Death tosses and rounds him slowly, as the sea rounds an angular stone.

At the time when the process of dying is incomplete, when he is delirious and in great pain, in despair, although with lucid intervals, from his living face stands out a new, strange, and terrible one. And this *second face* so pushes aside and swallows up the first—the past life of the man, all his living thoughts, feelings, and actions come to appear so trivial—that in our memories there is fixed for ever not the life, but the death of Prince Andreï; not the living individual, but that in-comprehended, inhuman, unearthly second face of his.

Then take Natasha Rostov, who seems wholly alive, native, national, akin to ourselves, yet individual and unique. How tenderly and firmly is tied the knot of her human personality! Of what evasive, fine, and various gradations of spiritual and physical life is woven this "chastest model of the purest charm!" Like Pushkin's Tatiana, she embodies the Muse of the poet, and reflects his own view of the "eternal feminine."

And yet, just at the time when the figure of Natasha, ripening, attains its highest charm, the artist introduces one fleeting, but strikingly subtle and unforgettable trait. The thing happens in the fields during coursing: the dogs have just run down a hare, and one of the sportsmen gives the hare the *coup de grace* and shakes it about so that the blood may run out. All are excited, flushed, panting; in unusual exultation they boast of and recount the circumstances of the coursing. Just then Natasha, without drawing breath, in her delight and enthusiasm, gave so piercing a yell that their ears tingled. In this yell she gave expression to what the other sportsmen gave vent to by all talking at once. And this yell was so strange and so wild that she herself would have been ashamed of it, and all the others astonished, if it had happened at any other time.

In this wild sportsman's yell of the primordial instinct to slay, in this woodcraft of the satyr, the charming features of Natasha, stamped with primal passion, are almost unrecognizably disfigured. It is her "second face," and recurs for ever.

Is not something similar to this wild yell heard by Pierre Bezukhov? The same sound is heard in the inhuman howl and roar of Kitty when in childbirth. It is in the epilogue to *Peace and War*, when Natasha becomes a spouse and a mother, "bears, brings forth, and nurses," that her figure at the end of the vast epic arrives at final perfection. But it does so in unexpected fashion.

After seven years of marriage Natasha "had grown stout and broad, so that it was difficult to recognize in the stalwart mother the slender, active Natasha of old." "She had run wild to such a degree that her costumes, her way of doing her hair, her inept remarks, her jealousy—she was jealous of Sonia, of the governess, and of every woman, good-looking or ugly—were the staple jokes of those about her." Now "she troubled herself no longer, either about her manners, or the delicacy of her speeches, or about showing herself to her husband in becoming attitudes, or about her toilet. Nor did she try to avoid annoying her husband by her exactingness. She violated all these rules."

"To untidiness and neglect she added stinginess." There was no intellectual bond between her and her husband. Of his scientific occupations "she understood nothing." "She has no words of her own," says Nicolai Rostov in astonishment, though he himself does not excel in intelligence or abundance of speech. Everything human, except concern for her husband and children, is lost to her. She, as it were, has grown wild in family life; avoids people, and takes delight "only in the society of her own children, in which, slipshod and in a dressing-gown, she could stride from the nursery with a face of delight to inspect swaddling clothes with a yellow instead of a green stain on them, and hear comforting reports that 'now the child was much better.'" She frequently seems to have lost her soul in her body, and become a mere prolific she-animal.

Has then the artist abandoned the importance he formerly attached to Natasha? Has the figure shrunk and grown dim? Is there something unforeseen which did not enter into his first conception, a contrast between Natasha the girl, full of innate grace and mysterious charms—the sister of Pushkin's Tatiana, the pure and prophetic Muse of Tolstoy—and this merely conceiving child-bearing animal-mother in whom "you can see face and body, but soul not at all?"

Between these two figures, in the eyes of their creator, there is not only no discrepancy, but actually an inevitable bond of organic consistency and development. It was just to this, the transformation of her into a female, the change of all that was characteristic, yet conventional and limited, into the elementally impersonal, unconventional and universal, that he was leading her throughout his vast epic. So Nature leads the bud to the fruit; and it was only for that that he loved her. Her figure has neither shrunk nor grown dim, but on the contrary has only now attained its greatness—the greatness of motherly nature. That "ceaselessly burning fire of animation" which formed the charm of Natasha the girl has not died out in Natasha the mother, but sunk deeper, remaining divine; not divinely spiritual, only divinely *fleshly*. It is a state, not lower than the first, but merely the first contemplated from another side. The mystic music and aroma were merely a chrysalis, a brilliant spring garb, which Nature gave her, as she gives to flowers perfume, to the birds voice and plumage, and to fish their magically kaleidoscopic colouring, for the time of their sexual existence. But this *passing* charm is at the same time *lasting*; for here, in the dawn, in the perfection of sex, in Love, in the winged and all-winging Eros-desire, is most deeply and brightly disclosed the divine meaning of all creation; the prophetic union of every breathing creature with the spirit of the life of the world. The original figure of Natasha is not lost, but only transformed and swallowed up in the second. "She felt," Tolstoy tells us, "that those charms which instinct had taught her to use before would not only be ridiculous in the eyes of her husband, to whom from the first moment she had given herself wholly, with her whole soul, not leaving a single nook hidden from him; she felt that the bond between her and her husband was maintained, not by those poetic sentiments which had attracted him to her, but by something different, undefined but strong, like the *link between her own soul and body*."

Here you see Tolstoy, as everywhere and at all times, reduces everything to this "link between the soul and body," the connexion of flesh and spirit, the "natural man," and that golden chain of Eros as Desire, which the gods, in Homer's phrase, have let down from heaven to earth to link together earth and heaven and one sex with the other.

The spring pairing-season is over: lives already fructified, assuaged, are silently collecting their forces for parturition and alimentation. All the time Natasha's power over her husband, formerly given her, did not diminish, but increased. "Natasha, in her own house," Tolstoy tells us, "though she put herself on the footing of the slave of her husband, and directly it is a question of judgment, has no words of her own, uses *his* words." "Yet the general opinion was," adds Tolstoy on his own account, "that Pierre was under the thumb of his wife; and it really was so."

Pierre may philosophise, aim at Christian "revival," dream of the good of his fellows and of the good of the people as much as he likes. But if matters had gone as far as putting the dream into execution, or come near a real distribution of the property, Natasha would have sooner "put him under guardianship" than agreed to anything of the kind. Then "the slave of her husband," the mate defending her young, would have shown her lord her talons, and doubtless subdued him, because behind her was—all Nature.

Matters, however, never come to such a pass. Natasha is easy; Pierre will always merely dream, merely "theorize," and his life passes unruffled away. He is more moderate and reasonable than he seems. Let him philosophise—you must do anything to soothe a child, thinks the prudent Natasha. Or again:

"The soul of Countess Maria always aimed at the endless, the lasting, and the perfect, and therefore she never could be quiet." She had "a secret lofty suffering of the soul, overweighted by the body." She remarks, however, with naïve cynicism, with regard to the Christian dreams of Pierre as to giving away his property: "He forgets that we have other and nearer obligations, which God Himself has shown us, *that we may run risks ourselves, but not for our children.*"

All the heroes of Tolstoy either die or come to this—there is no other issue.

Pierre and Levine, philosophising rationalism and the Christian conscience, are under the thumb of their wives. Kitty and Natasha to all their "philosophisings" retort with a silent and irrefutable argument, the bringing into the world of a fresh child. "And this good thing will always be, must always be," the great seer of the body seems to say in these characters, *against his own will and reason.*

Natasha has "no words of her own." But, like the statue crowning the very pinnacle of some huge elaborate building, the figure of Natasha, the mother, silently and majestically reigns over the whole vast tale of *Peace and War.* So that the effect of worldwide tragedies, wars, the upheaval of nations, the grandeur and the downfall of heroes, seem only the pediment to this mother and mate. Austerlitz, Borodino, the burning of Moscow, Napoleon, Alexander the Blessed, may be or may not be—all passes by, all is forgotten, is wiped off the tables of universal history by the next wavelike letters written on the sand. But never will mothers cease to delight in their babies. On the very summit of this work, one of the greatest edifices ever raised by men, Natasha triumphantly waves—"swaddling clothes, with a yellow stain instead of a green," as the guiding banner of mankind.

XII

The swallowing up of the human individual in the universal and non-human is one of the prevalent "burdens" of the Tolstoyan method.

As Nature swallows up Uncle Yeroshka ("I die and—the grass grows") Death swallows Platon Karataev and the Prince Andreï, childbearing absorbs Natasha, so the element of unfruitful extra-conjugal, destroying Love—which from Tolstoy's standpoint is the wicked and sinful "death-bearing Eros"—swallows up Anna Karénina. From her first sight, almost her first silent glance, at Vronski, to her last sight of him, Anna loves, and only loves. We scarcely know what she has felt and thought, how she has lived; it would seem that she had really no existence until Love came: it is impossible to imagine her as not loving. She is all love, as if her whole being, soul and body, were compact of love, as the Salamander is of fire, or Undine of water. Between her and Vronski, as between Natasha and Pierre, Kitty and Levine, there is no express and, generally speaking, no spiritual bond. There is only the dark and strong physico-spiritual bond, "the bond of the soul on its bodily side." She never talks to him about anything but Love. Even her love speeches are poor.

"'I danced more at Moscow at that one ball of yours than all the winter through at St. Petersburg. I must have a rest before travelling.'

"'And you are certainly going tomorrow?' asked Vronski.

"'Yes, I think so,' replied Anna, as if astonished at the daring of his question. But the unrestrained quivering flash of her eyes and smile inflamed him as she said this."

In this society small talk the words express nothing, but the eyes and smile complete what is left unsaid. It is the deciding moment of their passion.

When Vronski confesses his love for Anna the words again are poor. "Do you not know that you are all my life to me? You and I to me are one. And I do not foresee the possibility of peace either for myself or for you. I see the possibility of despair, of misery; or I see the chance of happiness, such happiness! Is it really impossible?" he ended, only shaping the words, yet she heard him.

"She strained all the powers of her mind to say what she ought, but instead of that she fixed on him her glance, full of love, and made no other reply."

If we compare the awkward, commonplace, wretched babble of Vronski with the "triumphant hymns of Love" of the Sakuntâla, of Solomon and the Sulamite, or Romeo and Juliet, how poor it seems! But this voiceless gesture and language of Love is much more effective than any words.

Moreover in Tolstoy the artistic centre of gravity, the force of delineation lies, not in the dramatic, but in the descriptive part, not in the dialogues between the characters or in what they say, but in what is said of them. Their speeches are hurried or senseless, but their silence is unfathomable and pregnant. "She was one of those animals," says Tolstoy of Frou-frou, Vronski's horse, "who seem not to speak, only because the mechanical construction of their mouths does not admit of it." We may say of some of his characters—of Vronski and Nicolai Rostov, for instance—that they only *do* speak because the mechanical conformation of their mouths admits of it.

Anna too "has not words of her own," like Natasha, who uses those of her husband, and Platon Karataev, who uses those of the people, apothegms and proverbs. How many unforgettable, personal feelings and sensations of Anna's are preserved in our memory, but not a single thought, not a single particular or personal expression, even with regard to Love. Yet she never seems stupid; on the contrary, we gather that she is mentally more complex and significant than Dolly, Kitty, or Vronski, and perhaps (who knows?) even more so than Levine, who talks so much. But her position in the working out of the story, her complete absorption in the element of passion, are such that they draw her away from us on the side of intelligence, will, and the highest, most selfless, and passionate life of the spirit. Who or what is she, apart from Love? We only know that she is a St. Petersburg woman in high society. But, apart from her rank, where do the roots of her being find their way into the soil of Russia? For that being is deep and primitive enough to have such roots. What does she think about in general, about children, people, Duty, Nature, Art, Life, Death, and God? On this we know nothing, or almost nothing. But, on the other hand, we know exactly how her curls wave and flutter on her neck and temples, how her slender fingers taper at the end, and what a round, firm, polished neck she has; every expression of her face, every movement of her body we know. Her body, where it touches the primitive animal point, soul—*her nightly soul*—we see with startling distinctness. With not less distinctness we also see the primitive and elemental personality

DMITRY MEREZHKOVSKY

and character of Vronski's horse Frou-frou, and the horse is one of the characters of the tragedy. If it is true that Vronski is like a horse in an aide-de-camp's uniform, then his mare is like a charming woman. And it is not for nothing that Tolstoy emphasizes the marked similarity, full of mysterious foreshadowings, of the "eternally feminine" in the charm of Frou-frou as of Anna Karénina.

Frou-frou "was not perfect according to the canons," but it is just these irregular "personal" characteristics that attach Vronski to her. When he first looks at Anna he is struck by the "race," the "blood" in her appearance. Frou-frou too "had in the highest degree this 'blood,' this 'race'—a quality which made you forget all defects," this aristocracy of the body. They have both, the mare and the woman, the same *definite expression* of bodily presence, which combines strength and tenderness, delicacy and energy. The bones of Frou-frou "below the knee, looked at in front, were no thicker than your finger, but sideways seemed to be very broad." They both have the same active lightness, sureness, as it were wingedness of movement, the same over-stormy and passionate excess of vitality. Between Frou-frou and her master there was a strange "spiritual" bond. She knows and loves him for his affection, desires and yet fears it. Directly Vronski came in she drew a deep breath, and rolling her prominent eye so that the white showed the blood, from the opposite side gazed at the newcomers, shaking her headstall and nimbly changing her feet.

"Oh, you beauty, oh!" cried Vronski, going up to the mare and coaxing her.

"But the nearer he went the more excited she got. Only when he went to her head she suddenly became quiet and the muscles quivered under the fine delicate skin. Vronski gazed at her strong neck, set right on the sharp bit the bar which had shifted, and put his face to her nostrils, soft as a bat's wing. She noisily drew in and let out again the air, with dilated nostrils, quivering, then pricked a sharp ear and put out her powerful black muzzle towards Vronski, as if meaning to take him by the sleeve. But remembering the headstall, she shook it and began again to change her polished feet."

Vronski loves the mare almost as a woman.

"Quiet, my pet, quiet!" said he, again stroking her. The excitement of the mare communicated itself to him, and he felt the blood rush to his heart. Like the mare he wanted to be in motion, to have his fling—he felt both ill at ease and lively.

Frou-frou too loves the dreadful mastery of her lord, and, like Anna, is submissive, even to death. And on both of them is wrought the cruelty of love, the boyish sport of death-bearing Eros. At the races, when Vronski had distanced every one and is nearing the winning-post, Frou-frou, gathering her last strength together, flies beneath him like a bird. "Oh, my beauty!" he thinks, with infinite affection and tenderness. "She anticipates every movement, every thought, every feeling of her rider. In the exultation of almost supernatural speed, in the glorious intoxication of their flight, man and animal are as one body. And then one false irremediable movement: not keeping time with the motion of the horse, he jerked back in the saddle, and suddenly lost his balance." He felt that something dreadful had happened. He came to the ground with one foot, and the mare rolled on it. Scarcely had he succeeded in freeing the foot when she fell on one side, breathing heavily and making fruitless efforts to raise her slender perspiring neck, rolled over on the ground at his feet, like a bird shot on the wing. The awkward movement that Vronski had made had broken her back. But this he only realized much later. For the present he stood trembling in deep sticky mud; and before him, panting heavily, lay Frou-frou. Bending her head towards him, her beautiful eyes looked at him. Still not realizing what had happened, Vronski dragged at her by the rein. She again struggled like a fish, shaking the flaps of the saddle, and got free her fore feet; but, unable to raise her quarters, at once sank down again and fell on her side. With a face distorted by passion—pale, and his lower jaw quivering—Vronski struck her with his heel in the side, and again began to tug at the rein. She did not stir, but, burying her nose in the ground, simply stared at her master with speaking eyes.

"'Ah, ah!' groaned Vronski, clapping his hands to his head; 'Oh, oh! what have I done, what have I done?' he cried. 'And the race is lost too! And it is my fault, my shameful, unpardonable fault!'

"For the first time in his life he experienced misery—misery incurable, and of his own making."

And who knows, did not Fate send him a warning in the death of Frou-frou? Was he not to destroy Anna in just the same way? Here, as there, it was "one wrong movement"—false and irremediable. He is driven on by that love which, full of hate—the thirst of physical possession akin to murder—finds expression in the most passionate endearments of lovers.

When he looked at the living Anna Vronski "felt what a murderer

DMITRY MEREZHKOVSKY

must feel when he sees the body of his victim. Repulsive to him was the remembrance of that for which all this terrible price of shame had been paid. Shame of spirit overcame her and was imparted to him. But in spite of all the horror of the murderer in face of the *corpse* of his victim, he must take advantage of what he has gained by the murder. And so with fury he rushed at this body; covers it and her shoulders with kisses."

After Anna's suicide (she threw herself, you remember, before a railway train) Vronski sees this same body "on the barrack table, shamelessly exhibited before strangers, blood-stained, yet full of the life that had scarcely left it—the head, which was intact, bent backward with its heavy plaits; the hair waving at the temples; and on the charming face, with the half-open rosy mouth, a frozen, strange, pitiful aspect of the lips, and a terrible look in the glazed, unclosed eyes, as if uttering anew the harrowing words of parting, 'that he would repent of it,' which she had used to him at the time of their quarrel."

Again a misery incurable. Again the blame lay with himself. Again the eternal wrong of the strong towards the weak, the crime of Eros the passionate against Another, who said: "Be ye all one, as Thou, my Father, art in me and I in Thee, so that they may be one in us."

Thus, after probing the human till he reaches the animal, and the animal, Frou-frou, till he reaches the human, Tolstoy finds in the inmost recesses of both a "symbolical," a uniting first principle. But before he digs his way to these depths through what stormy abysses of pain he has to pass! From Anna Karénina, full of involuntary and innocent excess of life, to this "blood-stained body, shameless on the barrack table," how fearful the journey!

With Tolstoy the utter denudation of man, the bringing of the likeness of God to the image of the beast—in sensuality, in illness, in childbirth, in death—sometimes verges on deliberate cruelty. He sometimes, like Dante's merry demons, strips despair till it becomes cynical and ridiculous.

Take the swart face of the grunting Tartar, whose back is being probed by the surgeons after the battle of Borodino. That snub-nosed, dark face, with its gnashing teeth—is it not a vision of "Hell," of "The Last Judgment"? Or take poor Anatole, the pampered darling, and Adonis, sobbing a convulsive farewell to his own white leg—still in its boot, but amputated.

Take the sprawling, dead, ox-like attitude of the body of the merchant Brekhunov—frozen to death, in *Master and Man*, to save his servant's life; "to rise again," thinks Tolstoy perhaps, "at the last trump," but meanwhile to lie monstrously kicking and ridiculous. Might not the heroic face of death, as with the Greeks, have been decently covered? Might not the insult to the sanctuary of the human body have been spared?

Or take the account of the illness of Ivan Ilyich. Here the artist purposely dwells on the unconquerable human habit of deceiving oneself, of shutting one's eyes to the ultimate animalism of one's own body, which is perhaps a trifling, but how ineradicable and touching, symptom of our super-animal spirituality.

With what pitiless insistence the artist dwells on the contrast between the young, healthy, fresh, wholesome, active, powerful, good, simple peasant Gerasim, and the unclean, evil-smelling gentleman Ivan, decayed to the loss of all human dignity, and put to shame by his illness!

The ingenuity and subtlety of the devices—"burnings, as of fire, with appetence," "rearings," and "throbbings" of complaints, prickings, repentances, and terrors—through which Tolstoy with a Christian motive takes Ivan Ilyich, his hero or victim, recall the inquiries of the Most Holy Inquisition or the secret Commission, presided over by one of Tolstoy's ancestors, one of the instruments of the Tsar Peter, head of the Secret Chancery—the famous Count Peter Tolstoy.

Tolstoy has in his books no heroes, no characters, no personalities, but merely contemplative victims, who do not struggle or resist. They are swallowed by the elements.

Therefore there is no tragedy. Everywhere isolated tragic *nodi* are tied; but, not being untied by human intervention, these pass once more into the impersonal, the inarticulate, the involuntary, and the non-human. There is no *catastrophe*. In the ocean of that shoreless *Epos* everything fluctuates wavelike—is born, lives, and dies, and is born again, without end and without beginning.

There is no redeeming horror, and there is no redeeming laughter. The air is stifling, low, heavy; there seems nothing to breathe.

The principal victims, or "characters" of Tolstoy, are all clever people, and honourable and good, or good-hearted, simple, or naïve; and yet we never feel completely at home with them, for they have something disturbing, painful, about them. At times it seems as if they all, even the most innocent girls, "the chastest models of the chastest charm," had that satyr-like animal savour which characterizes the old savage, Uncle Yeroshka. Whether this is their own doing, or that of the artist that created them, you can never be sure but that from out a familiar human face will look something different, alien, and primally animal, that, to repeat Voltaire's jest on the "social contract" of Rousseau, his most charming girls "will not get on all fours—run off into the woods, and begin to grunt like the Tartar."

Even Turgeniev remarked on this sensation of *crampedness* in the works of Tolstoy, a sort of absence of the highest liberty, of a certain mountain air, freshening the spirit's breath and all the mental faculties. He tried to explain this defect by Tolstoy's deficiency of *knowledge*. But would not "consciousness" be the better word? "I wish you liberty, spiritual liberty," he wrote once to Tolstoy. *Peace and War* he considered one of the greatest productions of the world's poesy, but at the same time "the most lamentable example of the absence of true comprehensive, spiritual liberty, resulting from the absence of true knowledge." "Without that atmosphere you cannot breathe at ease."

Before Borodino, Prince Andreï sees soldiers bathing by the hot roadside in a muddy pond. They were pelting one another, yelling and shouting. "On the banks, on the dam, in the pond—everywhere white, healthy, muscular bodies. 'It's not half bad, your excellency—if you would condescend,' suggested one of the bathers. 'Dirty,' said the prince, frowning and filled with repulsion at the sight of so much *chair à canon*."

Tolstoy's world must have often appeared to him like that muddy pond with the many naked bathers disporting themselves under the low heavy sky and the red ball of the blazing sun; or like the low and stifling marquee for the wounded.

If we feel suffocated—stifled, as by impending thunder—it is because of Tolstoy's *too great sense of the body* and too little sense of the spirit.

Sometimes even his hero-victims rebel, and struggle towards abstract Christian "musings." But what a pitiful, wingless flight it is! "We may run risks ourselves, but not for our children." So the family bond of blood speaks, and scarcely have the heroes risen, when plump! they fall still more heavily into that rollicking muddy pond.

XIII

G od's creature: there's not only 'God's man,' but 'God's beast.'" In this popular juxtaposition of words, apparently so commonplace, lies a mystery.

Man, too, is "God's creature," and God's beast. The whole living animal creation is the God-beast.

"Love all God's creation—every grain of sand," says the holy old man Zosima in Dostoevsky's book, "every leaf, every ray of God, you should love. *Love animals, love plants,* love everything. Love everything, and you will arrive at God's secret in things."

"God's creature"—a peasant phrase, half-pious, almost ecclesiastical, but there is something pre-Christian, pre-historic, Pan-aryan in the idea. With what careless ease the old Greeks, purest of Aryans, transform the god-man into the god-beast! The limbs of the divinely fair, civilized human body are so knit together and interwoven with the limbs of animals and plants—Pan with the goat, Pasiphae with the bull, Leda with the swan, Daphne with the laurel—that it is difficult to decide where the human or the divine ends in a man, and the animal, the bestial, the vegetable begins: one is fused into the other. The Greeks are amused by these metamorphoses, as by sensual and merry fables; and play with erstwhile awful religious blendings or "symbols," as with toys.

But a people as bright and joyous as the Greeks, yet more earnest and calm (I mean the Egyptians) began pondering over the conjunction in man of the divine and the animal, and never ceased to ponder over it during a culture of, perhaps, six thousand years. Their strange deities, sculptured out of black, shining, indestructible diorite, half men, half beasts, human bodies with the heads of cats, dogs, apes, or crocodiles, or beasts' bodies as those of the Sphinxes with the subtle and spiritualized human smiles, bear witness to this immovable, unsatisfied, terrible, and yet lucid contemplation.

Then another insignificant race, a handful of wandering Semites, shepherds and nomads—alien to all, persecuted by all, hated and despised, lost in the wilderness, and for thousands of years seeing nothing above it but the sky, or around it but bare dead regions, and before it the solitary horizon—set to thinking over the unity of the external and inward creation.

With incredible arrogance this paltry tribe declared itself the chosen one of all tribes and nations, the single people of its God, the one true God. And in all living bodies it saw only a soulless body, for blood-sacrifices and holocausts to the one God of Israel. The face of man, its own face, it fenced off and separated as the likeness and image of God from all animal beings by an impassable gulf. In this idea of terrible loneliness and solitude, in the idea of a jealous God, destroying like fire, there is something of the breath of that fiery wilderness from which this tribe issued: a breath instantly heated, and therefore at times startlingly productive, but also death-dealing and parching.

Judaism at the end of its fight with polyglottism and polytheism, at its terrible extreme of exclusiveness, came in contact with late Hellenism in the schools of the Alexandrine Neo-platonists, Neo-pythagoreans, and Gnostics, the crucible in which was fused, like Corinthian brass from a number of metals, the amalgam called Christian philosophy. Here for the first time the spirit of Semitism, the spirit of the waste and of laying waste, breathed on the magnificent, wild, many-foliaged, magic wood of the Indo-Europeans, and infected one of its branches with a powerful and infectious poison.

The freshly arrived and simple northern semi-barbarians, who had scarcely left the forest defiles, received the ancient and subtle cult with childish simplicity and coarseness. By Christianity they were captivated as by fear, attracted as by a precipice. They seized upon that side of Christianity which was most alien and opposed to their own nature, namely, the exclusively Semitic side; mortification of the irredeemably sinful body, and fear, became their faith, and primitive wild nature their Devil

This spirit of revived Judaism, the spirit of the desert in which Israel had wandered, grew stronger and stronger in the Middle Ages. It passed like a fiery whirlwind over all European civilization, withering the last blossoms and fruits of Graeco-Roman antiquity, until the very Renaissance, when apparently it fell palsied. It recovered, and is rampant today.

We are poisoned by the purely Semitic dread of nakedness, of our bodily selves.

The blighting Eastern simoon passed, however, only over the tops of the Aryan forest: in the thick of it, nearer to the soil, to the people, enough of the old Western moisture and freshness remained partially to revive; there, in the legendary shade, in the storied twilight, still teemed and swarmed the many-tongued, many-deitied "creature of God." In the national Aryan Church legends of the Middle Ages, so akin to the Indo-European Epos, this "creature of God" constantly appears, God's animal, the sacred animal—the mystic stag of St. Hubert, with the cross shining between its antlers; the sheep entering a church, and during the elevation of the "Host" bending its knees with devout bleatings, a lamb before the Lamb; St. Antony of Padua blessing the fish; St. Francis of Assisi preaching to the birds; our own Russian hermit, St. Sergius of Radonej, taming bears with the cross; Sts. Blasius, Florus, and Laurus protecting domestic animals; the holy martyr Christopher, who, even now, is reverenced by the Russian people, and of whom it is said in an illuminated missal of the seventeenth century, "This wondrous martyr, who had a dog's head, came out of the country of the man-eaters," that is Ethiopia or Lower Egypt.

All these bore witness to the pathetic recognition of Man's fellowship with the animal.

It is an immemorially old and ineradicable religious idea in man, this sanctity of the animal and of himself as animal. It is also a prophetic idea, full of dread and glamour. Man, remembering the beast in his own nature (that is, the incomplete, the progressive element, transmuted and unlike the inorganic, and easily transferable from one physical mould to another) has a presentiment that he, himself, man, is not the last attainable goal, the final crown of Nature, but merely a means, a transition, a mere temporary bridge thrown across the chasm between the pre-human and the superhuman, between the Beast and the God.

The dark face of the Beast is turned earthwards, but he has wings, which Man has not.

Prometheus, rebel against Heaven, the "Forethinker," breath of the infernal snake-bodied Titans, also "called down fire from heaven to earth." Nowhere, perhaps, was the old Semitic dread of the animal seen as in the writer of the Revelation—who allows the unexhausted force, the unrevealed knowledge of the Beast-shaped, Antichrist, to rebel and contend with the risen Christ.

Animals at least know much that we, having forgotten, arrogantly call animal instinct. It is a nocturnal sight, an innocent direct knowledge "on the far side of good and evil."

"Human musing of the cradle, the deathbed meditation of Man": this is the most recondite speculation of Tolstoy. Here lie the hidden

Titanic roots, the secret sources of his creations. Here is the loophole and the issue to some other depth, some other sky.

"And you have killed men?" asks Olenine of Uncle Yeroshka. The old man suddenly raised himself by both elbows and put his face close to Olenine's. "The Devil!" he shouted at him. "What are you talking about? You mustn't say that! It is hard work to take a life, ugh! hard work!"

Yes, Uncle Yeroshka, the old hunter, not only "knows," but "pities" and "loves" the moths and the beasts. He knows them because he loves them. He loves even that boar which he stalks in the reeds and strikes down. Here is the purely Aryan paradox, an elemental offshoot of the tangled Aryan forestage, alien and unintelligible to the pitiless straight line, the desert spirit of the Semite, bare as the limit of the horizon.

Tolstoy, like Yeroshka, knows the Animal because he loves him. For the first time after thousands of years of Semitic desolation and isolation this great Aryan has ventured fully and fearlessly to combine by "symbolism" the tragedy of the Animal and the Man, Anna Karénina and Frou-frou.

One of his most marvellous pieces of description is of a visit to a slaughter-house.[1]

"Man, you are king of the beasts—*re delle bestie*—for in truth your bestial nature is the greatest," writes in his diary Leonardo da Vinci, another great Aryan, who did not feed from the "slaughter-house," and had pity for every living creature. A Florentine traveller of the sixteenth century, in the depths of India, in speaking of the Buddhist recluses, remembers his countryman Leonardo, who, even as they, "did not allow harm to be done in his presence to any animal or even plant."

There is an old Indian legend that once, to tempt Buddha, the Saviour of the world, the Evil Spirit in the guise of a vulture, pursued a dove; the dove hid in Buddha's bosom, and he wished to protect it, but the Spirit said, "By what right do you take away my prey? One of us must die, either it by my talons or I of hunger. Why are you sorry for him and not for me? If you are merciful and wish none to perish cut me a piece of flesh from your own body of the same size as the dove." Then he showed him two scales of a balance. The dove settled on one. Buddha cut a piece of flesh from his own body and laid it in

---

1. In a pamphlet called *The First Step.*

the other scale. But it remained motionless. He threw in another piece, and another and another, and hacked his whole body, so that the blood poured out and the bones showed, but the scale still did not sink. Then with a last effort he went to it and threw himself into it, and it sank, and the scale with the dove rose. We can only save others by giving, not a part of ourselves, but the whole.

Out of this ancient unreasoning Aryan pity for live creatures proceeded Buddhism; and, like a flood which bursts the dams, swept away the strongest and firmest of the barriers of human society, the pitiless caste of India separating Brahmin from pariah as widely as God from an animal.

The shedding of blood, the butchery of numberless animals, "where blood flows below and drips from above"—such is the service acceptable to the "jealous God, consuming like a fire," the God of Semitism: such is "the sweet savour, pleasing to the Lord." All tongues, tribes, and nations of the earth are merely flesh for sacrifice. "I will enter My winepress and tread the nations like corn, and make red My garments with blood." Messiah was to come and reign by extermination.

And Messiah came, a babe laid among the cattle. He came "sitting on an ass and a colt, the foal of an ass." "The beasts have their holes and the birds their nests, but the Son of Man hath not where to lay His head." He teaches men the simplicity and wisdom of animals, and the glory of lilies.

What a change, what a transition towards Aryanism from the parched, desolate wilderness of Israel, from the smoking remains of victims to the blossoming garden of God! What an incredible change from the mortification of the flesh to *the resurrection of the body*!

It is as if on reaching its furthest summit Semitism broke down, and overcame itself, and reverted to its first state. It was as if the two opposing geniuses of the world's progress, the Semitic and the Aryan spirit, the spirit of Death and the spirit of Life, had, through all ages and races, sought each other, and finally coalesced.

None of the Aryans has approached so near (though unconsciously, like a mole, by the nocturnal sight of instinct) to this last blending mystery of the spirit and body—the spiritualized body, as Tolstoy.

The never-ending last thoughts and tortures of Prince Andreï, the unsavouriness, uncleanliness, and terrible cry of Ivan Ilyich, "I don't want to—o—o!" and this silent oscillating and the dying of the branch on the tree that is being felled![2] Gradual is the descent of the ladder. Man to animal; animal to plant; plant to the cloud, melting in the sky, ever stiller and stiller, to the last stillness. But even then there is not nothingness, but the beginning of life: there is the issue to a new sky: there there is "*the boundless gloom which is more beautiful than any light*," in the words of Plotinus. "In thy nothing I shall perchance find everything," replies Faust to Mephistopheles as he falls into the abyss below with the keys of the kingdom of "the Mothers."

"For five years our garden had been neglected," records Tolstoy. "I hired labourers with axes and shovels, and worked myself in the garden with them. We cut and hacked at the dead wood and rubbish, superfluous bushes and trees. The trees that had become overgrown and too dense were the poplars and the cherries. The poplar grows away from its roots, and it is no use digging it up, but you must cut the roots out of the ground. Beyond the pond was a huge poplar two armsful in girth. About it was a field, all overgrown with offshoots of poplars. I wanted to dig them up, for I wished the place to be more cheerful, and besides I wanted to relieve the old poplar, because I thought all these young trees came from it and drew the sap from it. When we were getting rid of these young poplars it sometimes went to my heart to see them dug out of the ground, their roots full of sap, and how afterwards we pulled four at a time and could not get out the poplar we had dug up. It held on with all its might, *and did not want to die. I thought, it is plain they want to live, if they cling so hard to life.* But we had to get rid of them, and I did. Afterwards, when it was too late, I realized that there was no occasion to make an end of them. I thought the offshoots sucked the sap from the old tree, but the reverse was the case. When I took them down the old poplar was already dying. When the leaves came out I saw (it had been split into two stems) that one stem was bare, and that same summer it withered. It had been dying for a long time, and *knew* it, and passed on its life to the offshoots. That was why they ran wild so soon, and I wanted to relieve him, and only killed all his children." The trees have their wisdom.

"One wild cherry had grown up on the trunk of a nut tree and choked the hazel bushes. I thought for a long time whether to cut it down or not, *for I was sorry for it.* It was not a shrub, but a tree four or five inches in thickness and four toises in height, spreading and bushy, and covered

2. In *The Three Deaths.*

with bright white fragrant blossom. From a distance you caught its perfume. I was not for cutting it down, but one of the workmen (I had spoken to him before about it) began to do so in my absence. When I came he had already cut some three inches into it, and the sap flowed under the axe, when he came upon a blade imbedded in it. 'There is nothing to be done—it is evidently Fate,' I thought, took an axe myself, and set to help the man. All work makes one cheerful, and so does tree-felling. It is merry work to drive the axe deep sideways and then make a clean cut on top of that, further and further back into the tree. I quite forgot about the tree itself, and thought only of how to get it down. When I got hot I laid down the axe, leant with the man against the tree, and tried to push it down. We shook it, and its leaves quivered and sent down a shower of dew and covered us with the white fragrant petals of its blossoms. It broke off at the incision, and with a stagger fell, foliage and blossom, on the grass. The branches quivered, and the blossom was done for after the fall.

"'Ha! a fine piece of stuff!' cried the man; 'but I'm bitterly sorry.' And I too felt so sorry that I hastened away to the other workmen."

He is sorry for man, he is sorry for the beast, he is sorry for the tree, he is sorry for everything, because all is one live whole, all God's creatures. What is to be done? It is sinful to eat from the slaughter-house—"virtue is incompatible with a beefsteak," says this vegetarian—we may only eat harmless vegetable food. But then he is sorry for plants too. "It was as if something cried out and wept" when there was a crack in the middle of the tree. "Bitterly sorry!" "Will they not have to answer for this?" "No, they will not answer," the vegetarian reassures us. "This is a senseless, exaggerated, Buddhistical pity." Yet did not pity for animals seem, in former ages, senseless and excessive?

Perhaps the time is coming when all men will renounce the slaughter-house.

To live means to cause death. "We make our life out of others' deaths"—*facciamo la nostra vita delle altrui morte*—says Leonardo da Vinci. *The limit of love is the limit of life itself, the end of the world.* And I, for my part, believe that the existing world is drawing to a time when, by its own free choice, it will reject slaughtered flesh as food.

"When did I begin to be?" says Tolstoy in the fragment *Earliest Recollections*. "When did my life commence? Did I not live when I had learnt to see, to hear, to understand, to speak; when I slept and drank, and kissed the breast, and laughed, and delighted my mother? Yes, I lived, and lived happily. Did I not then acquire all that by which I now live, and acquired so much, so quickly, that all the rest of my life I have not acquired a hundredth part of the same? *From the five-year-old child to me there is but a step. Between the newborn child and the five-year-old there is a terrible distance. Between the embryo and the newborn is a gulf. And between the non-existent and the embryo lies far, far more—a distance utterly inaccessible to our conceptions.*"

This inaccessible retreat, this gloomy, lower depth—the ante-natal "journey" of all living things, animal and vegetable ("Consider the lilies of the field, how they grow")—always attracted and drew Tolstoy. Sagely and fearlessly has he looked into this gulf, and into the last mystery of Flesh and Blood.

The mystery, the secret of Flesh and Blood. When Christ revealed it to His disciples it frightened yet tempted them? "He that eateth My Flesh and drinketh My Blood has eternal life, and I will raise him up at the last day, for My Flesh is meat indeed, and My Blood is drink indeed. He that eateth Me shall live in Me." What strange words! Who can understand them? But, like Tolstoy's, these words aim at unifying body and spirit—divinizing the body. They were spoken, we remember, by Him who turned water into wine, and wine into blood. And I would have you notice that by the false view of later Christian asceticism we have carved out the reverse process of blood being turned into wine and wine into water, the sacred Body into bodiless sanctity, the spiritual Flesh into fleshless spirituality, the resurrection of the Flesh into the mortification of the Flesh. This is a second betrayal as great as the first.

If ever the religious thirst of men goes back to this blighting source, then maybe they will remember that Tolstoy, though unconsicously, even in many cases against his own judgment, trod this path towards this Symbol.

Apparently with cynical cruelty—in reality with shamefaced pity—he has laid Man bare of all that is human: he seeks in him the animal in order to make that animal divine.

"To every true artist," he says, "there comes what came to Balaam, who, wishing to bless, found himself involuntarily cursing what he *ought* to have cursed and blessing what he *ought* to have blessed."

The same thing has happened to Tolstoy himself as an artist. Precisely where he sees his shame and shortcoming lies his glory and justification.

XIV

I f in the literature of all ages and nations we wished to find the artist most contrary to Tolstoy we should have to point to Dostoevsky. I say contrary, but not remote, not alien; for often they come in contact, like extremes that meet.

The "heroes" of Tolstoy, as we have seen, are not so much heroes as victims. In them the human individuality, without being perfected to the full, is swallowed up in the elements. And as there is not a single heroic will ruling over all, so there is not one uniting tragic action: there are only separate tragic *nodi* and situations—the separate waves which rise and fall in purposeless motion, not guided by a current within, but only by external forces. The fabric of the work, like the fabric of humanity itself, apparently begins nowhere and ends nowhere.

With Dostoevsky there is throughout a human personality carried to the extremes of individuality, drawing and developing from the dark animal roots to the last radiant summits of spirituality. Throughout there is the conflict of heroic will with the element of moral duty and conscience, as in Raskolnikov; with that of passion, refined, deliberate, as in Svidrigailov and Versilov; in conflict with the will of the people, the State, the polity, as in Peter Verkhovenski, Stavrogine, and Shatov; and lastly in conflict with metaphysical and religious mystery, as in Ivan Karamazov,[1] Prince Myshkine, and Kirillov. Passing through the furnace of these conflicts, the fire of enflaming passions and still more enflaming will, the kernel of human individuality, the inward *ego*, remains undissolved and is laid bare. "I am bound to display self-will," says Kirillov in the *Dæmons*, to whom suicide, which seems the limit of self-abnegation, is in fact the highest pitch of the assertion of his personality, the limit of "self-will." All Dostoevsky's heroes might say the same. For the last time they oppose themselves to the elements that are swallowing them up, and still assert their *ego*, their individuality and self-will, when their end is at hand. In this sense even the Christian resignation of the Idiot, of Alesha, and old Zosima is an insuperable resistance to evil forces about them; submission to God's will, but not to man's, that is the inversion of "self-will." The martyr dying for his

---

1. In *The Brothers Karamazov* (trad. into French E. Halperine et Morice, Paris, 1887).

DMITRY MEREZHKOVSKY

belief, his truth, his God, is also a "hero": he asserts his inward liberty against outward tyranny, and so of course "displays self-will."

In accordance with the predominance of heroic struggle the principal works of Dostoevsky are in reality not novels nor epics, but tragedies.

Peace and War and *Anna Karénina*, on the other hand, are really novels, original epics. Here, as we have seen, the artistic centre of gravity is not in the dialogue between the characters, but in the telling of the story; not in what they say, but in what is said of them; not in what we hear with our ears, but in what we see with our eyes.

With Dostoevsky, on the contrary, the narrative portion is secondary and subservient to the construction of the whole work. And this is apparent at the first glance; the story, written always in one and the same hasty, sometimes clearly neglected language, is now wearisomely drawn out and involved, heaped with details; now too concise and compact. The story is not quite a text, but, as it were, small writing in brackets, notes on the drama, explaining the time and place of the action, the events that have gone before, the surroundings and exterior of the characters; it is the setting up of the scenery, the indispensable theatrical paraphernalia—when the characters come on and begin to speak then at length the piece begins. In Dostoevsky's dialogue is concentrated all the artistic power of his delineation: it is in the dialogue that all is revealed and unrevealed. There is not in all contemporary literature a writer equal to him for mastery of dialogue.

Levine uses just the same language as Pierre Bezukhov or Prince Andreï, Vronski or Pozdnyshev: Anna Karénina the same phrases as Dolly, Kitty, or Natasha, If we did not know who was talking, we should not be able to distinguish one person from another by the language, the sound of the voice, as it were, with our eyes shut. True, there is in Tolstoy a difference between the language of the common folk and the gentry, but this is not external or personal, but merely internal and according to class, In its essence the language of all the characters in Tolstoy is the same, or all but the same: it is colloquial parlance, as it were the sound of the voice of Leo himself, whether in gentleman's or peasant's dress. And merely for this reason we overlook the fact that in his works it is not what the characters *say* that matters, *but how they are silent*, or else groan, howl, roar, yell, or grunt: it is not their human words that matter, but their half-animal, inarticulate sounds, or exclamations—as in Prince Andrei's delirium "i titi-titi-titi," or the "bleating of Vronski" over the dead horse, or the sobbing of Anatole over his own amputated leg. The repetition of the same vowels, a—o—u, seems sufficient to express the most complex, terrible, heart-rending, mental and bodily emotions.

In Dostoevsky it is impossible not to recognize the personage speaking, at once, at the first words uttered. In the scarcely Russian, strange, involved talk of the Nihilist Kirillov we feel something superior, grating, unpleasant, prophetic, and yet painful, strained, and recalling attacks of epilepsy—and so too in the simple, truly national speech of "holy" Prince Myshkine. When Fedor Karamazov, suddenly getting quite animated and ingurgitating, addresses his sons thus: "Heigh, you, children, bairns, little sucking pigs, for me—all my life through— there were no such thing as touch-me-nots. Even old maids, in them sometimes you would make valuable discoveries if you only made them open their eyes. A beggar woman, and a touch-me-not: it is necessary at the first go off to astonish—that is the way to deal with them. You must astonish 'em to ecstasy, to compunction, to shame that such a gentleman has fallen in love with such a slut as she." We see the heart of the old man, but also his fat, shaking, Adam's apple, and his moist, thin lips; the tiny, shamelessly piercing eyes, and his whole savage figure— the figure of an old Roman of the times of the decadence. When we learn that on a packet of money, sealed and tied with ribbon, there was also written in his own hand "for my angel Grushenka, if she wishes to come," and that three days later he added "and the little darling," he suddenly stands before us wholly as if alive. We could not explain how, or why, but we feel that in this belated "and the little darling" we have caught some subtle, sensual wrinkle on his face, which makes us feel physically uncomfortable, like the contact of a revolting insect, a huge spider, or daddy-longlegs. It is only a word, but it holds flesh and blood. It is of course imaginary, but it is almost impossible to believe it is *merely* imaginary. It is just that last little touch which makes the portrait too lifelike, as if the painter, going beyond the bounds of his art, had created a portrait which is ever on the point of stirring and coming out of the frame like a spectre or a ghost.

In this way Dostoevsky has no need to describe the appearance of his characters, for by their peculiar form of language and tones of voices they themselves depict, not only their thoughts and feelings, but their faces and bodies.

With Tolstoy the movements and gestures of the outward bodily frame, revealing the inward shapes of mind, often make profoundly significant most paltry words of his heroes. Not less distinctness in the physical appearance does Dostoevsky achieve by the contrary process: from the internal he arrives at the external, from the mental at the physical, from the rational and human we guess at the instinctive and animal. With Tolstoy we hear because we see, with the other we see because we hear. Not merely the mastery of dialogue, but other characteristics of his method bring Dostoevsky near to the current of great tragic art. At times it seems as if he only did not write tragedy because the outward form of epic narration, that of the novel, was by chance the prevailing one in the literature of his day, and also because there was no tragic stage worthy of him, and what is more, no spectators worthy of him. Tragedy is, of course, composed only by the creative powers of artist and audience; it is necessary that the public, too, should have the tragic faculty in order that tragedy may really be engendered.

Involuntarily and naturally Dostoevsky becomes subject to that inevitable law of the stage which the new drama has so thoughtlessly abrogated, under the influence of Shakespeare, and by so doing undermined at the root the tragic action. It is the law of the three unities, time, place, and action, which gives, in my opinion, such incomparable power, as against anything in modern poesy, to the creations of the Greek drama.

In the works of Tolstoy there always, sooner or later, comes a moment when the reader finally forgets the main action of the story and the fate of the principal characters. How Prince Andreï dies, or how Nicolai Rostov courses hares, how Kitty bears children, or Levine does his mowing, are to us so important and interesting that we lose sight of Napoleon and Alexander I, Anna, and Vronski. It is even more interesting, more important to us at that moment whether Rostov runs down his hare than whether Napoleon wins the battle of Borodino. In any case we feel no impatience, we are in no hurry to learn the ultimate fate of these persons. We are ready to wait, and have our attention distracted as much as the author likes. We no longer see the shore, and have ceased to think of the destination of our voyage. As in every true epic there is nothing unimportant: everything is equally important, equally leading. In every drop there is the same salt taste, the same chemical composition of water as in the whole sea. Every atom of life moves according to the same laws as worlds and constellations.

Raskolnikov kills an old woman to prove to himself that he is already "on the wrong side of good and evil," that he is not "a shuddering being," but a "lord of creation." But Raskolnikov in Dostoevsky's conception is fated to learn that he is wrong, that he has killed, not "a principle," but an old woman, has not "gone beyond," but merely wished to do so. And when he realizes this he is bound to turn faint, to get frightened, to get out in the square and, falling on his knees, to confess before the crowd. And it is precisely to this extreme point, to this one last moment in the action of the story, that everything is directed, gathers itself up and gravitates; to this tragic catastrophe every thing tends, as towards a cataract the course of a river long confined by rocks.

Here there cannot, should not be, and really is not, anything collateral or extraneous, arresting or diverting the attention from the main action. The events follow one another ever more and more rapidly, chase one another ever more unrestrainedly, crowd together, are heaped on each other, but in reality subordinated to the main single object, and are crammed in the greatest possible number into the least possible space of time. If Dostoevsky has any rivals they are not of the present day, but in ancient literature the creators of Orestes and Œdipus: I mean in this art of gradual tension, accumulation, increase, and alarming concentration of dramatic action.

"How well I remember the hapless day," Podrostok cries wonderingly; "it always seems as if all these surprises and unforeseen mishaps conspired together and were showered all at once on my head from some cornucopia." "It was a day of surprises," remarks the narrator of *The Dæmons*, "a day of untying of old knots and tying of new, sharp elucidations, and still worse confusions. In a word, it was a day when astounding events happened together." And so it is in all his stories—everywhere that infernal "cornucopia," from which are poured on the heads of the heroes unexpected tragedies. When we finish the first part of *The Idiot*—fifteen chapters, ten printed quires—so many events have taken place, so many situations have been placed before us, in which are entangled the threads of the most varied human destinies, and passions and consciences have been laid bare, that it would seem that long years had passed since the beginning of the story: in reality it is only a day, twelve hours from morning to evening. The boundless picture of the world's history which is enfolded in *The Brothers Karamazov* is condensed, if we do not count the intervals between the acts, into a few days. But even in one day, in one hour, and that almost on one and the same spot—between a certain seat in the Pavlovski Park and the Terminus, between Garden Street and Haymarket Square—the heroes

　　　　　　　　　　　　　　DMITRY MEREZHKOVSKY

of Dostoevsky pass through experiences which ordinary mortals do not taste in a lifetime.

Raskolnikov is standing on the staircase, outside the door of the old female usurer. "He looked round for the last time, pulled himself together, drew himself up, and once more tried the axe on the lock. 'Shall I not wait a little longer, till my heart ceases to throb?' But his heart did not cease. On the contrary, as if to spite him, it beat harder and harder. *And he scarcely felt the presence of the rest of his body.*"

To all the heroes of Dostoevsky there comes the moment when they cease "to feel their bodies." They are not beings without flesh and blood, not ghosts. We know well what sort of body they *had*, when they still felt its presence. But the highest ascent, the greatest tension of mental existence, the most burning passions—not of the heart and the emotions, but of the mind, the will, and the conscience—give them this divorce from the body, a sort of supernatural lightness, wingedness, and spiritualization of the flesh. They have the very "spiritual, ethereal bodies," of which St. Paul spoke. These are the men who are not suffocated by flesh and blood, or the Tolstoyan "human bubble." It seems as if, at times, they were bodily invisible, only their intense souls could be seen.

"We look at you and say, 'She has the face of a kind sister,'" says the Idiot, describing the beauty of a certain woman. It is curious to compare these instantaneous, supersensual descriptions of Dostoevsky with those of Tolstoy—for instance, the figure of Anna Karénina, so full of deep-seated sensuality; the living souls of Dostoevsky with the overgrown beef of Tolstoy. All Dostoevsky's heroes live, thanks to his higher spirituality, an incredibly rapid, tenfold accelerated life: with all of them, as with Raskolnikov, "the heart beats harder and harder and harder." They do not walk like ordinary mortals, but fly; and in the intoxication of this flight fly into the abyss.

In the agitation of the waves we feel the increasing nearness of the whirlpool.

At times in Greek tragedy, just before the catastrophe, there suddenly sounds in our ears an unexpectedly joyous chant of the chorus in praise of Dionysus, god of wine and blood, of mirth and terror. And in this chant the whole tragedy that is in progress and almost completed, all the fateful and mysterious that there is in human life, is presented to us as the careless sport of the spectator god. This mirth in terror, this tragical play, is like the play of the rainbow, kindling in the foam of some cataract above a gulf.

Dostoevsky is nearest of all to us, to the most inward and deeply-seated principles of Greek tragedy. We find him depicting catastrophes with something of this terrible gaiety of the chorus.

Tolstoy's "still heat" before thunder is here broken, into what roaring of thunder, what lightning of terror! It is no longer, as in Tolstoy, difficult to breathe; in that dragging, deathly heaviness which weighs down the heart in everday life. All expands and expands. At times, even in Dostoevsky's work, we lose our breath from the rapidity of the movement, the whirl of events, the flight into space. And what reviving freshness, what freedom there is in this breath of the storm! The most petty, paltry, and commonplace features of human life here become splendid under the lightning.

We may say of the Muse of Tolstoy what Pierre Bezukhov once said of Natasha. "Is she clever?" asked Princess Maria. Pierre hesitated. "I think not," he said at last, "or rather, she is. *She does not condescend to be clever.* No, she is resourceful, but no more."

The resourcefulness of Tolstoy's Muse lies precisely in this, that she, as it were, "does not condescend to be clever," that with her you sometimes forget the existence of the human mind.

As for Dostoevsky's Muse, we may doubt any other qualities of hers we please, only not her intelligence. He remarks in one place that an author ought to have *a sting*; "this sting," he proceeds to explain, "is the rapier point of deep feeling." I consider that no Russian writer, except Pushkin, was such a master of "the mental rapier of feeling" as Dostoevsky himself.

In contradistinction with the favourite heroes of Tolstoy, who are not so much intelligent as "philosophising," the principal heroes of Dostoevsky—Raskolnikov, Versilov, Stavrogine, Prince Myshkine, and Ivan Karamazov—are clever men first and foremost. Indeed it would seem that, taken on the whole, they are the cleverest, most rational, cultured, and cosmopolitan of Russians, and are European because they "in the highest degree belong to Russia."

We are accustomed to think that the more abstract thought is, the more cold and dipassionate it is. It is not so; or at least, it is not so with us. From the heroes of Dostoevsky we may see how abstract thought may be passionate, how metaphysical theories and deductions are rooted, not only in cold reason, but in the heart, emotions and will.

There are thoughts which pour oil on the fire of the passions and enflame man's flesh and blood more powerfully than the most unrestrained licence. There is a logic of the passions, but there are also passions in logic. And these are essentially *our* new passions, peculiar to us and alien to the men of former civilizations.

Raskolniskov "sharpened his casuistry like a razor." But with this razor of abstractions he cuts himself almost fatally. His transgression is the fruit, as the public prosecutor Porphyry puts it, "of a heart outraged theoretically." The same may be said of all the heroes of Dostoevsky: their passions, their misdeeds, committed or merely "resolved on by conscience," are the natural outcome of their dialectic. Icy, razor-sharp, this does not extinguish, but kindle and inflame. In it there is fire and ice at once. They feel deeply because they think deeply; they suffer endlessly because they are endlessly deliberate; they dare to will because they have dared to think. And the further, apparently, it is from life— the more abstract, the more fiery is their thought, the deeper it enters into their lives. O strange young Russia!

And the most abstract thought is, at the same time, the most passionate: the burning thought of God. "All my life God has tortured me!" owns the Nihilist Kirillov. And all Dostoevsky's heroes are "God-tortured." Not the life of the body, its end and beginning, death and birth, as with Tolstoy, but the life of the spirit, the denial or affirmation of God, are with Dostoevsky the ever-boiling source of all human passions and sufferings. The torrent of the most real, the most "living" life, falling only from these very highest summits of metaphysics and religion, acquires for him that strength of flow, that turbulence of action and striving, which carries him to his tragical catastrophes.

The great poets of the past ages, in depicting the passions of the heart, left out of consideration the passions of the mind, as if they thought them a subject out of the reach of the painter's delineation. If Faust and Hamlet are nearest to us of all heroes, because they think more than any, yet they feel less, they act less, precisely because they think more. The tragedy of both men lies in the contradiction which they cannot solve, between the *passionate heart and passionless thought*. But is not a tragedy of *thinking* passion or passionate *thought* possible? The future belongs to this tragedy and no other. And Dostoevsky was one of the first to make an approach to it.

He has overcome the superstitious timidity, common to modern artists, of feeling in presence of the mind. He has recognized and showed us the connexion there is between the tragedy of our hearts and that of our reason, our philosophical and religious consciousness.

This, in his eyes, is preeminently the Russian tragedy of today. He has observed that cultivated Russians have only to come together—be it in fashionable drawing-rooms like the hearers of Prince Myshkine, or in dirty little inns, like Podrostok with Versilov, in order to begin to dispute about the most abstract of subjects—the future of European civilization, the immortality of the soul, the existence of God. In reality it is not only men of culture, but the whole Russian people (witness, for instance, the history of our dissenters), from the Judaizers of the fifteenth century to the present day Skoptsy and Dukhobortsy, who are absorbed in these thoughts. "All men philosophize, all make inquiries about belief on the roads and in the places of commerce," complained even the holy Joseph Volotski. And it is just by reason of this innate philosophical and religious animation (so Dostoevsky thought) that Russians are, "in the highest degree, Europeans"—I mean the Europeans of the future. This insatiable religious thirst is the presage that Russia will share, and perhaps lead, the universal civilization of the future.

As in our bodily impressionability something is altered after reading Tolstoy, so after reading Dostoevsky something is changed in our spiritual impressionability. It is impossible to forget, to either reject or accept him with impunity. His reasonings penetrate not only into the mind, but into the heart and the will. They are momentous events which must have consequences. We remember them some time or other, and perhaps precisely at the most decisive impassioned crises of our lives. "Once touch the heart," he says himself, "and the wound remains." Or, as the Apostle Paul puts it, he "is quick and powerful, sharper than any two-edged sword, piercing even to the dividing asunder of soul and spirit, of joints and marrow."

There are simple-minded readers, with the effeminate, sickly sentimentality of our day, to whom Dostoevsky will always seem "cruel," merely "a cruel genius." In what intolerable, what incredible situations he places his heroes! What experiments does he not play with them; through what depths of moral degeneracy and spiritual trials (contrast the bodily trials of Ivan Ilyich) does he not lead them, to crime, suicide, even idiocy! Does he not give expression in the humiliating situations in which he places human souls to that same cynical malice which Tolstoy finds expression for by terrible and humiliating physical conditions? Does it not sometimes seem as if he tortures his "dear victims" without object, in order to enjoy? Yes, of a truth he is one who delights in torture, a grand Inquisitor, "a cruel genius."

DMITRY MEREZHKOVSKY

And is all this suffering natural, possible, real? Does it occur? Where has it been seen? And even if it occurs, what have we sane-thinking people to do with these rare among the rare, exceptional among the exceptional cases, these moral and mental monstrosities, deformities, and abortions, fancies of fever and delirium?

Here is the main objection to Dostoevsky, one that all can understand, unnaturalness, unusualness, apparent artificiality, the absence of what is called "healthy realism." "They call me a psychologist," he says himself; "it is not true, I am only a *realist in the highest sense of the word*, i.e. I depict all the soul's depths." This is what Turgeniev meant in objecting to Dostoevsky's "psychological mole-runs."

But he is a searcher into human nature; also at times "a realist in the highest sense of the word"—the realist of a new kind of experimental realism. In making scientific researches he surrounds in his machines and contrivances the phenomena of Nature with artificial and exceptional conditions. He observes how, under the influence of those conditions, the phenomenon undergoes changes. We might say that the essence of all scientific research consists precisely in deliberately "artificialising" the surrounding conditions. Thus the chemist, increasing the pressure of atmospheres to a degree impossible in the conditions of nature as known to us, gradually densifies the air and changes it from gaseous to liquid. May we not call unreal, unnatural, supernatural, nay miraculous, that transparent liquid, dark blue as the clearest sky, evaporating, boiling and yet cold, inconceivably colder than ice? There is no such thing as liquid air, at least in terrestrial nature as it comes within our scrutiny. It seems a miracle. We do not find it; yet it exists.

But is anything of the sort done by Dostoevsky in his experiments with human souls? He also places them in extraordinary and artificial conditions, not knowing himself, but waiting to see, what will become of them. In order that unforeseen aspects, the powers hidden "in the depths of man's soul," may be revealed he needs a degree of pressure of the moral atmosphere rarely met with today. He submits his characters either to the rarefied icy air of abstract dialectics or the fire of elemental animal passion, fire at white heat. In these experiments he sometimes arrives at states of the human mind as novel and seemingly impossible as liquefied air. Such a state of mind *may* exist, because the spiritual world, like the material, "is full," to use Leonardo da Vinci's words, "of countless possibilities, as yet unembodied." It has never been known, yet it is more than natural that *it should be*; to give the unembodied a body is a natural proceeding.

What is called Dostoevsky's psychology is therefore a huge laboratory of the most delicate and exact apparatus and contrivances for measuring, testing, and weighing humanity. It is easy to imagine that to the uninitiated such a laboratory must seem something of a "devil's smithy."

Some of his scientific experiments are dangerous to the experimenter himself. We sometimes feel alarmed for him. His eyes are the first to see the unpermitted. He ventures into "depths" into which no one yet ventured before. Will he come back? Will he be able to manage the forces he has called up? In this daring of inquiry there is something especially modern and characteristic, it may be, of European science in general. It is also a Russian quality that we find in Tolstoy as well. With the same audacious curiosity Tolstoy scrutinizes the body and its past. The two writers supplement each other's work: "deep calleth unto deep."

In Dostoevsky's novels there are peculiar passages as to which it is difficult to decide (compare some poems of Goethe's and drawings of Leonardo da Vinci's) whether they are Art or Science. At any rate they are not pure Art nor pure Science. Here accuracy of knowledge and the instinct of genius are mingled. It is a new "blend," of which the greatest artists and men of science had a prevision, and for which there is, as yet, no name.

And yet we have here "a cruel genius." This reproach, like some feeling of vague yet personal vexation, remains in the hearts of readers blessed with what is called "mental warmth," which we sometimes feel inclined to call "mental thaw." Why these sharp "shafts," these extremes, this "ice and fire"? Why not a little more good-heartedness, a little more warmth? Perhaps these readers are right; perhaps he really is "cruel," yet he is assuredly more merciful than they can conceive, for the object of his cruelty is knowledge. There are poisons which kill men, but have no effect on animals. Those to whom Dostoevsky seems cruel will probably survive.

There remains the question, more worthy of our attention—the question of the cruelty of Dostoevsky towards himself, his morbidity as an artist.

What a strange writer, in good sooth, with insatiable curiosity exploring only the maladies of the human soul, and for ever raving about plagues, as if he could not, or would not, speak of anything else! And what strange heroes these "lucky dogs," hysterical women, sensualists, deformed creatures possessed of the devil, idiots, lunatics! Perhaps it is not so much the painter as the healer of mental diseases we have here, and withal such a healer that to him we must say, "Physician, heal thyself." What have we that are whole to do with these, this plague-stricken collection of clinical cases?

But then we know tests of shameful disease have proved permanent sources of healing. Of a truth, it is only "by his sickness that we are healed." Ought not we, who have had such a warning from the history of the world, though we are only nominally Christians, to deal with less careless self-confidence, with more civilized caution, with all maladies?

For instance, we see too clearly the connexion between health and strength, an *abundance* of vitality on the one side and between disease and weakness and the *loss* of vitality on the other. Yet does there not exist a less obvious but not less real connexion between disease and strength, between what seems disease and real strength? If the seed does not sicken and die and decay, then it does not bear fruit. If the wingless insect in the chrysalis does not sicken, then it never gets wings. And "a woman when she is in travail suffereth pain because her hour is come." There is a sickness, not unto death, but unto life. Whole generations, civilizations, and nations are like to die for pain, but this too may be the birth-pang and the natural and wholesome sickness. In societies, true, it is immeasurably more difficult to distinguish apparent from real sickness, Decay from New Birth. Here we must feel our way. But there are dangerous diseases of society, which depend not on the want, but the excess of undeveloped life, of accumulated and unvented inward power, from the superabundance of health. Our national champions have sometimes felt "burdened with strength," as with a load, and seemed ailing because too strong.

The reverse is, of course, also true. Temporary excess of vitality and the sharpening of the natural capacities is the outcome of real sickness. The too strained cord sounds more loudly before it snaps.

Yes, the more deeply we ponder it the more difficult and enigmatical becomes the question of social maladies, and of the "sacred," or not sacred, malady of Dostoevsky in particular. Yet it seems clear that whether he be great or little, at any rate he is unlike any of the family of world-famous writers. Does his strength come from his ailment, or his ailment from his strength? Is the real holiness—if not of the author himself (though those that were about him declare that there were times when he, too, seemed almost a saint) yet that of the *Idiot*—the result of apparent disease? Or does undoubted disease result from the doubtful sanctity?

"'Go to the doctor,' Raskolnikov advises Svidrigailov, who has told him about his 'presentiments.'

"'I know, without your telling me,' is the reply, 'that I am out of health, though really I don't know in what way. *In my own way*, I feel sure, I am five times as well as you.'

"I asked, 'Do you believe in previsions—presentiments?'

"'No; nothing will induce me to believe in them,' cried the other, with a touch of anger.

"'Well now, what is the usual remark on the subject?' growled Svidrigailov, as if to himself, looking on one side and hanging his head down. 'They say, "You are ill: it is all your fancies—nothing but imagination, delirium." *But there's no strict logic in that.* I admit that previsions only appear to sick men, but then that only argues that previsions appear only to sick men, and not that they have no existence in themselves.'

"'Certainly they have none,' persisted Raskolnikov irritably.

"'No? You think so?' resumed the other, slowly gazing at him. 'Well, how if you settle it this way (there, help me): previsions are, so to say, fragments—pieces of other worlds, beginnings. The healthy man, of course, can't see them anyhow, because a healthy man is the most earthly man. He must, of course, live only the life of this world for completeness and order's sake. But no sooner does he fall ill, no sooner is the normal earthly order broken in his organism, than straightway the possibility of another world begins to dawn on him. The more ailing he is, the closer, I suggest, his contact with the other world.'"[2]

We can understand why Raskolnikov is irritated: although he himself has a dialectic on which he places his whole reliance, "sharpened like a razor," he feels that Svidrigailov, whom he despises as a moonstruck dreamer, has one still keener. Is Svidrigailov simply laughing at Raskolnikov? Is he merely teasing him with his previsions? Or is he exceedingly serious? Has he arrived at finally doubting even *un*belief? He once admits that the idea of eternity sometimes seems to him discomforting: "a chamber something like a village bathhouse, long neglected, and with spiders' webs in all its corners."

---

2. From *The Crime and the Punishment* (English translation, Vizetelly, 1886).

DMITRY MEREZHKOVSKY

It is curious that Dostoevsky in his last diary, when expressing his stray thoughts about Christianity, repeats almost word for word the expression of Svidrigailov: "The firm belief of mankind in the contact with other worlds, obstinate and enduring, is also very significant." Not only so, these words of Svidrigailov's are also echoed by the "saintly" old Zosima in *The Brothers Karamazov*: "Grown creatures live and are kept alive only by the sense of contact with other and mysterious worlds."

In his thoughts about illness as the source of some higher life, or at least a state of insight not attainable in health, Svidrigailov and the *Idiot* agree with the "holy" Prince Myshkine.

"He thought, amongst other things, how, in his epileptic condition, there was one stage, just before the actual attack, when suddenly in the midst of sadness, mental darkness, and oppression, his brain, as it were, flamed up, and with an unwonted out-burst all his vital powers were vivified simultaneously. The sensation of living and of self-consciousness at such moments was almost decupled. They were moments like prolonged lightning. As he thought over this afterwards, when in a normal state, he often said to himself that all these flashes and beams of the highest self-realization and self-consciousness and doubtless 'highest existence' were nothing but a disease, the interruption of the normal state; *and if so, it was by no means the highest state, but on the contrary must be reckoned as the very lowest.* And yet he came at last to the exceedingly paradoxical conclusion, '*What matter if it is a morbid state?*' Finally he decided, '*What difference can it make that the tension is abnormal, if the result itself, if the moment of sensation, when remembered and examined in the healthy state, proves to be in the highest degree harmony and beauty; and gives an unheard of and undreamed of feeling of completion of balance, of satisfaction, and exultant prayerful fusion with the highest synthesis of life?*' If at that, the last instant of consciousness before the attack, he had happened to say to himself lucidly and deliberately 'Yes, for this moment one might give one's whole life,' then certainly that instant of itself would be worth a lifetime. However, he did not stand out for dialectics: obfuscation, mental darkness and idiocy stand before him as the obvious consequence of these loftiest moments."

It is a pity that Prince Myshkine did not stand out for the dialectical part of his deduction. For there is a vast importance attaching to the question, whether it is worth while to give for "a moment of the highest existence" the life, not merely of a man, but of all mankind? In other words, "*Is the goal of the world's evolution an endless continuation in time, in the succession of civilizations*, in the sequence of the generations, or some *final culmination* of all the destinies of history, all 'times and seasons,' *in a moment of 'the highest existence'*; *in what Christian mysticism calls 'the ending of the world'*?" This question seems mystical, abstract, aloof from actuality, but cannot fail, sooner or later, to have an effect on social life of the whole of mankind.

Before Christianity came mankind lived as the beasts live, without thought of death, with a sense of animal perdurability. The first, and so far the only religion which has felt the *imperativeness of the thought of the end*, of death—not only for man in particular, but also *for the whole of mankind*—has been Christianity. And perhaps it is just in this that lies the main distinction of the influence of Christianity (an influence that, even yet is not complete) on the moral and political destinies of Europe.

And here the idea of the end of world, the last consummation of all earthly destinies in a moment, when the angel of the Apocalypse "shall declare to all living that there shall be no more time," the moment of the highest harmony of "higher existence"—last pinnacle of all the civilization of the world—draws near to another idea. To the crowning idea of the religion of Christ the God-man draws near from another shore the religion, the solution of the man-God. Its preacher in Dostoevsky's pages is the Nihilist Kirillov in the book called *The Possessed*—Kirillov whom all his life "God has tortured," who repeats even to the startling coincidence in the turns of expression the "extreme paradox" uttered on this point by Prince Myshkine.

"Have you moments of eternal harmony, my friend? There are seconds—five of six of them at most go by at a time—and you feel suddenly the presence of eternal harmony. It is not earthly, and I do not say that it is heavenly, but man in his earthly guise cannot bear them. *It is necessary to be transformed physically or to die.* This is a distinct feeling and one that cannot be disputed. It is as if you suddenly had the sense of all Nature and exclaimed 'Yes, it is true'; just as God, when He created the world, at the end of every day said, 'Behold, it is good.' It is not softening of heart, but just a kind of delight. You do not forgive anything, for there is nothing to forgive. Neither do you 'love,' for it is a feeling higher than love. The most terrible part is that it is so terribly distinct and joyful. For more than five seconds the mind cannot bear it, and must break down. In those five seconds I live a lifetime, *and for them I would give my lifetime.*

"In order to hold out ten seconds you must be transformed physically.

I think men ought to cease to propagate. What is the use of children, or of progress, seeing the goal has been attained? In the New Testament it is written that in the resurrection they shall not have children, but be as the angels of God."

Here, in reality, Kirillov merely carries to its farthest consequences the dialectic of Prince Myshkine when he says "For that moment a man might give his whole life." Kirillov carries it on and concludes, *"For that moment you might give the life of all mankind."* However, Prince Myshkine too at times seems to approach this pinnacle. He dreads it, but it is nevertheless inevitable. "At that moment," he says to an intimate old friend, "there somehow became intelligible to me that hard saying, *'There shall be no more time.'*"

"Seriously, of course, he would not have maintained it," unexpectedly and timidly concludes Dostoevsky. "In his appreciation of that minute doubtless there was an error." What error? "Obfuscation, mental darkness, and idiocy stood before him as the evident consequence of these loftiest minutes." But is not this obfuscation, this mental darkness, the prospect for every man living? Might not all mankind voluntarily give up its continued life for a brief epoch of intensest harmony with God? Would not that be a solution of both Pagan and Christian doctrine? This question is rooted in the very heart of Christian, nay, of *all* religion.

"Does this state often come to you?" asks Shatov of Kirillov, after his admission as to his moments of eternal harmony.

"Once in three days, or once in a week."

"Have you not got epilepsy?"

"No."

"Well, it means that you will have it. Take care, Kirillov; I have heard that is just the way epilepsy begins. An epileptic described to me in detail his sensations before an attack, exactly as you have; he mentioned the five seconds, and declared he could not stand more."

In Prince Myshkine[3] also the spiritual beauty of nature (undoubted in Dostoevsky's eyes) results from these very flashes of "eternal harmony."

Kirillov anticipates a gradual but literal "physical transformation of man." We seem actually to hear echoes of apocalyptic prophecies:

---

3. In *The Idiot* (English translation, Vizetelly, 1887). "The theory put forward in *The Idiot* is, that a brain in which some of those springs which we consider essential are weakened may yet remain superior, both intellectually and morally, to others less affected."— WALISZEWSKI.

"Behold, I make all things new. There shall be a new heaven and a new earth." "In Christ Jesus—*a new creature.*" The "physical transformation of man" is the new birth of the flesh—the real "resurrection of the body." "I tell you a mystery. We shall not all die, but we shall all be changed."

"Then there will be a new life on earth," says Kirillov. "*Then History will be seen divided into two vast epochs, the first from the gorilla to the annihilation of the conception of God, and, secondly, from the extinction of God to—*"

"To the gorilla?" suggested Stavrogine, with cold mockery.

"*To the transformation of the earth and of man physically,*" resumed Kirillov calmly. "Man will be a god, and be physically transformed in his powers. The world will be changed, and all things will be changed, including thought and emotion."

The idea of the physical transformation of man gives Kirillov no rest, and haunts him like a fixed idea.

"I begin and end and open the door. And I save," he says to Peter Verkhovenski just before his suicide, in prophetic and pitiful enthusiasm. "Only this one thing can save all men, and in the next generation regenerate them physically; for in his present physical guise, as far as my conceptions take me, it is impossible for man to exist anyway without a previous God. I have sought for three years the attributes of my deity, and have found it: his attribute is self-will! That is the only way I can materially show my insubmission and my new and terrible liberty."

To Dostoevsky Kirillov is a madman, "possessed, perhaps, of some spirit," one of those possessed that even Pushkin had foresight of:

> *Endless, shapeless, soundless,*
> *In the moon's dim rays*
> *Demons circled, many*
> *As the leaves of November.*

Not for nothing were these lines of Pushkin's taken by Dostoevsky as a motto for his *Possessed.* He tried to discover in Kirillov to what monstrous extremes it is possible for the Russian nature to carry the logical dialectics of atheism.

But then, even Prince Myshkine is also a madman, possessed of devils, though only in the eyes of "this world," the wisdom of which is "foolishness with the Lord," and not in the eyes of his Creator. The "moments of highest harmony" which light up the figure of the *Idiot* with such a glow of unearthly beauty and sanctity are due also, according to his own admission, to the "sacred," or dæmonic, sickness. The most profound and vital thoughts of Kirillov and Prince Myshkine both are in connexion with the prophecy. "There shall be no more time," i.e. that the aim of universal, historical evolution is not an endless, earthly continuance, *but the ending of mankind*. Here Dostoevsky hesitates. He will not fully utter his own thoughts; he draws back before some gulf, and closes his eyes: the thinker is lost in the artist. The Idiot and Kirillov are two sides of his own being, his two faces—one open, the other mysterious. Kirillov is the double of the Idiot.

"To recognize that there is no God, and at the same time not to recognize that you yourself have become a God, is folly; otherwise you would infallibly kill yourself." So says the daring Kirillov. "If there *is* a God, how can I bear the thought that *I* am not that God?" So says Friedrich Nietzsche. "There is no God. He is dead. And we have killed him. Ought we not to turn ourselves into deities? *Never was a deed done greater than this. He who shall be born after us by this alone will belong to a higher stage in history than any that has gone before.*" Who says this? Kirillov again? No, Friedrich Nietzsche. But Kirillov, as we have seen, says the same, with his two main epochs of history—including the extinction of the present conception of God. He too foretells the transformation of the earth and of the "physical nature of man," i.e. in other words, the appearance of the "Man-god," the "Uebermensch."

Although Nietszche called Dostoevsky "his great master," we know that the principal ideas of Nietzsche were framed independently of the latter, under the influence of the Hellenic world, and mainly of ancient Tragedy, the philosophy of Kant and Schopenhauer on the one hand, and on the other the conclusions of modern experimental science, the ideas of Darwin, Spencer, and Haeckel on the biological transformation of species, the world's progress, natural metamorphosis, and Evolution, as it is called. Nietzsche merely carried on these scientific deductions and applied them to questions of sociology and universal history. *Man to him is not the end, the last link of the chain, but only one of the links of cosmic progress: just as man was the outcome of the transmutation of animal species, so a new creature will result from the transmutation of civilized human species.* This very being, the "new creature," is the "more than man," or, as with ingenious cynicism Dostoevsky's Nihilist puts it, our world proceeds "from the gorilla to the man, and from man to the extinction of God," to the Man-god.

Here, of course, we have only the generally accessible, obvious, and outward aspect of Nietzsche—one which, in the long run, seemed to himself a coarse outer shell. He has also another more profound and hidden aspect. "As regards my complaint," he owns in one place, "I am undoubtedly more indebted to it than to health. I am indebted to it for *the highest kind of health*, the kind *in which a man is the stronger for whatever does not kill him.* I owe all my philosophy to it. Great pain alone is the final emancipator of the soul. Only great agony—that long-drawn, slow torture in which we seem to be burning over damp faggots, a pain which is in no hurry—only such lets us who are philosophers descend to our lowest depths and makes us rely on nothing of faith, good will, concealment, softness and directness, on which, perhaps, we previously based our humanity." This Nietzsche, like *The Idiot* and Kirillov, finds in the birth-pang, in his illness, "moments of eternal harmony," the source of "the highest state." *In the death of the human* he finds the first lightnings and glimpses of the "superhuman."

"Man is what must be overcome," says Zarathustra. Only by overcoming, by mortifying, both in his spirit and in his flesh, all that is "human, too human," only by casting off "the old man" with the animal serpent-like wisdom as an old dead slough, can man rise to incorruptibility, attain to the divine existence for which "there is a new heaven and a new earth."

Pushkin certainly—the most healthy and sane of our countrymen—had already pondered on this "physical transformation of man," physical and spiritual at once, this regeneration and turning of the "fleshly" flesh into spiritual flesh.

> *And to my lips he stooped,*
> *Removed my sinful tongue:*
> *(Idle of speech and crafty)*
> *And placed with his blood-stained hand,*
> *Within my palsied lips,*
> *The serpent's sting of wisdom.*
>
> *Clove my breast with his glaive,*
> *My fluttering heart drew forth,*
> *And a burning fiery coal*
> *Forced into my bared breast.*
> *Like a corpse in the desert I lay—*

DMITRY MEREZHKOVSKY

Then God's voice called to me:
"Prophet, arise!"

But the Man lying in the desert will arise *no longer man* as we know him.

If the seed does not die, then it does not germinate. The constructive agony of birth is like the destructive agony of death.

"There come, as it were, unnecessary and gratuitous sufferings," says Tolstoy in *The Kingdom of God*, with regard to the inward state, "passing into a new form of life, untried as yet by man as he is today. Something happens akin to childbearing. All is ready for the new life, but this life still does not make its appearance. The situation seems one from which there is no issue." And a few lines later he speaks *of the flight, the wings, of the new man*, who "feels himself perfectly free, just as a bird would feel in a fenced-round close, *as soon as it chose to spread its wings.*"

Who knows? In others (not in himself) Tolstoy has sometimes found this illness of the present day—the pang of birth, the pain of the bursting of wings. Is he himself as free from such pain as he avers, as he would wish to be? Or is he only more skilful than others in hiding weakness by reproving the weakness of others?

"Every man of our day, if we penetrate the contrast of his judgment and his life, is in a desperate condition," he says, as usual speaking of others, of the people of "this world." But is there another "man of our day" whose reason and life are at greater variance than his own? In him the old struggle still continues in the subterranean quakings and echoes, like the dull roar of earthquake. In Tolstoy's *Resurrection* old Akim celebrates his "new birth" and the death of the "animal" in him— what he believes to be his final victory over the Beast. But if it be a victory, what a poor one! Docs not Tolstoy realize in the penetralia of his artistic conscience that it is just here, at the decisive moment, that something has broken down and betrayed him? In this "regeneration" the mortification of the flesh has led to what it always leads to, the mortification of the spirit. Before our eyes is taking place the suicide of a man's genius.

Was this the "Resurrection" that we expected of him, that he expected of himself? It is not for nothing that he abjures those of his works which he owes to his "world-wide fame." *In him there was, or might have been, a prophet, though by no means such a one as he considered himself to be.* He must content himself with his fame as mere artist.

Tolstoy has human fame, but not God's fame, which is man's absence of fame, the persecution of prophets. His pride must be scourged by the servile praises of "innumerable pigmies." The spectacle recalls the torments of those wretches who, stripped naked, bound and smeared with honey, were exposed in the sun for insects to devour.

He is always silent. Silence is his last refuge. He will not admit his sufferings. But yet he knows that the hour is at hand when One, to whom nothing can be refused, will demand an account. We owe pity to this man of the day in his most desperate condition, the most lonely, deserted, and unregarded, in spite of all this fame. But sometimes one fancies that, being so great, he deserves no pity. In any case, only those who do not *love* him will believe in the health, the peace, and happiness, the "regeneration" of this man.

His illness is shown by a gradually increasing silence, callousness, decline, ossification, and petrification of the heart, once the warmest of human hearts.

It is because his ailment is inward, because he himself is scarcely conscious of it, that it is more grievous than the malady of Dostoevsky or the madness of Nietzsche. Pushkin carried to the grave the secret of his great health; Dostoevsky that of his great sickness. Nietzsche, the corpse of the "more-than-man," has gone from us, carrying the secret of his wisdom into the madhouse. And Tolstoy, too, has deserted us.

This generation is thrice-deserted, timid, ailing, ridiculous even in its own eyes. We have to solve a riddle which Gods and Titans could not solve—to draw the line which separates health in us from sickness, life from death, resurrection from decay. We can evade this riddle. Have we courage to solve it?

An almost unbearable burden of responsibility is thus laid on our generation. Perhaps the destinies of the world never hung so finely in the balance before, as if on the edge of a sword between two chasms. The spirit of man is faintly conscious that the beginning of the end is at hand.

Woe to them who awake too early, when all others are still asleep. But even if we wished we can no longer deceive ourselves and ignore the blinding light we behold.

Among the common people, far down out of hearing, there are those who are awaking as we.[4] Who will be the first to arise and say

---

4. Merejkowski is thinking of Maxim Gorki.—ED.

DMITRY MEREZHKOVSKY

that he is awake? Who has overcome the fine delusion of our day, which confounds in each of us, in minds and life, the withering of the seed with its revival, the birth-pang with the death-pang, the sickness of Regeneration with the sickness of Degeneration, the true "symbolism" with "decadence"? Action is first needed; and only when we have acted can we *speak*. Meanwhile here is an end of our open course, our words, our contemplation; and a beginning of our secrecy, our silence, and our action.

XV

Tolstoy has simply ignored St. Petersburg: he has retired not only from St. Petersburg, but from the Moscow the Slavophiles love into the country, the backwoods, the body of Russia. And if in the country he encounters Petersburg, "Peter's Creation," in the shape of the new manufacturing "civilization" of concertinas, brandy, and infectious diseases, it is only to show that to him the spirit of commerce, as of the great world, seems "the power of darkness." The action of *Peace and War* and *Anna Karénina* takes place, it is true, partly in St. Petersburg, but there is none of the Petrine spirit there. In all Tolstoy's works we have only the country, the land, only the body, or dark primitive soul of Russia. But of the spirit as the power of light, as the new social and national consciousness, the quest of the future Russian city, which is beyond St. Petersburg—the, as yet, unrevealed front and head of Russia—there is no trace in Tolstoy. Dostoevsky, with a different, but not inferior sensitiveness, realizes both St. Petersburg and Moscow.

In his *The Brothers Karamazov* Alesha in the monastery by the coffin of old Zosima awakes from a portentous dream of Cana of Galilee, and goes forth from the cell into the garden. "Above him spread wide and boundless the vault of heaven, thick with still, shining stars. From the zenith to the horizon the as yet dim milky way spread double. The fresh yet motionless night enwrapped the earth. *The white towers and gilded pinnacles of the cathedral gleamed in the hyacinthine sky*. The luxuriant flowers of the autumn in the parterres were slumbering till the morning. The stillness of the earth seemed blended with that of the sky; its mystery in contact with the mystery of the stars."

These white towers and golden pinnacles of the Cathedral, shining in the hyacinth-coloured sky, remind us of the mysterious mountains and towns depicted with magical detail in the dim background of old icons.

And here is a still more icon-like bit of nature; from the *Possessed*, where Lizaveta the deformed tells about her life in the nunnery.

"I used to go to the shore of the lake: on one side was our nunnery, and on the other our peaked mountain, and they call it the Peak. I go up this mountain, turn my face to the East, fall on the ground, and weep, I forget how long, and then I forget everything, and know nothing of it. I get up by and by and turn back, but the sun comes up—such a great, fiery, splendid sun. Do you like looking at the sun? It is fine, yet sad. I turn back again towards the east, but the shadow, the shadow from our mountain, runs far over the lake like a shaft, narrow and long, very long; and a half mile further, right to the island in the lake, and this stony island is cut in half by the shadow, and as it cuts it in half the sun goes down altogether, and all suddenly grows dark. Then I begin to be altogether weary, and then suddenly my memory comes back:—I am afraid of the dark, Shatushka."

Here is the free charm of the knightly legends. The ballad note is mingled with the peaceful and dim monastic legend, with a national music as yet unheard.

There is a notion current that Dostoevsky did not love Nature. But though he certainly but little and rarely describes it, that is, perhaps, just because his love for it is too deep not to be restrained. He does not wear his heart on his sleeve, but all the more in his rare descriptions there is more vigour than in anything of the kind in Tolstoy.

No, Dostoevsky loved the land not less than he loved the "body" of Russia, but less the "tangible" frame than the spiritualized face of that land.

Holy Russia lies to him in the past, and in the yet distant future. Neither for the future nor the past does he forget the near Russia of St. Petersburg today. It is for him "the most fantastic of towns, with the most fantastic history of any town on the globe"; that boasted "Paradise" of Peter the Great, built as if on purpose with "Satanic intent," as a mock at men and Nature.

On one occasion Raskolnikov,[1] after the murder, is passing on a summer's day over the Nicolaev Bridge, and stops and turns his face towards the Neva in the direction of the Palace. "The sky was without the slightest speck of cloud, and the water almost a deep blue, a rare thing in the Neva. The cupola of the Cathedral, which does not show up better than from this point, from the bridge, shone so that through the pure air you could clearly distinguish each single ornament. *An inexplicable chill* breathed on him always from all this magnificent panorama: this gorgeous picture was to him full of *a deaf and dumb spirit.*"

From this terrible spirit, which seems alien and Western, but really is native, the old Russian, pre-Christian, "Varangian" spirit of Pushkin

---

1. In *The Crime and the Punishment.*

and Peter, came Raskolnikov, and in no small measure Dostoevsky himself.

The "burgh of Peter" is not only the "most fantastic," but the most prosaic of human cities.

Who knows St. Petersburg better, and hates it more, and feels more overcome by it, than Dostoevsky? Yet, as we see, there are moments when he suddenly forgives everything, and somehow loves the place, as Peter loved his monstrous "Paradise" and as Pushkin loved "Peter's handiwork." "The foundling of nature," the most outcast of towns, of which even its inhabitants are secretly ashamed, Dostoevsky makes it, by the force of his affection, pathetic, piteous, almost lovable and homelike, almost beautiful; though curelessly diseased, yet with a rare "decadent" beauty not easily attained.

"If I know of some happy places in St. Petersburg," admits Podrostok, "that is, places where, for some reason or other, I have been happy, I save up those places, and refrain from going to them for as long as possible, for the express purpose of afterwards, when I am quite lonely and miserable, going there to be sad and remember."

He says: "I love it when they sing to the barrel-organ of a cold, dark, and damp autumn evening—particularly when it is damp and all the passers-by have pale-green and suffering faces; or, still better, when a damp snow is falling, quite straight, and the air is windless, you know, and the gas lamps glimmer through it."

"He took me," says another character, "to a small inn on the canal, down below. There were few customers. A rickety, squeaking organ was playing, and there was a smell of dirty napkins. We took our seats in a corner. No doubt you do not know the place. I like sometimes, when I am bored, terribly bored and worried, to go into such dog holes. The whole scene, the squeaking *aria* from 'Lucia,' the waiters in national costumes that are scarcely decent, the smoke-room, the cries from the billiard-room—*all that is so commonplace and prosaic that it actually borders on the fantastic.*"

Precisely such dirty slummy inns, the "servants' halls" of St. Petersburg cosmopolitanism, are to be found in all Dostoevsky's stories. In them take place his most important, speculative, and impassioned conversations. And however strange it may be, yet you feel that it is just the platitude of this "cosmopolitan servants' hall" atmosphere, the sordid realism and the commonplaceness, that give to these talks their peculiarly modern, national flavour, and make their stormy and apocalyptic brilliance, like that of the sky before thunder, come into full relief.

The granite pedestal of the Bronze Horseman of St. Petersburg, rearing and reined in with an iron bit, though it seems so firm, yet stands on a shifting putrid morass, from which spring ghostly mists. "Sometimes," he writes, "it has occurred to me, 'What if, when this fog scatters and lifts, there should depart with it the whole rotten flimsy town—vanish like smoke—and only the old Finnish swamp remain, with the Bronze Horseman for ornament?'"

He was the first of us to feel and realize that Peter's Russia, "pulled to her haunches by an iron bit," like a plunging horse, "had reached some boundary, and is now rearing over an abyss." "Perhaps it is some one's dream. Some one will awake of a sudden, who has dreamed all this—and then it will all disappear." Ah, Dostoevsky *knows*, for a certainty, that it *will* disappear; knows that Russia will abandon St. Petersburg; yet will never go back to Moscow for a capital, whither the Slavophiles call her. Nor will she resort still further back to Tolstoy's rural Yasnaia Poliana and the plebeian, but really squirearchal "Kingdom of God." He knows that Russia will not continue at St. Petersburg.

Dostoevsky saw in the later years of his life where lies the new and final Russian capital. He quite definitely realized that Petersburg, the second capital of Russia, is merely a spectral and transitional capital. That third, imperial, and final Russian Rome will be Constantinople and the Oecumenical Russian Cathedral, the Church of St. Sophia.

What he says about Petersburg, "the most fantastic of cities," Dostoevsky says about his own works, all his artistic creations. "I am dreadfully fond of realism in Art, when, so to speak, it is carried to the fantastic. What can be more fantastic and unexpected than reality? Nay, what can, at times, be more improbable? What most people call fantastic is, in my eyes, often the very essence of the real."

All his heroes may be divided into two families, opposite, yet having many points of contact. Either, like Alesha, the Idiot, and Zosima, they are the men of "the city that is to come," of the holy Russia that is at once too old and too new, not yet in existence; or, like Ivan Karamazov, Rogojine, Raskolnikov, Versilov, Stavrogine, and Svidrigailov, they are the men of the existing city, of contemporary actual St. Petersburg, Petrine Russia. The first seem spectral, but are real; the second seem real, but are spectral—mere "dreams within a dream," a pitilessly fantastic dream, which has now, for two centuries, been dreamed by Peter the Brazen Horseman.

Raskolnikov sees in a dream the room in which he murdered the old woman; the huge, round, copper-red moon was looking straight in at the windows. "It is so quiet because of the moon," he thought. He stood and waited, waited long, and the stiller the moonlight was the harder beat his heart, till it ached and stopped; and still there was silence. Suddenly there came a momentary dry cackle, as if some one was breaking a piece of wood; then all was silent again. A fly woke up and suddenly knocked in its flight against the glass, and buzzed a complaint. He saw the old usurer-woman, and struck her with the axe on the crown once and again, but she broke out into a low, noiseless laugh. The more he struck her the more she shook with laughter. "He wanted to cry out, and—awoke. He drew his breath hard, but, strange to say, *his dream seemed still to go on.* His door was opened wide, and in the doorway stood a man totally strange to him, and looked steadily at him. 'Am I still dreaming or not?' he thought. Some ten minutes passed. It was still light, but evening was coming on. In the room there was perfect stillness. Even from the staircase not a single sound came. There was only the buzzing and flapping of a large fly, beating its wings against the glass."

This realistic, connecting "symbolic" trait, the fly buzzing in both the rooms ("all that you have, we have too," says the Devil to Ivan Karamazov, that is, all in the world of phenomena is also in the world of realities—"in both rooms"), so knits together dream and reality that the reader can hardly tell where vision ends and reality begins.

"At last it grew intolerable. Raskolnikov suddenly sat up on the sofa. 'Well, tell me, what do you want?'

"'Why, I knew that you were not asleep, but only pretending,' was the strange answer of the unknown, who laughed calmly. 'Allow me to introduce myself, Arkadii Svidrigailov.'"

So ends the third part of *Crime and Punishment.*

"'Is this a continuation of my dream?' thought Raskolnikov"; such is the beginning of the fourth part.

Cautiously and suspiciously he looked at the unexpected visitor.

"'Svidrigailov? What nonsense! It is impossible!' he at length cried aloud in amazement."

And when, after a long interview, partly on business, the visitor went away, Raskolnikov asks his comrade, Razumikhin the student, "Did you see him?"

"'Well yes, I noticed him, noticed him well.'

"'You saw him distinctly? Quite clearly?' insisted he.

"'Why, yes, I remember him distinctly. I would know him in a thousand—I have a good memory for faces.'

"Again there was a pause.

"'Hm—so—so,' muttered Raskolnikov. 'Well, you know—I thought—it still seems to me—that it was, perhaps, my fancy. Perhaps I am really under a delusion and only saw a ghost.'"

Svidrigailov is the result of his dream, and he himself is all a sort of dream, like a thick, dirty-yellow St. Petersburg fog. But if it is a ghost, then it is one with flesh and blood. In that lies the horror of it. There is nothing in it romantic, vague, indefinite, or abstract. In the action of the story Svidrigailov more and more takes form and substance, so that in the long run he proves more real than the sanguine, beefy heroes of Tolstoy. Gradually we learn that this "most vicious of men," this rascal, is capable of chivalrous magnanimity, of delicate and unselfish feelings: when Raskolnikov's sister Dunya, the innocent girl whom he has enticed into a trap in older to seduce her, is already wholly in his power he suddenly sets her free, although he knows for a certainty that this violence to himself will cost him his own life. Just before his death he concerns himself simply and self-sacrificingly, as if for his own daughter, on behalf of the orphan girl who is a stranger to him, and secures her fortune. Are we to believe that he has no existence? We hear the tones of his voice, we see his face so that we should "know him at once in a thousand." He is more living and real to us than most of the people we meet every day in so-called "real life."

But see, when we have grown finally to believe in him, then, just as he emerged from the fog, so, most prosaically, he vanishes into it.

"It was early morning. A milky, thick fog lay over the town. Svidrigailov went off along the slippery, muddy wood pavement in the direction of the Little Neva. Not a passer-by, not a cab, did he meet along the Prospect. Unlovely and dirty looked the little bright-yellow houses, with their closed shutters. The cold and damp seized hold of his whole frame. He came in front of a large stone house. A tall watch-tower flashed in sight to his left. 'Bah!' he thought, 'there is the place. At any rate I have an official witness.' He almost laughed at the novel idea. At the closed great gates of the house stood, leaning his shoulder against them, a little man, muffled in a grey soldier's cloak, with a brass Achilles helmet. His sleepy eyes rested indifferently on the approaching Svidrigailov. On his face appeared the everlasting, sulky discontent which is bitterly imprinted on the faces of all Hebrews without exception. They both, Svidrigailov and the Achilles, for some time looked at each other in silence. At last it occurred to Achilles that it was irregular for the man not to be drunk and stand in front of him three paces off, looking point blank at him and saying nothing.

"'Hey, what do you want here?' he cried, still not stirring or changing his posture.

"'Why, nothing, brother. Good morning!' replied Svidrigailov.

"'Here is no place for you.'

"'I am going to other countries, lad.'

"'To other countries?'

"'To America.'

"'To America?'

"Svidrigailov drew out his revolver and cocked it. Achilles raised his eyebrows.

"'Ah, well, this is no place for that sort of shoke' (joke).

"'And why is it not a place?'

"'Becosh it *is* not a place.'

"'Well, lad, it is all the same to me. The place is a good one; when you are examined, answer that I said I was going to America.'

"And he put the revolver to his right temple.

"'But you mushn't here—here is no place!' protested Achilles, opening his eyes still wider.

"Svidrigailov pulled the trigger."

This phantasm Svidrigailov is convincing. And we, too, "are such stuff as dreams are made of."

The terror of "ordinary apparitions" lies partly in the fact that, as it were, they are conscious of their own paltriness and absurdity.

Does Science profess to exhaust all the actual possibilities of human consciousness? Science answers, "I do not know." But then it is just with these "I don't knows" that the terror of phenomena begins; and the deeper the "*ignoramus*" (and when was it deeper than now?) the more our disquiet. We had hoped that all the shadows of the non-scientific would vanish in the light of Science, but, on the contrary, the brighter the light, the blacker, more distinctly defined and mysterious are the shadows become. We have but extended the field of our ignorance. Men have become scientific, and their shadows, the ghosts, imitating and hurrying after them, grow scientific too. The phantasms themselves do not believe, or at least affect disbelief in their own reality, and laughingly style themselves delirium, or hallucination.

Not only do Dostoevsky's spectres pursue the living, but the living themselves pursue and terrify each other like spectres, like their own shadows, like their doubles. "You and I are fruit off the same tree," says Svidrigailov to Raskolnikov, and in spite of all his resistance, his callousness, the latter feels that it is true; that they have certain points in common; that, perhaps, even their personalities have a common centre. Svidrigailov has only gone immeasurably further along the road which Raskolnikov has barely begun; and shows him the inevitable super-scientific deductions from his own logic about good and evil—stands him in stead of a magic mirror. And being conclusively convinced that Svidrigailov is not a delusion or a ghost, but living, he is just for that reason far more afraid than ever of his own shadow, his own double. "I dread that man," he says. "Do you know what?" Ivan Karamazov tells his footman Smerdiakov, "I am afraid you are a vision, a phantom that is sitting there before me."

"'There is no ghost here, no,' answers Smerdiakov, 'except us two, and some third, other person. The third man is *between us two.*'

"'Who is? What other? What third?' cried Ivan in alarm, looking about him and hurriedly searching all the corners with his eyes."

This "third" link, in Smerdiakov's opinion, Providence, or God, turned out later for Ivan's benefit the earthly incarnation of the Smerdiakov spirit, the Devil.

"*You* have killed," says Smerdiakov to him ("for you are the murderer, and I only the faithful accomplice). It was at your order that I did it."

Peter Verkhovenski, another character, is also the faithful accomplice of his master, his demigod, his legendary "Ivan the Tsarevich," Stavrogine. The latter plainly says "I laugh at my ape." And this dark, withered, monkey-like mask, still an endlessly deep and faithful mirror, is not only ridiculous to Stavrogine, but terrible. When he chances to call Peter a buffoon, the latter retorts with terrific vigour, and what seems justifiable heat, "I *am* a buffoon, but I do not wish you, my larger half, to be one. Do you understand me?"

"Stavrogine understood, and he alone, it may be," adds Dostoevsky significantly. Stavrogine alone understands Verkhovenski, as God alone understands the Devil, his everlasting "ape."

Thus with Dostoevsky we often get tragical contrasted *couples* of lifelike, realistic people, who seem to themselves and others integral personages—*halves of some third divided being*, halves that seek one another, doubles that shadow one another.

Says one half to the other what Ivan, with such unwarrantable fervour, says to the Devil, "Not for a moment do I take you for an actual fact. You are a lie, you are my illness; only I do not know how to exorcise you. You are my hallucination, my other mask. You are only one side of me: my thoughts and feelings, but only the most contemptible and foolish ones. All that there is of foolish in my nature," groans he spitefully, "is long since over, recast, thrown aside as rubbish, and you bring it to me as a discovery. You say just what I think, and *are unable to say anything new to me.*"

Ah! there's the rub! Can the Demon really say anything *new* or not? All the terror of this apparition to Ivan—nay, to Dostoevsky himself—lies just in this. Well, what if he can? In any case there is no doubt that the Familiar of *Ivan Karamazov* is one of the greatest national creations of Dostoevsky, unlike anything else in the world's literature, a creation that has its roots seated in the inmost recess of his consciousness and of his unconsciousness. It is not for nothing that he expresses by the mouth of the Familiar his own most oracular thoughts. We might trace how Dostoevsky arrived at him all through his characters. As regards his essence, the Demon speaks in almost the same words as Dostoevsky himself of the essence of his own artistic creations, of the first source of that generative power from which all his works proceeded.

"*I am dreadfully fond of realism—realism that is, so to speak, carried to the fantastic. What most people call fantastic to me forms the very essence of the real,*" says the Demon, "and therefore I love your earthly realism. Here with you everything is marked out, here are formulas and geometry, but with us all is a matter of indefinite equations. I walk about here and dream. I love to dream. Besides, on earth I become superstitious—don't laugh, please: I like it. I accept all your habits here: I have got to like going to the tradesman's baths, that you may imagine, and I like steaming in company with tradesmen and priests. *My dream is to be incarnated,* but finally, irrevocably, and therefore in some fat eighteen-stone tradesman's wife, and to believe in all that she believes in."

This seems coarse and absurd, but we must remember that the keenest and sharpest pain ever felt by Dostoevsky was hidden under this empty mask: the weariness and revolt of the Devil against all that is ghostly or fantastic, against all "indefinite equations," are the weariness and revolt of himself: it is his own longing for "earthly realism," for "incarnation," for the health he had lost, the disturbed equilibrium of spirit and flesh. For this earthly "geometry," for his clear, precise formulas, for his "immutable" adherence to the senses, he loved Pushkin as he did; constantly torn from the earth, carried away by the whirlwind of his spectral visions, he sought in Pushkin points of support, and convulsively clung to him as to his native soil. He went still further, for in his gravitation towards the "sons of the soil" and the Moscow Slavophiles (also in their way "eighteen-stone tradesmen's wives") he found a refuge for himself from the terrible, sincere, inhuman reality.

"People take all this comedy" (the world of phenomena) "for something serious, in spite of all their undoubted wit," says the Demon further on in his talk with Ivan. "In that lies the tragedy. Well, they suffer, no doubt, but still *they live, they live really, not in fancy*: for suffering, too, is life."

But yet the Devil is not for nothing "the third between the two," the link between the Russian, half-cosmopolitan, "squireen" Ivan, and the national yet cosmopolitan valet, Smerdiakov. The Demon smacks of the most modern cosmopolitan frivolity: he seems at times old-fashioned, well-born, very economical ("has a look of neatness on very slender means"), and also recalls the suspicious "gentleman" of the latest minor press. And the apparition seems to take a pride in this "human, too human" trait, in this "immortal frivolity of mankind," and teases Ivan with it.

Only at rare intervals, as if by accident, does he let slip some word which reminds Ivan with whom Ivan has to do. And then there looks out from behind the human face "Another": "*All that you have, we have*; that one secret of ours I reveal to you as a friend in confidence, although it is against the rules."

Here is an incomplete revelation from the region of *Noumena*, a glimpse of something further and darker than eye of man has ever reached. This is abstract dialectics, the "critique of knowledge" embodied in flesh and blood, laughter and terror. Such "noumenal" thoughts, or mere shadows of thoughts, must have been puzzling Goethe when he created the "Mothers" in the second part of *Faust*, and Kant when thinking out his *Transcendental Aesthetics*.

Ivan, at times, cannot restrain himself; suddenly forgets that the Demon "cannot tell him anything new," and gets curious.

"Is there a God, or not?" he cries with savage persistence. "Oh, so you are in earnest? My dear fellow, by the Lord *I don't know*. There's a big admission for me to make!"

"You don't know, and yet you see Him? No, I forgot, you have no existence of your own—you are merely my own imagination."

Ivan is angry because he secretly feels himself wrong; for, in spite of the wretched pun, the Devil, by this cynical "I don't know," has answered his question about God, an idle "unscientific" question, with the final agnostic verdict of science. This "I don't know" is the inevitable fruit, the dead and deadening fruit of the Tree of Knowledge, ungrafted on the Tree of Life.

Nietzsche, even at the time when he had overcome, as he fancied, all the metaphysical "survivals" could not get rid of one of them—the most ancient, feared, and obstinate of all. On one occasion there appears to Zarathustra a dwarf, a repulsive hunchback, the spirit of "earthly heaviness," and reminds him of this inevitable metaphysical illusion, the "eternal revisitings." Zarathustra, without answering, is seized with fear and consternation, and falls to the ground as one dead.

Compare Dostoevsky: "You are always thinking of our present earth," the Devil says to Ivan. "Why, you know, our present earth has been renewed, perhaps, a billion times. It has been worn out, frozen, cracked, split up, dissolved into its component principles, water has again flooded the face of the dry land; then whack! a comet again. Sun again, and the sun has brought back the land; you see this is evolution, *already repeated an endless number of times, and always in one and the same form to a hair*. It's a terrible bore." "I tell you candidly," Svidrigailov once owns to Raskolnikov, with a wonderful air of simplicity, "*I am very bored.*"

"I *like* to be magnificently bored." And he orders "Lucia di Lammermoor" on the barrel organ.

This metaphysical ennui is the most terrible of human misfortunes and sufferings. In this "earthly heaviness," in this terrestrial tedium, there is something unearthly, not of this world, as it were primitive, connected with the similar, likewise "metaphysical," delusion about "immortality," for instance. "Eternity" may be sometimes imagined as something by no means vast. Say a neglected village Turkish bath-room, with musty cobwebs in all its corners.

Svidrigailov, no doubt, is not less aware than the Positivists that "spiders" and "a bath-room" are merely "phenomena," things seen, and that bathrooms cannot, of course, exist in the region of the *Noumena*. But then phenomena are merely symbols, *only the names for what is behind them.*

Sometimes in reading Dostoevsky a sort of chill comes over me: a chill, perhaps, that is not of this earth—as it were the chill of the expanses of the universe where

> *'Tis fearsome, fearsome, in will's despite,*
> *Amid the viewless plains. . . . .*

This is the terror of the "eternal revisitings," of the endless *repetitions* of which the Demon speaks to Ivan and the dwarf to Zarathustra; it is the weariness of the "neglected bath-room with spiders in the corner"— the endless monotony in variety of cosmic phenomena, risings and settings, ebbings and flowings, the kindling and dying out of the suns—it is that weary "Lucia" on the cracked organ, the "solemnity of boredom" felt at times, even in the roar of the sea waves and the voices of the night wind:

> *Of what is thy crying, wind of the night?*
> *Of what dost thou plain thee so wildly?*
> *O sing not these terrible strains*
> *Of chaos in which thou wast born!*
> *How eager the world in the night-mood*
> *To list to the tale that she loves.*
> *From a mortal's lorn bosom it bursts,*
> *Longing to mix with the boundless,*
> *To wake the storms from their sleep,*
> *For beneath them stirs chaos and heaves.*

The Demon confesses: "I was there when the Word that died on the Cross entered into Heaven, bearing on His bosom the soul of the thief that had been crucified on His right hand. I heard the joyous outcries of the Cherubim, singing and shouting 'Hosanna!' and the thunderous roar of exultation of the Seraphim, which shook the sky and the fabric of the world; and I swear by all that is holy I wished to join the choir and cry with them all 'Hosanna!'; there already escaped, there already broke from my breast—"

But at this point, sparing his victim for the time, he again hides behind his "human, too human mask," and concludes with levity: "I am very sentimental, you know, and artistically susceptible. But common sense—my most unfortunate quality—kept me within due limits, and I let the moment pass. For what, I asked myself at the time, what would have resulted after my 'Hosanna!'? That instant all would have come to a standstill in the world, and no events would have taken place. And so, simply from a sense of duty and my social position, I was forced to suppress in myself the good impulse and stick to villainy. Some one else takes all the honour of doing good to himself, and I am left only the bad for my share."

"I know, of course, there is a secret there, but They will not reveal it to me at any price, because, forsooth, if I found out the actual facts I should break out into a 'Hosanna!' and instantly the indispensable minus quantity would vanish. Reason would begin to reign all over the earth, and with it, of course, there would be an end of everything. But as long as this does not happen, as long as the secret is kept, *there exist for me two truths, one up yonder, Theirs, which is quite unknown to me, and another which is mine.* And it is still unknown which will be the purer of the two."

These words concerning the two co-existent Truths, eternally-correlated, yet distinct, as immediately afterwards the Fiend explains, to conclude the interview, are the truths of the God-man and that of the Man-god, Christ and Antichrist.

From the contact and collision of these "two Truths" came Dostoevsky's fire of doubt. "Really I do not believe in Christ and His creed as a boy believes, but my Hosanna has passed through a great furnace of doubt, as the Devil says in my pages in that very story"; so runs one of his latest diaries.

These "two Truths" have, of course, always existed for Tolstoy too, not in his deliberate judgment, but in his instinct. But he never had the strength or courage, like Dostoevsky, to look them both straight in the face.

However, even in Dostoevsky, the strongest of his heroes cannot stand this view of the two Truths, side by side: Ivan throws a glass at the Fiend like a woman, as if in dread that he will in the end really tell him something new, too new. And it would seem that he himself could not bear the theory, and never spoke his last decisive word on the subject.

His Principle of Evil, of Loss, says merely: "*I am leading you between alternate waves of belief and disbelief, and that is the object I have in view.*"

Does it not seem as if this Fiend, in spite of his tail, like a "Great Dane's," and the fact that "philosophy is not his strong point," had read to advantage the *Critique of Pure Reason*? The Voltaireans of the eighteenth and our own century (for there *are* not a few of them in our day, though under other names), these "philosophers without mathematics," as Halley, the friend of Newton, put it, would certainly have managed to deal with him without much difficulty. But perhaps minds of more exactitude and judgment than theirs, minds of the stamp of Pascal and Kant, would have had to wrestle in the same way, to "put forth their manhood" against this phantom, in order to drive out the "ten-thousandth part" of doubt or belief, which he still inspires.

Leaving the Romanticists out of the question, even such a lover of all that was realistic as Goethe sometimes felt that the paltriness of the Europe of his day was getting too much for him; and in his search after the supernatural, which, if it did not quench, at least assuaged the religious thirst, went to the Middle Ages or classical antiquity. Dostoevsky first, and so far alone, among writers of modern times, has had the strength, while adhering to present-day actuality, to master and transform it into something more mysterious than all the legends of past ages. He was the first to see that what seems most trivial, rough, and fleshly marches with what is most spiritual, or, as he called it, "fantastic," i.e. religious. And he was the first that succeeded in finding the sources of the supernatural, not in the remote, but in penetrating the ordinary.

Not in abstract speculations, but in exact experiments, worthy of our present science, in human souls did Dostoevsky show that the work of universal history, which began with the Renaissance and the Reformation, the method of strictly scientific, critical, discriminating thought, if not already completed, is approaching completion; that "this road has all been traversed to the end, so that there is no further to go," and that not only Russia, but all Europe has "reached a certain final point and is tottering over an abyss." At the same time he showed with an almost complete clearness of judgment that we must inevitably turn to the work of the new thought, creative and religious.

All the veils of obsolete, theological, or metaphysical dogmatism have been removed or torn away by the criticism of knowledge. But behind these veils there proved to be not barren emptiness, not unvarying ineptitude (as the facile sceptics of the eighteenth century supposed, with their light incredulity), but a living and attracting deep, the most living and the most attractive ever laid bare before men's eyes. The overthrow of dogmatism not only does not prevent, but more than anything tends to the possibility of a true religion. Superstitious, fabulous phantasms lose their substance, but reality itself beomes merely *conditional*, not superstitious, but only *unbelieving*, and for some reason, all the more it does so, more than ever a phantom. Religious and metaphysical dreams lose their reality, but waking itself becomes "as real as dreams." How much more terrible, much more monstrous than Dante's Hell, in which rules a certain kind of wild justice, that is religious Cosmos, are these "waking dreams," no longer sanctified by any kind of religion, and all chaotic: as fantastical and yet as real is the raving of Zarathustra about "eternal revisitings." Is it possible, in fact, to live with such blind ravings, to which science replies only with her cynical "Go to a doctor," or with the dry and laconic "I don't know," like knocking one's forehead against a wall? No, after four centuries of labour and critical reflection the world does *not* remain as terrible and mysterious as it was. It has become still more awe-inspiring and enigmatic. In spite of all its unspeakable outward dulness and poorness, in spite of this commonplaceness, the world has never yet been so ripe for religion as in our day, and withal for a religion that is final and will complete the world's evolution, partly fulfilled at the first, and predicted for the second coming of the Word.

In fact present-day European man has before him the unavoidable choice between three courses. The first is final recovery from the disease which in that case men would have to call the "idea of God." This would be recovery to a greater blank than the present, because now at least men suffer. Complete positive recovery from "God" is possible only in the complete, but as yet only dimly foreshadowed, vacuity of a social tower of Babel. The second course is to die of this complaint by final degeneration, decay, or "decadence," in the madness of Nietzsche and Kirillov, the prophets of the Man-god, who, forsooth, is to extirpate the God-man. And, lastly, the third resort is the religion of a last great union, a great Symbolon, the religion of a Second Coming, the religion of the voluntary end of all.

Here, by the bye, it is necessary to make a reservation. Dostoevsky was not fully conscious, or pretended not to be conscious of the importance to his own religious ideas of the most cherished and profound idea in Christianity, the idea of the end, of the Second Kingdom, which is to complete and supplement the first—of the Kingdom of the Spirit, which is to come after that of the Son. Dostoevsky thought more of the first than of the second, more of the reign of the Son than of that of the Spirit; and believed more in Him who was and is than in Him who was, is, *and is to be.* That which men have *already received* in his eyes outweighed that which *they, as yet, cannot receive.*

He only put his riddles to us. From the necessity of solving them he himself was divided only by a hair's breadth. But we are face to face with them; we must either solve them, or gradually perish.

XVI

What is the true relation between Art and Religion? It is a difficult subject. But I may venture to say that, in the view taken of beauty by the so-called aesthetes in their doctrine of "Art for Art's sake," there is something that is, perhaps, true, but insufficiently modest. Beauty loves to be seen, but does not love to be pointed at. Beauty, I say, is modest: she seems altogether the most modest thing in the world, covering herself as God does, who covers His inmost spirit with the half-transparent veil of phenomena.

In the aesthetes' view of beauty there is also a certain lack of pride. Beauty loves to be served, but loves also to serve. The great artists sometimes make her a slave, or victim, as if they were sacrificing or were ready to sacrifice her to higher powers, because they know that at the very last minute, before the act of sacrifice, like Iphigenia under the knife of her father Agamemnon, beauty will become fairer than ever; in sooth, at that last moment, for the most part the gods save her by a miracle, and, like Iphigenia, carry her to inaccessible coasts, where she becomes their immortal daughter.

Tragedy, the most perfect creation of the Hellenic spirit, was the outcome of a religious mystery, and throughout its evolution, preserved a living connexion with religion, so that the action of the drama was half a religious service, the theatre half a temple. Just in the same way all great art in its prime was the handmaid of religion. It was only when, by contact with the coarser and more outward Roman culture, this link of Art with Religion was snapped, when they began to collect the gods (from whom life had already fled) into Pantheons and museums and palaces of the Caesars as objects of luxury and gratification, when the phenomena of the beautiful were exhausted, that talk about beauty began, and Alexandrian "aestheticism," "Art for Art's sake," Art as a religion in itself, came into vogue. And this doctrine, begotten in a sterile time and generating nothing, was the precursor of Roman decline and "decadence."

In the untutored "symbolic" prattle of Christian wall-painting in the catacombs the severed bond between Art and Religion is again knit and becomes more vital, more binding; from the first subterranean basilicas, the Galilean legends of the Good Shepherd, to the Gothic spires rising into the sky of mediaeval cathedrals, and "the consecrated gestes," the Mystery plays, from which came the new drama.

DMITRY MEREZHKOVSKY

The Italian Renaissance seemed once more to destroy, but in reality only transformed this bond. The face of Christ in Leonardo's *Last Supper* is not the face of the Christ whose vicegerent is the Pope, whether he be Gregory, Hildebrand, or Alexander Borgia: the "prophets and sibyls on the ceiling of the Sistine Chapel are the Old Testament ancestors and ancestresses of the New Testament, which has no place in the Catholic Church, and cannot have. Both the great propagators of the religious spirit of the Renaissance, Leonardo and Michael Angelo, are nearest to us, and will probably be nearer to our descendants than to their own contemporaries. They both deepened and strengthened the connexion of Art with Religion, but with the Religion not of the present, but of the future.

In any case, neither of them enters the territory of "Art for Art's sake": they are more than artists. Michael Angelo is a sculptor-painter, a sculptor even in his painting, the designer of St. Peter's, the builder of Florentine fortifications, the favourite of Vittoria Colonna, poet, scholar, thinker, prophet. But even he seems almost limited compared with Leonardo. The artistic creations and immense scientific notebooks of Leonardo, until quite lately not explored or appreciated, for want of a similarly all-embracing intelligence, give only a feeble idea of the actual extent of his powers. Apparently no man ever carried with him to the grave such a store of well-nigh superhuman possibilities.

Raphael, as if alarmed at this incredible inheritance, took for his province only the smallest and least weighty part of it. He immensely contracted and narrowed the sphere of his contemplation: he confined himself to aiming at the possible, and for his pains actually achieved it: he wished only to be an artist, and so really was one in a more complete measure than the two others. But at the same time through Raphael, this "fortunate lad"—"*fortunato garzon*," as Francia calls him—was accomplished the passage of the great world-historical mountain-barrier of the Renaissance—the ascent was at an end, the descent began. He made possible the phenomenon of such an "asthete," the precursor of our present-day asthetic repletion and monotony, as Pietro Aretino, who scowled at Leonardo, laughed at Michael Angelo, and defied Titian, as the incarnator of "pure beauty," *Art, not for Religion, but as a Religion*, the purely material, positive, epicurean, godless religion of self-gratification, of "Art for Art's sake."

Now Tolstoy and Dostoevsky have two characteristics which approximate them to the great initiators of all "Renascence." In the first place the art of both is in communion with religion, but that not of the present, but the future. In the second they do not dwell within the bounds of Art as a self-sufficing religion, what is called "pure Art." Their feet cannot but transgress these bounds and pass out beyond them.

The weakness and the error of Tolstoy lie not in the fact that he wished to be more, but merely in this, that in his efforts to be more he sometimes became less than an artist; not in his wishing to serve God by his art, but in his serving not his own, but another's God.

And yet in him and such as him we feel the real, though not yet realized, possibility of a profounder, a more religious theory of Art than the purely artistic. Is it not just in this constant inward struggle and suffering, in this insatiate and insatiable thirst for fame *merely* as an artist, in this unheard-of self-mortification and suicide of genius that lies the true tragic greatness and glory of the man? For even merely to will is sometimes a mark of greatness: one must first merely will in order that another may both will and achieve.

As regards Dostoevsky then, it is already, I fancy, quite plain that his creations as little satisfy the "aesthetic," the worshippers of "pure beauty," of "Art for Art's sake," as their opponents who look for the useful and the good in the beautiful, to whom Dostoevsky will always seem a "cruel genius." He not only had in him to fulfil, but in a considerable measure realized, one of the greatest possibilities of our day. He had not the special gift of Tolstoy, yet had one that was not less important. He not only wished to be, but was, the proclaimer of a new religious view, and a prophet indeed.

We can understand the consternation of one of the worthy Popes at the countless number of bare bodies painted by Michael Angelo on the ceiling and wall behind the throne of the Sistine Chapel. He could not see that these bodies were sacred and spiritual, or at any rate might be spiritualized. Perhaps he experienced a feeling like Prince Andrei at the sight of "the number of soldiers stripped and disporting themselves" in the muddy pond on the Smolensk road, a feeling of terror and aversion.

In fact it is just here in the Sistine Chapel that Michael Angelo, with unheard-of boldness, stripped Man of his thousand-year-old Christian covering and, like the ancients, again looked into the mystic depths of the body—that inaccessible "gulf," as Tolstoy calls it. And in the faces of the naked, weeping, seemingly intoxicated youths, the elemental Demons round the Old Testament frescoes in the Sistine, as in the face of Moses at San Pietro in Vincoli, that dread, inhuman face, with the monstrous horns instead of a nimbus, Pan-like, Satyr-like, goatish, we see revived the Aryan idea, immemorially old, yet ever new, of the union of the divine and the animal, of "God's creature," of the God-beast. These half-gods, half-beasts, by whom the natural is carried into the supernatural, these beings, huge-sinewed and muscular, in whom "we see only the face and the body, but the soul at times seems absent," are pregnant with an electric, Bacchic excess of animal life, like the "Night" and "Morning" of the Medici monument, the "Cumaean Sibyl," or the "Scythian captives," as if they wished, but could not awake out of a trance, and with vain, incredible effort were striving after thought, consciousness, spiritualization, deliverance from the flesh, the stone, the matter which binds them. There is nothing that has less desire to be Christian than they.

Now, as Michael Angelo looked into the abyss of the flesh, so Leonardo contemplated its opposite, the not less deep abyss of the spirit. He, so to speak, started at the point which Michael Angelo had just reached. All his productions are "spiritual bodies," carried to a degree of ethereality and transparency at which it would seem the spirit within burns through them: they "scarcely feel that they have bodies on them." Leonardo's caricatures of men and animals, those faces full of diabolical distortion, like the other faces in his drawings, full of angelical charm, in which, as Dostoevsky puts it, "the secret of the earth mingles with the mystery of the stars," are like visions or phantoms, but they are phantoms of mathematically-defined and exact construction, phantoms with flesh and blood, most fantastic, and at the same time most life-like. "I love realism when it is carried to the fantastic," says Dostoevsky. Seemingly both he and Leonardo might say with the greatest truth, "I love the fantastic when it is carried to the point of realism." To them both *the fantastic sometimes constitutes the very essence of the actual.* *They both seek and find "what is substantial as a dream" by pushing to the extremest limits the realistic and the actual.* The creator of *Monna Lisa*, too, is a great psychologist, "a realist in the highest sense," because he "explores all the depths of the human soul." He, too, makes cruel, even criminal "experiments with human souls." In these experiments we find our modern scientific curiosity that shrinks from nothing, a combination of geometrical exactness with enthusiastic insight. His most abstract thought is his most passionate thought; it is of God, of the First Mover within the divine mechanism, *Primo Motore.* Mechanics and religion, learning and love, ice and fire, go together. "Love is the daughter of Learning: the more exact the learning, the more fiery the love." Leonardo was the first to depict the new tragedy—the tragedy not only of the heart, but of reason—in his *Last Supper*, in the birth of Evil, by which God died in Man, through the opposition of the passionate, "human, too human," figure of Judas and the calm superhuman figure of the Lord. Who was nearer than he to the first secret appearance of the Word made Flesh, to the reign of the Son? Was it not only a step that divided the maker of the figure of Christ in the *Last Supper* from the second incarnation in which I believe, from the ever-intensifying reign of the Spirit? But Leonardo never took that step; and so he never finished the face of Christ on the wall of Maria delle Grazie. His dream—"to be incarnated finally and without recall"— thus remained only a dream. And, in spite of all his love for Euclidian formulae, for earthly "realism," he yet passed over the earth, scarcely leaving a trace: like a shadow, a phantom, a bloodless spirit, with silent lips and face averted.

The excess of spiritual sensitiveness, the acuteness of it which we find in Leonardo, expressed as much morbidity, decadence, incompleteness, as the excess of the bodily, the animal, the elemental "whirl of chaos" in Michael Angelo.

Such are these two gods or Demons of the Renaissance in their external contradiction and their eternal oneness.

> *They were two likenesses of Daemons twain:*
> *One like the Delphian image, a young form,*
> *Angered and full of awful majesty*
> *And breathing all of power beyond these realms.*
> *The other, womanlike, and formed for passion,*
> *A dubious phantom and deceptive,*
> *A witching Demon, fair as he was false.*

Raphael not only failed to reconcile, but failed to feel this contradiction. But the truce in him between the two chimeras was too facile and superficial, *too cheaply purchased, safe and rational*—"both ours and yours." This feminine submission with regard to Christianity and Paganism, the prophetic vision of Ezekiel and that of Pope Leo X, this insinuating flattery of the "fortunate lad," opened in the end the door to the hypocritical, cold Philistine and unoriginal convention of "secentism" which ruined the Renaissance and prevented its "ripening" and succeeding. Even now it is awaiting completion.

But this contradiction could not be evaded. It awoke with the spirit of the Renaissance in men like Goethe and Nietzsche. It could not fail also to affect the two latest exponents of national Renaissance, Tolstoy and Dostoevsky.

We have seen that Tolstoy is the greatest portrayer of the human animal in language, as Michael Angelo was in colours and marble. He is the first who has dared to strip the human frame of all social and historical wrapping and again entertain the Aryan idea. Tolstoy is the Russian Michael Angelo, the re-discoverer of the human body, and although we feel all over his works the Semitic dread of the body, yet he has felt the possibility of a final victory over this dread, complete as in the days of Praxiteles and Phidias.

Just as Tolstoy has explored the depths of the flesh, so Dostoevsky explored those of the spirit, and showed that the upper gulf is as deep as the lower, that one degree of human consciousness is often divided from another, one thought from another by as great an inaccessibility as divides the human embryo from non-existence. And he has wrestled with the terrors of the Spirit, that of consciouness over-distinct and over-acute, with the terror of all that is abstract, spectral, fantastical, and at the same time pitilessly real and matter-of-fact. Men feared or hoped that some day reason would dry up the spring of the heart, that knowledge would kill emotion, not conscious that they are coupled and that one is impossible without the other. That fact embodies our last and highest hope.

Raphael, the uniter, or would-be uniter of the two opposite poles of the Italian Renaissance, followed after Leonardo and Michael Angelo. The order of trinity of our Russian Renaissance is reversed. Our Raphael is Pushkin. And he precedes Tolstoy and Dostoevsky, who have consciously divided and fathomed what was by nature in Pushkin unconsciously combined. If Tolstoy be the thesis, Dostoevsky the antithesis, there must, by the law of dialectical evolution, follow a final, harmonizing Symbolon, higher than Pushkin's, because more profound, religious, and deliberate.

Yet, while thinking of the future, it is impossible to leave out of the question the present of our national culture. And that is just where our doubt, our humility begins. Can we, in fact, disguise from ourselves that this present is more than painful, that it seems almost hopeless? It is hard to believe that present Russian culture is the same which a generation and a half ago gave to the world at once in quick succession two such phenomena as Peter and Pushkin, and in the following half century Tolstoy and Dostoevsky. It is hard to believe that scarcely a quarter of a century ago, almost within the memory of the present generation, the two greatest works of the European literature of the day were produced in Russia—*Anna Karénina* and *The Brothers Karamazov.* After these two great national attainments, what a sudden falling away, what an abrupt descent!

Russia may be proud of her geniuses, but would these geniuses have been proud of their country today?

On all the phenomena of our modern spirit is set the seal of philosophic and religious impotence and unfruitfulness.

Would Dostoevsky the prophet, if now alive,[1] have abjured his prophecy concerning the worldwide destiny of the Russian spirit? A friend of his, once a passionate believer in that destiny, wrote at last:

> *And lo! the Lord inexorably*
> *Has rejected thee, my country!*

The political and outward social helplessness of that social order is vaster still. Nietzsche is the culminating point—none can go further—of the revolt against that society. We Russians cannot, as we have so often done before, evade the responsibility—put it off our shoulders on to those of Western Europe. We must look to ourselves for salvation, if salvation of Europe there is to be.

There is a handful of Russians—certainly no more—hungering and thirsting after the fulfilment of their new religious Idea: who believe that in a *fusion* between the thought of Tolstoy and that of Dostoevsky will be found the Symbol—the union—to lead and revive.

A child's hand may unseal the invisible will in any one of us; may unseal the spring of immense and exploding waters—living forces of destruction and regeneration. It needs, perhaps, but that the meanest of us should say to himself: "Either I must do this thing, or none will," and the face of the earth will be changed.

Note.—*The author has continued the above subject in a Study of the Religion of Tolstoy and Dostoevsky. Whether this Study shall be given to the English and American public will depend upon the reception accorded to his foregoing book.*—Ed.

---

1. He died in 1881.

A Note About the Author

Dmitry Merezhkovsky (1866–1941) was a Russian novelist and poet. Born in Saint Petersburg, Merezhkovsky was raised in a prominent political family. At thirteen, while a student at the St. Petersburg Third Classic Gymnasium, Dmitry began writing poetry. Soon, he earned a reputation as a promising young writer and enrolled at the University of Saint Petersburg, where he completed his PhD with a study on Montaigne. In 1892, he published *Symbols. Poems and Songs*, a work inspired by Poe and Baudelaire in which Merezhkovsky explores his increasingly personal religious ideas. In 1895, he published *The Death of the Gods*, the first novel in his groundbreaking *Christ and Antichrist Trilogy*. With these novels, Merezhkovsky was recognized as a cofounder of the Russian Symbolist movement. In 1905, his apocalyptic Christian worldview seemed to come to fruition in the First Russian Revolution, which he supported through poetry and organizing groups of students and artists. Formerly a supporter of the Tsar, Merezhkovsky was involved in leftist politics by 1910, but soon became disillusioned with the rise of the radical Bolsheviks. In the aftermath of the October Revolution, Merezhkovsky and his wife, the poet Zinaida Gippius, were forced to flee Russia. Over the years, they would find safe harbor in Warsaw and Paris, where Merezhkovsky continued to write works of nonfiction while advocating for the Russian people. Toward the end of his life, he came to see through such leaders as Benito Mussolini, Francisco Franco, and Adolf Hitler a means of defeating Communism in Russia. Though scholars debate his level of commitment to fascist and nationalist ideologies, this nevertheless marked a sinister turn in an otherwise brilliant literary career. Nominated for the Nobel Prize in literature nine times without winning, Merezhkovsky is recognized as an important figure of the Silver Age of Russian art.

A Note from the Publisher

Spanning many genres, from non-fiction essays to literature classics to children's books and lyric poetry, Mint Edition books showcase the master works of our time in a modern new package. The text is freshly typeset, is clean and easy to read, and features a new note about the author in each volume. Many books also include exclusive new introductory material. Every book boasts a striking new cover, which makes it as appropriate for collecting as it is for gift giving. Mint Edition books are only printed when a reader orders them, so natural resources are not wasted. We're proud that our books are never manufactured in excess and exist only in the exact quantity they need to be read and enjoyed.

Discover more of your favorite classics with Bookfinity™.

- Track your reading with custom book lists.
- Get great book recommendations for your personalized Reader Type.
- Add reviews for your favorite books.
- AND MUCH MORE!

Visit **bookfinity.com** and take the fun Reader Type quiz to get started.

Enjoy our classic and modern companion pairings!

9 781513 283104